1

Contributor Comments about the ProdBOK® Guide

"I immediately recognized the value of the ProdBOK Guide in order to create an international standard to guide our profession, much as PMBOK® has for the field of project management and BABOK® has for the discipline of business analysis."
— **Greg Cohen, Author, *Agile Excellence for Product Managers***

"The ProdBOK Guide finally provides a collaborative view across the profession for the role of product management and the value it can deliver to organizations. For anyone at any level or title who wants to improve the effectiveness of their product management activities in delivering market-driven products, this is the place to start." — **Don Vendetti, Founder and Principle, Product Arts**

"The ProdBOK Guide will become a vital addition to every manager's library and will sit proudly on the shelf next to the PMBOK."
— **Lee Lambert, CEO, Lambert Consulting Group**

"The ProdBOK Guide will be on the bookshelf, desktop, and Kindle of every product manager in the country. I learned a ton when I read it and was able to apply that knowledge to my day-to-day activities immediately. I'm sure that this will be an amazing success and a valued resource for product managers in all stages of their careers." — **David Radzialowski, President, Chicago Product Management Association**

"The ProdBOK Guide is essential for professional development purposes, for defining who's qualified to practice, and for communicating the value of the product management profession to the world." — **Rich Gunther, President, User Experience Professionals Association (UXPA)**

"The ProdBOK Guide is a major step forward in standardizing what product management is, and the key practices it entails. The Guide will help product managers and marketers adopt practices that lead to greater professional success." — **Linda Merrick, Principle, Pivotal Product Management**

"We think that it's very important for the product management community to have a common reference point for the roles and responsibilities of product management. The ProdBOK Guide will provide additional credibility to the product management function in organizations." – **Nick Coster, Co-Founder and Head of Training, Brainmates**

"The ProdBOK Guide will further legitimize the role of product management and lead to more attention and study of the field. I'm proud to have been a contributor to its development." – **Jeff Lash, *How to Be a Good Product Manager***

"The ProdBOK Guide connects the roles of product and project managers and paves the way for improved communication and smoother delivery of products by providing needed guidelines and explanations that improve performance." –**Frank Saladis, Owner, Blue Marble Enterprizes, Inc.**

"The ProdBOK Guide defines the requirements, orientation, and basic foundation of product management, which are desperately sought after by individual product management professionals, product teams, decision-makers, HR departments, and organizations of all sizes seeking to increase market share and product success." – **Cindy F. Solomon, Founder, Global Product Management Talk**

"In my 30+ years managing projects and products, I have seen the subject of product management treated many different ways. But for me, ProdBOK stands alone as THE definitive guide."
– **Gary R. Heerkens, President, Management Solutions Group, Inc.**

The Guide to the

Product Management and Marketing Body of Knowledge

(ProdBOK®)

Edited by

GREG GERACIE AND STEVEN D. EPPINGER

**Product Management Educational Institute
Carson City, Nevada**

ISBN: 978-0-9845185-0-0
Library of Congress Control Number: 2011927728

Product management
Product management — Textbooks, handbooks, manuals, etc.
New products — Management
Marketing
Project management
Body of knowledge

Table of Contents

List of Tables and Figures

Foreword

This project began when we received a call from the president of the Association of International Product Marketing and Management (AIPMM) inquiring whether we would be interested in channeling the leading voices in product management —analysts, authors, academics, consultants, bloggers, and practitioners—to create a formalized body of knowledge. This would be no easy task, and it gave us pause.

Part of what went through our minds as we considered the opportunity was that most of what exists in the product management literature has been authored by insightful *individuals* who stepped in to help fill the gap that existed because there was no *collective* body of knowledge. Although these individuals, ourselves included, have done an admirable job helping practitioners broaden their knowledge and work more effectively, a compendium of the different voices did not yet exist.

We also found ourselves asking why so many other professions, including adjoining ones like project management and business analysis, had documented their bodies of knowledge while product management had not? As we researched other professional bodies of knowledge, it became clear that the one thing they had in common was the sponsorship of an industry association. These sponsoring bodies act as the central catalyst to drive the development of a body of knowledge. The call we received from AIPMM was this first step.

Developing a body of knowledge requires collaboration from a wide swath of the professional community in question. We are tremendously grateful for the generous participation of the many members of the product management community who contributed time, energy, and material to this body of knowledge. With very few exceptions, members of the community gave freely of their expertise. We are truly grateful for their generosity.

We would also like to thank the various thought leaders from outside the product management community who contributed to this effort. Many of the leading voices in the project management, business analyst, and user experience communities contributed their thoughts to ensure that our material and the best practices from the adjoining professions aligned for the betterment of our collective process.

Which brings us to the material itself. Because this is the first edition of *The Guide to the Product Management and Marketing Body of Knowledge*, the editorial team has tried to keep the information concise. However, in a number of instances our research indicated that we needed to go deeper than we might have otherwise desired, had the nomenclature been universally understood. So to establish broader understanding, we have provided greater detail on the topics of value creation processes, Agile, and the importance of utilizing project management within the product lifecycle.

This brings us back to the opening question of whether we would take on this project. After careful consideration, our response was, "Sign us up!" We couldn't think of a nobler pursuit than to help this profession—one that we believe adds such value for customers, organizations, and practitioners—develop a solid foundation for learning and creating value.

Editor-in-Chief

President

Actuation Consulting

Editor

Professor of Management Science and Innovation

Massachusetts Institute of Technology (MIT)

The Product Management Lifecycle

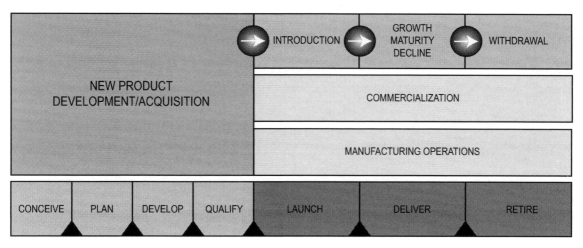

Source: The Association of International Product Marketing and Management (AIPMM)

The ProdBOK Guide contains information that is meant to be applied across the product management lifecycle, a term that describes the lifespan of a product – from conception through retirement. Once the product has been developed or acquired, it moves into commercialization, manufacturing, and operations phases, where the product is introduced, grows over time to reach maturity, and then declines, eventually leading to withdrawal from the market. This process can be further broken down into seven distinct phases: Conceive, Plan, Develop, Qualify, Launch, Deliver, and Retire. This entire "cradle-to-grave" process is generally considered to be universal and will be discussed in detail in Section Two.

The ProdBOK Guide does not prescribe an order in which individual tasks are performed. Some ordering of tasks is inevitable, as certain tasks produce outputs that are required inputs for other tasks. It is important to keep in mind that the ProdBOK Guide only prescribes that the input must exist. The input may be incomplete or subject to change and revision, which may cause the task to be performed multiple times. Agile or Iterative methodologies may require that tasks be performed concurrently. Tasks may be performed in any order, as long as the necessary inputs to a task are present.

SECTION 1:
Understanding Product Management

This section provides a basic foundation for understanding product management. It defines key terms, concepts, processes, and basic context for the rest of the ProdBOK Guide. It also provides key integration points on how this BOK can be used and aligned with other industry standards and marketplace processes.

Chapter 1

Introduction

Over the last 15 years, the product management community has grown from a handful of thought leaders to dozens. But this growth has done little to solidify a standard body of knowledge or skill set needed to succeed as a product manager. Bodies of knowledge lead to greater understanding. Although product management is clearly understood in a company like Procter & Gamble, which defined brand management decades ago, there are many companies that, being unsure what product management involves, hire an "experienced" product manager to lead.

There is no single course or university program that one can take to become a professional product manager. Therefore, it's fair to say that product management is an on-the-job experience. Using the experience accrued via trial by fire or on-the-job training, a career product manager moves from company to company, bringing his or her own uniquely shaped perspective.

This "on-the-job" education of product managers has led hiring organizations to believe that domain experience is required because hiring managers are unsure what skills are transferable from industry to industry. And the lack of a defined foundational skill set has left the field open to interpretation and improvisation. The editors of this book believe it is important, therefore, to establish a basic standard of knowledge on product management as a profession.

1.1 What Is *The Guide to the Product Management and Marketing Body of Knowledge* (ProdBOK®)?

A Body of Knowledge (BOK) conveys a commonly accepted standard of concepts, definitions, processes, and activities that make up a profession, as defined by the participating thought leaders, academics, and practitioners in the field. A BOK is not an encyclopedia of all things product management but a *guide* that spurs practitioners to seek additional knowledge, resources, and certification. *The Guide to the Product Management and Marketing Body of Knowledge* (ProdBOK) is that sum of knowledge within the product management profession.

ProdBOK represents knowledge and practices that are applicable to most product managers, most of the time, based on a consensus of their value and usefulness. This BOK provides the fundamental knowledge required to be an effective product manager. It was developed to give product managers information that would motivate them to look deeper into the subject and research the far greater body of knowledge that exists within the product management domain. It is a living reference that is constantly evolving.

1.2 Introducing a New Standardized Product Management Framework

A product management framework (PMF) creates a consistent language encompassing the innovation, creation, delivery, and ongoing management of products. A PMF is applicable to all products developed and managed throughout their lifecycle—from emerging growth products to well-established, mature products in the market. The goal of this PMF is to define the activities that a product manager must perform to innovate, design, and manage a product that meets customer and business needs and expectations and can be properly managed in terms of budget, schedule, scope, quality, and resources.

The PMF organizes and guides cross-functional development activities through various stages, and it incorporates design controls to optimize the execution and effectiveness of resulting products. It is scalable and maintainable, and can be applied to the full range of goods and services.

Today's business environment is challenging and complex. Product managers can use a framework to address issues, such as managing products, that are integrated combinations of goods and services, globalization, changing legislation, and increasing regulations. A PMF enables organizations to adopt a holistic, system-level approach. The PMF is not meant to be a standard operating procedure. That is, it's not meant to be prescriptive, where completing all deliverables within the framework is a requirement. Rather, it promotes critical thinking about the activities needed to support any product initiative. The critical thinking allows the team to decide which activities make sense, and it fosters the necessary agility that teams need to deliver in this quickly changing, competitive environment.

1

1.3 The ProdBOK's Audience

This guide provides a singular reference for anyone interested in product management, from senior executives establishing expectations for their product managers to those simply interested in learning more about the field. This includes, but is not limited to:

- Senior executives

- Managers of product management professionals

- Brand managers

- Product managers

- Product owners

- Product marketing managers

- Portfolio managers

- Program managers

- Project managers

- Business analysts

- Educators and trainers developing educational programs and teaching product management or related topics

- Consultants and other specialists in the field of product management

1.4 Laying the Groundwork for Certification and Academic Learning

Bodies of knowledge define a standard for discussing, writing, and applying a common lexicon to a professional field. They provide an excellent opportunity for professional domains to standardize the fundamental understandings, language, and skills needed for individuals and organizations to be successful. Earning a certification by using this standard body of knowledge demonstrates to peers the qualitative and quantitative ability to perform the job. Certification also demonstrates a dedication to learning and advancing product management skills.

This BOK is the basis for developing questions for the exam that individuals must pass to become a product manager certified by the Association of International Product Marketing and Management (AIPMM). Applicants for AIPMM certification undergo a rigorous and comprehensive examination of their knowledge in each area. A professional certification and licensure testing company helped construct this examination. AIPMM follows the International Standard ISO/IEC 17024, General Requirements for Bodies Operating Certification of Persons, in creating the certification and examination processes.

1.5 The ProdBOK Guide Structure in Summary

The ProdBOK Guide is organized into three sections:

Section 1: Understanding Product Management

This section provides a basic foundation for understanding product management. It defines key terms, concepts, processes, and basic context for the rest of the ProdBOK Guide. It also provides key integration points on how this BOK can be used and aligned with other industry standards and marketplace processes.

Section 2: The Product Management Lifesycle Framework

This section identifies the framework used to manage a product. It describes the seven different phases of product management; Conceive, Plan, Develop, Qualify, Launch, Deliver, and Retire.

Section 3: Key Product Management Tools by Product Lifecycle Phase

This section provides a detailed description of the major product management tools contained within each product management lifecycle phase.

Chapter 2

Product Management and Product Marketing Management

2.1 The Current State of Product Management

Today's business challenges are causing product management to evolve and become more structured. These challenges have also created intense competition and sophisticated consumers. As a result, organizations now demand highly skilled individuals who can immediately impact the bottom line, develop the next "must have" product or service, and execute a winning plan.

During an interview with *Harvard Business Review* on the topic of growth, Jeffrey Immelt, CEO of General Electric, once stated that the company did not "have enough sophisticated product managers and system engineers to put in charge of high-visibility programs."[1] Because Immelt saw this as an "organizational weakness," General Electric immediately began to address this problem.

This increased demand for product management professionals has created a continuing growth in product management training and certification.

2.2 The History of Product Management

To see where product management as a profession is going, it helps to look at its origins.

Product management was born from intense, sustained, and rigorous trial and error in the market research department at the giant consumer packaged goods company Procter & Gamble (P&G). In 1931, D. Paul "Doc" Smelser, a PhD economist from Johns Hopkins University and the head of the new unit at P&G—the market research department—hired female college graduates to conduct fieldwork. He used an anthropological approach, sending the graduates door to door to survey homemakers about their use of all kinds of household products. Within several

---

[1] Stewart, T.A. (2006, June). Growth as a Process, An Interview with Jeffrey R. Immelt. *Harvard Business Review*, 63–64.

years, the department's staff grew to around 34, in addition to dozens of field researchers. The first product group, commonly called a *brand*, to incorporate these market research methods in the product design process was Camay soap.

Camay soap was the catalyst for defining brand management, and P&G's Neil McElroy led the charge. Procter & Gamble's perfumed beauty bar, Camay soap, challenged the purity positioning of another P&G product, Ivory soap. The two products targeted very different markets and competed for resources within P&G. This convinced McElroy, then a young advertising manager, of the need to establish assignments for its marketers in brand-specific teams so those teams would have a measure of autonomy in running marketing campaigns.[2]

In a P&G company memo dated May 13, 1931,[3] McElroy outlined the duties and responsibilities of the "brand men." They were tasked with analyzing the brand history and instructed to "study the territory personally," including the dealers and the customers. Both Smelser and McElroy understood the importance of fieldwork. They both advocated getting out of the office and talking face to face with customers. Not unlike anthropologists, they knew that the most valuable data about people are how they behave in their own environment. They recognized that surveys, scheduled interviews, and focus groups only give a partial picture.

McElroy's memo laid the groundwork for a shift from a geographically aligned sales perspective to a brand orientation. The result was a fundamental restructuring of P&G. John Pepper, former P&G chairman of the board, president, and CEO, said, "responsibility and accountability for discreet business units were assigned to separate organizations...by Neil McElroy, when he helped create the brand management system in the 1930s."[4] Procter & Gamble brand managers assumed responsibility for coordinating all activities and tasks involving their brand. Far more than just marketing, the brand managers would also coordinate product development and field sales.

From McElroy forward, every one of P&G's chief executives would hold the positions of assistant brand manager and brand manager on their way up the executive ladder.

2.3 The Evolution of Brand and Product Management

"A product is made in the factory. A brand is made in the mind."[5]

This might be overly simplistic, but it does highlight the differences between brand and product management.

---

[2] Dyer, D., Dalzell, F., & Olegario, R. (2004). *Rising Tide: Lessons from 165 Years of Brand Building at Procter & Gamble.* Boston, MA: Harvard Business School Press.
[3] McElroy, N. (1931). Procter & Gamble company memo, May 13, 1931.

2

What exactly does "a brand is made in the mind" mean? A brand is a name, term, design, or symbolic representation of the seller's goods or services. In other words, a brand is the sum of the perceived psychological and emotional factors that exist in the relationship between a company and its customers. Brands have meaning and help to establish a personal and emotional connection with the customer.

Companies build goods and/or services and then add value by creating brands to convey functional, economic, and psychological benefits for the customer in terms of quality, price, and image. Products serve as the delivery mechanism of the brand promise. This promise encapsulates a company's reputation and overall value proposition and communicates what customers can expect beyond what the product delivers.

Many companies have a single brand and therefore structure the organization around the products. When a company has multiple brands, such as the case with P&G, the brand is at the pinnacle of the product hierarchy. An excellent example is Disney's focus on creating "magical" customer experiences.

In the brand management model developed by P&G and adopted by many packaged goods companies, the brand management structure was the center of the wheel and the career path for future CEOs at P&G. In fact, a number of brand managers from P&G became leading CEOs in other industries, such as eBay (Meg Whitman), Intuit (Scott Cook), Microsoft (Steve Ballmer), and AOL (Steve Case), to name a few.

The noticeable success resulting from P&G's focus on brands and their underlying products led organizations outside the consumer product segment to adopt a similar model — product management. It was in this way that what began as brand management evolved into the *distinct* profession called *product management* and became more comfortably acclimated into a wide range of industries, including consumer products.

---

[4] Pepper, J. (2005). *What Really Matters*. Cincinnati, OH: Procter & Gamble Company.
[5] Rutherford, D., & Knowles, J. (2007). *Vulcans, Earthlings and Marketing ROI*. Waterloo, ON, Canada: Wilfrid Laurier University Press.

Chapter 3

What Is a Product?

Products are the result of a process of effort or thought. At their core, products are the sum of benefits that satisfy a customer's need or desire. The word "product" is commonly used to describe durable or tangible goods. However, more correctly, products can be goods or services, and are distinguished by tangibility: goods are tangible and services are intangible.

From the customer's perspective, the product is the overall experience provided by the combination of goods and services to satisfy the customers' needs before they use it, while they use it, and after they have stopped using it.

3.1 Goods and Services

3.1.1 Goods

There are a number of types of physical products, as follows.

Consumer Products: items that are used daily. Consumer products are commonly identified as goods purchased for personal use. There are four types of consumer products:

Convenience products: goods that are purchased immediately and frequently with little comparison or decision time.

Shopping products: goods that require research and analysis before purchasing (e.g., gold, silver, automobiles, and clothing). Generally, each purchase requires an examination of price, quality, durability, and resale value.

Specialty products: goods and services that are either unique or have such a clear brand identification that a consumer is willing to make a significant effort to purchase them. Examples include luxury goods, exotic vacations, and collector items.

Unsought products: goods and services that a consumer either doesn't know about or doesn't want to think about. Examples include funeral items, such as caskets, headstones, or burial plots.

Business-to-Business: goods and services used for running a business or for selling directly to business customers.

Industrial Products: goods or services used by an industry or business, rather than by an individual.

Other Products: Other commonly used product classifications include:

Perishable products (also known as non-durable goods): goods that can be destroyed easily or do not have long shelf lives. Good examples are fruits, vegetables, dairy products, cosmetics, fuel, cleaning products, and paper.

Durable goods: the opposite of perishable products, these goods are in use for at least three years. Examples are furniture, electronic equipment, and hardware. Durable goods are also classified with industrial products such as copiers, machinery, and offices.

Finished goods: goods ready for immediate sale. Finished goods do not require further processing.

3.1.2 Services

According to Kotler and Keller (2008),[6] services are "any activity or benefit that one party can offer to another which is essentially intangible and does not result in the ownership of anything." The four characteristics of services are 1) intangibility, 2) perishability, 3) inseparability, and 4) variability.[7]

A common misconception is that services differ from what is often referred to as "products." Understanding that products are a mixture of goods and services in varying degrees is an important step in the value creation process (see section 6.2). Therefore, it is important to understand whether a product would be classified as a "pure good" (something that is not accompanied by a service, i.e., toothpaste) or a product that would result in only the delivery of a service (i.e., a dentist appointment).

Professional Services

Services are assistance, support, or benefits offered by one person to another. Examples are provided by professionals like plumbers, electricians, mechanics, attorneys, doctors, and cosmeticians.

---

[6] Kotler, P., & Keller, K. (2008). *Marketing Management* (13th ed.). Upper Saddle River, NJ: Prentice Hall.
[7] Kotler, P., & Armstrong, G. (2007). *Principles of Marketing* (12th ed.). Upper Saddle River, NJ: Prentice Hall.

Business Services

Business services are offerings that span all industries and organizations. These services include consulting, customer service, and information technology. Sometimes, business services are combined with complimentary goods. In these instances, services are closely aligned and can be difficult to separate from goods, particularly when they are part of augmented benefits in the case of warranties, service agreements, and support.

Technical Support Services

Technical support services accompany manufactured products. These services are offered either directly from the manufacturer or through a third-party provider.

Financial Services

Financial services are products offered by financial institutions for the facilitation of financial transactions and other related activities. Examples include loans, insurance, credit cards, investment opportunities, and money management.

Service Warranties

A service warranty provides protection against the cost of repair, replacement, or maintenance of a consumer product in return for payment of a premium. These services come in many forms, including warranties, guaranties, extended warranties, extended guaranties, or maintenance service contracts.

3.2 Brands

As previously noted, products are goods and services that offer a functional benefit. A brand, on the other hand, is a name, symbol, design, or mark that *enhances the value of the product* beyond its functional value. David Ogilvy, the founder of the advertising agency Ogilvy & Mather, defines a brand as:

"A complex symbol. It is the intangible sum of a product's attributes, its name, packaging, and price. Its history, reputation, and the way it's advertised. A brand is also defined by consumers' impressions of the people who use it, as well as their own experience."[8]

A brand can also be described as a strategic asset of an organization and the experience, perception, and reputation of an organization's values and beliefs, personality, and behavior. It also comprises the name and visual mark by which an organization is recognized.

---

[8] Ogilvy, D. (1985). *Ogilvy on Advertising*. New York, NY: Vintage Books.

3.3 Product Lines

According to the 12th edition of *Principles of Marketing*, "A product line is a group of products [categorized by a business unit or company] that are closely related because they function in a similar manner, are sold to the same customer groups, are marketed through the same types of outlets, or fall within given price ranges."[9]

3.4 Extensions

There is quite a bit of confusion about the definition of brand and product extensions. It is helpful to remember that a *brand lives in the mind*, and the product represents the delivery mechanism of the brand. The following definitions are intended to make the distinctions clear.

3.4.1 Brand Extensions

When a firm uses an established brand to introduce a new product, it is called a brand extension.[10] For instance, when celebrities use their brand (their name) in the creation of fragrances, clothing, restaurants, jewelry, vehicles, etc., they are creating brand extensions. During the creation process, the development teams for these categories are assuming that a particular brand identity will resonate with the consumer perceptions of the celebrity. Success is generally achieved when the brand and the category are closely aligned. To better illustrate that point, one can look over the past decade at the enduring brand of Harley-Davidson. Harley-Davidson has a strong male identity image. Therefore, it experienced a brand extension failure when it introduced a line of perfume. The image or identity of the strong male that lives in the mind for Harley-Davidson fans did not fit the product line of perfumes.

Brand extensions can be classified into two types: line extensions and category extensions.

3.4.2 Line Extensions

Product line extensions create new products in the same category using the existing brand name. These new products can include things like different formats, alternative packaging, new flavors, or new or additional ingredients. For example, Cherry COKE® is a product line extension of the Coca-Cola COKE® beverage.

[9, 10] Kotler, P., & Armstrong, G. (2007). *Principles of Marketing* (12th ed.). Upper Saddle River, NJ: Prentice Hall.

3.4.3 Category Extensions

Category extensions are the use of an existing or parent brand to launch products in other categories. For instance, Harley-Davidson® is a motorcycle, but the Harley-Davidson brand is used to distinguish a design styling used in Ford® F-series trucks.

3

Chapter 4

What Is Product Management?

Stated simply, product management is the process of conceiving, planning, developing, testing, launching, delivering, and withdrawing products in the market. It is the organizational function within a company dealing with the thoughtful and proactive management of a product or group of products throughout all stages of the product lifecycle.

As a discipline, product management provides *managerial* focus to products (goods and services) and brands as profit-generating systems within the context of the larger organization. Without effective product management, product development is prone to guesswork, misguided development projects, and missed opportunities. With world-class product management, companies develop products with robust knowledge of both customers and markets, increasing the likelihood of market success.

4.1 Internal and External Aspects of Product Management

Product management as a process has two distinct areas of focus: internal and external. Internal is defined as within the organization's environment, including such elements as current product teams, senior management, and required processes. The external environment includes such elements as the supply chain, distribution network, and markets. How each company defines, develops, and delivers products will be influenced by these factors.

4.2 Structure of Product Management

In practice, there is no single product management model. However, the strategic value of one trend has gained momentum and become increasingly clear: to have the product management function report directly to the CEO or the president of a strategic business unit. This trend is further supported by the results of a survey conducted by Tom Grant of Forrester Research, which indicated an increase in the effectiveness of the product management organization when the function reports directly to the senior executive.

Additionally, organizations report that product management performs best when it functions within a series of checks and balances. In other words, the process works best when the product management function balances the short-term needs of functions such as sales and customer care against the longer-term needs of the client base, market, and organization.

To achieve this objective, the product management function needs the autonomy to make the best overall decision on behalf of the organization, customer base, and target market. When these factors are in uneasy harmony, organizations report a high degree of market success.

4.2.1 The Upstream/Downstream Product Management Model

Linda Gorchels, in the 2011 edition of *The Product Manager's Handbook*, outlines two fundamentally different—though related—classifications of product management functions: upstream and downstream.

Upstream functions deal with the strategies of product roadmaps and new product development efforts. They usually include identifying critical portfolio needs and then providing leadership throughout the development process up until launch. Downstream functions deal with ongoing lifecycle management. Some medical device and diagnostic manufacturers, in particular, hire separate people for the two job categories. GE Healthcare, for example, has upstream product managers responsible for global product strategy and launch. Their downstream product managers handle the marketing and sales support necessary to manage the profitable sales of products after launch and beyond. Sometimes the downstream product managers are responsible for marketing the products in different countries. Health care product and services company Beckman Coulter has similar split positions, but refers to them as strategic and tactical product managers.

The split between upstream and downstream product management is not consistent across industries. For some companies, particularly in highly technical fields, upstream activities end before commercialization, with downstream product managers taking over at launch. And some companies shift from upstream to downstream at the start of a new product project (at the shift from R&D to development). The best practice for a company is what works best for their specific circumstances.

4.3 Product Management Structure within Organizations

Each company's stage of growth impacts the actual organizational structure of product management.

In startups and companies in the early stages of growth, where speed to market is emphasized, product management organizations tend to be small and nimble with a focus on direct customer interaction. The product manager is generally managing all aspects of a product or group of products from inception through launch. The organizational structure is very flat, with low degrees of specialization.

As a startup gives way to a successful midsized enterprise, resources shift to building scale and managing the resulting growth. As a result, the product management function is tasked with managing both growth and complexity. Product managers at this stage of growth are often surrounded by additional talent, particularly to assist with managing requirements, overseeing specifications, and ensuring appropriate levels of engagement with the cross-functional development and support teams. The product management organization is expanding during this stage as process implementation and specialization take hold.

More mature organizations have historically moved slowly and methodically to protect their existing market share while pursuing growth both organically and through mergers and acquisitions. As the business has increased in scale and complexity, product management organizations have grown significantly and now contain a high degree of expertise across a range of necessary skills with increased specialization.

Although growth stage often dictates product management's configuration, some organizations build cultures that defy convention and common logic.

Google's structure, for example, is built on a vice president (VP) of products leading a team of VPs of sector products, ultimately reporting directly to the CEO. Reporting to the VPs of the sector products are teams of product managers.

At Microsoft, there are many layers of senior VPs and VPs of business units to traverse before finding a VP of product management. Microsoft also has a team product management approach, using product managers, program managers, and product marketing managers. Facebook, a "software as a service" (SaaS) model company like Google, has a director of product management who reports directly to the CEO. Although there is not one magic formula, the decision on where product management sits in the organization comes down to these questions:

1. What is the overall product management objective?

2. Where in the organization can a product manager have the best strategic vantage point and be most effective?

3. Where is financial decision making for products located in the organization?

4. Where can those decisions be measured and benchmarked?

Clearly understanding the answers to these questions leads to designing the right product management structure within an organization. Product managers generally have the best opportunity to succeed when they report to a business leader at the enterprise or business unit level who must balance the short- and long-term needs of the customers, market, and organization.

4.4 Product Management's Relationship to General Management

General management encompasses strategizing, planning, organizing, staffing, executing, delivering, and providing the proper infrastructure associated with support and operational processes. Product management can include overall responsibility for managing the strategy, planning, revenue, cost, marketing, sales channel development, product delivery, operational rollout, and support of a product. Product management is essentially general management for a product. But there is a key distinction—general managers have full profit and loss responsibility and have functional leaders reporting to them, whereas product managers interact primarily through influence and by relying on shared organizational objectives.

4.5 Managing and Marketing Goods and Services across All Industries and Companies

The main objectives of marketing are identifying, satisfying, and retaining the customer. Although there are differences within industries on how each of those objectives is accomplished, some fundamental methods, skills, and programs exist. Unless otherwise noted, the processes and methods outlined in this body of knowledge are applicable to a broad range of industries and organizations, regardless of size.

4.6 Variations by Industry and Maturity

Product management spans a wide variety of industries. Listed below are examples that illustrate the emphasis on a specific subset of product management skills.

4

Consumer Packaged Goods

The consumer packaged goods industry requires product management that is nimble and responsive. The key to success in this market is to have effective innovation processes, faster time to market, brand recognition, and lower costs. There is a constant battle for the consumers' attention; therefore, the focus is on enhancing the consumer experience with the products.

Financial

Organizations offering financial services (e.g., banks, credit card companies, insurance agencies, consumer finance services, stock brokerages, investment fund organizations, and wealth management companies) usually separate the product management structure into business units by product lines and specialty. Product managers are augmented by subject matter experts who can focus on the government regulations and governance, while the product manager focuses on customer needs and the delivery mechanism of the service organization.

Hospitality

Hospitality is a service organization model covering lodging, restaurants, event planning, theme parks, transportation, cruise lines, and additional fields within the tourism industry. This industry favors product managers who also have aptitudes commonly associated with project management because of its focus on planning and shorter lifecycles.

Health care

Health care is the broad industry covering equipment and services in addition to pharmaceuticals, biotechnology, and life sciences. The particular sectors associated with these groups are biotechnology, diagnostics, drug delivery, drug manufacturers, hospitals, medical equipment and devices, diagnostic laboratories, nursing homes, providers of health care plans, and home health care. This broad range of products favors product managers who have science backgrounds as well as the ability to navigate through regulatory issues.

Manufacturing

Manufacturers today face global challenges. They must create rapid growth, introduce new products, and lower costs—all within the confines of an often competitive market. Product managers in this environment must understand the increased demand on innovation and must have the ability to work with offshore manufacturing teams and distributed supply chains. With short development times and real-time collaboration skills, product managers must learn to spot problems early.

Software

Software product management is very similar to that of other industries but has some issues that are more prominent. As in manufacturing, schedule slips are one of the biggest problems.

Telecommunications

In the telecommunications industry, time to market is crucial; as the market consolidates, the key players are forced to release product versions rapidly. Product management in telecommunication must identify the requirements and match those customer needs with the company's core software resources and technological assets to stay competitive. Pricing and licensing are also key issues for telecommunications.

Mature Industries

Mature industries are almost always dominated by a small number of large companies. This domination is caused by the industry consolidation and the competitive shakeout that accompanies these highly competitive industries during their growth. Product management within these organizations is generally more structured. An example of a mature industry would be the tobacco industry, which has continued sales but minimal growth.

Chapter 5

Common Product Management Roles

5

Product manager is the general term commonly used to describe team members that are responsible for managing one or more products within an organization. To bring more clarity and meaning to the role, the title is often enhanced to include the division, products managed, or function performed, i.e., product manager, beverage division; product manager, tools and metrics; or technical product manager.

5.1 Product Manager

Regardless of title, most product managers are tasked with channeling the needs of the market into the organization and ensuring that an optimal balance is struck between customers' needs and the organization's capabilities. Product managers therefore play an important role in maximizing the return on an organization's investment in goods and services over the entire product lifecycle.

The product manager role is a boundary role[11] that sits at the intersection of the market and the organization (Figure 5-1). Within the organization, the product manager must overcome diverse expectations from the various departments with which they must interact. Product managers also assume responsibility for product planning. In this role, the product manager is responsible for the ongoing process of identifying and articulating market requirements for a specific market or customer need.

---

[11] Lysonski, S. (1985, Winter). The Boundary Theory Investigation of the Product Manager's Role. *Journal of Marketing*, 29–41.

Figure 5-1. Product Managers Perform Their Role at the Nexus between the External Market and Internal Constituents

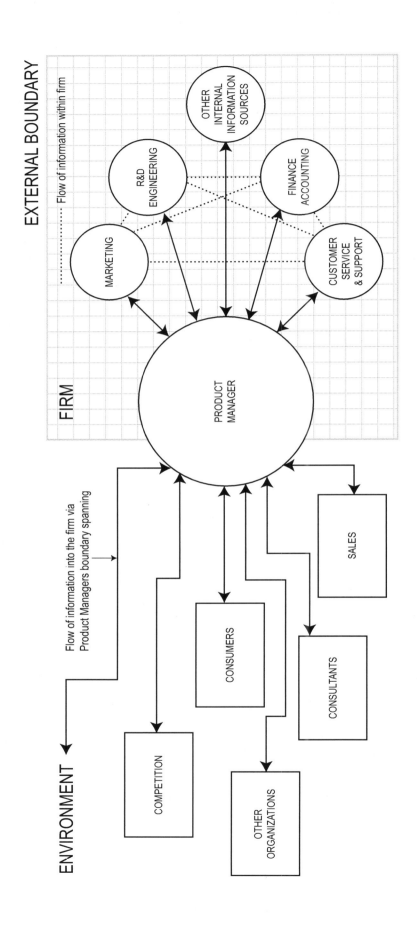

To perform this role, product managers must act as the voice of the customers, channeling their unmet needs. With this responsibility, the product manager initiates and participates in customer visits, organizes customer advisory panels, and performs customer interviews. Armed with this information, they can lead the process of improving in-market products and developing new ones.

The product manager must also possess keen influence and negotiation skills. In their article *The Product Manager as an Influence Agent*, Gemmill and Willemon state, "While product managers frequently are assigned total profit responsibility for their products, they often report that these responsibilities are not matched with commensurate authority over other organizational units on whom they are dependent for contributions in carrying out their marketing programs; i.e., sales, marketing research, manufacturing, research and development, and advertising."[12] The product manager's success often lies in the ability to use alternate methods of influence to gain support for his or her efforts.

5.1.1 Market-Facing

The market-facing product manager generally manages one or more products that have customers *outside* of their organization with whom they work closely to uncover unmet needs.

Market-facing product managers conduct market research to uncover unmet needs and articulate the needs of a target market or customer base. This position is not to be mistaken with the product marketing role, which will be covered later.

In this role, the product manager considers elements such as intended demographic, offerings from competitors, and the strategic fit of new products with the company's business model. The market information is used to gather intelligence for building the *right* products.

5.1.2 Internal

In contrast to market-facing product managers, internal product managers often represent products that are a component of a market-facing product *but whose customers are inside the organization*. Internal product managers are commonly found in technology or data industries, where a platform or database must be effectively managed to create value for products or services that are marketed to external clients via a market-facing product manager.

---

[12] Gemmill, G. R., & Willemon, D. L. (1972). The Product Manager as an Influence Agent. *Journal of Marketing*, 36, 26–30.

5.1.3 Technical

Technical product managers have a detailed understanding of the technological aspects of a product and commonly partner with market-facing product managers to serve the market's needs. It's not uncommon for technical product managers to spend significant time supporting the needs of colleagues—like the engineering team. A market-facing product manager, on the other hand, focuses on identifying customer or market needs.

Technical product managers also create detailed descriptions of product features, prioritization of features, use cases, system requirements, performance requirements, sales and support requirements, and, if necessary, market test plans.

5.1.4 Service

Service-oriented product managers are in market-facing positions with responsibility for managing the scope of an organization's services at all levels, including positioning, quality of experience, delivery, and pricing.

5.2 Product Marketing Manager

The product marketing manager role most often derives from a company's desire to increase the focus on "go to market" activities by dividing the product lifecycle into separate parts as the company grows. The product manager, who before the new role was managing the entire lifecycle, generally maintains responsibility for the pre-launch activities in the product lifecycle. The product marketing manager assumes responsibility for post-launch activities. The organization expects the product marketing manager to have or develop robust skills in supporting customer acquisition and in market activities.

One of the best ways to make a clear distinction is to delineate processes and roles. Product management and product marketing are processes. Product managers and product marketing managers are roles. This distinction places the bulk of the focus on the individual tasks.

A product marketing manager's role is primarily to help define and manage a product's image in the market. In other words, to announce the product to the world, build customer awareness, and support sales in turning prospects into profitable customers. A product marketing manager defines the product "promise" and ensures its successful execution in the market. That also means managing a successful launch, conducting sales training, and leading key programs through various distribution channels.

In addition to managing the finished product in market, the product marketing manager is uniquely positioned to gauge customer reactions to the product and therefore provide valuable input into future requirements, including revisions or major releases.

5.3 Product Portfolio Manager

Product portfolio manager is an umbrella term for a manager that's responsible for a business grouping of products. These products are often divided into logical portfolios, organized by business line or segment. Unlike product managers, who are concerned with the specifications and details of a product, the portfolio manager investigates higher-level details like investments, diversification, and risks. Product portfolio managers are also involved in managing the assets of intellectual property, patents, and trademarks. They are usually empowered to make buy/sell and transform, divest, or retire decisions while working closely with senior management, legal, and financial representatives.

5.4 Product Owner Outside of Scrum

The product owner role is a clearly defined subset of product management responsibilities focused on representing the business and customer stakeholders in the development process and ensuring the successful development of a product. They capture market requirements and customer acceptance criteria for the project. They prioritize the market requirements and make decisions about feature, function, and time tradeoffs. The product owner works with development to review product requirements and functional specifications and interacts with customers during development to ensure the product will meet their needs. In organizations with an established product owner structure, product owners may also develop business cases, release plans, and roadmaps—elements that have traditionally been thought of as the domain of product managers.

5.4.1 The Product Owner and Scrum

Scrum is an iterative, incremental process widely used for creating products. A detailed description of Scrum is provided in section 6.2.3. Although product owners can exist independent of the Scrum methodology, in Scrum, the product owner is one of three clearly defined roles (the other two are Scrum master and team member). The product owner is responsible for maximizing the business value of the output of the Scrum development team. The product owner can be viewed as the advocate for the business and the customer in the development process. Scrum empowers this individual as "the one and only person responsible for managing the product backlog,"[13] which is a prioritized requirements list, usually written as user stories. This authority prevents the team from having to deal with conflicting priorities.

In setting development priorities, the product owner applies knowledge of the market, the customer, and the business objectives. This individual will collaborate with the development team to understand the development cost and technical risk of each feature so risk-adjusted return can be maximized. Further, the product owner has a responsibility to socialize the product backlog to the rest of the organization to gather input from each department and build consensus around the plan.

In organizations where the product owner role has taken root, the product owner may perform tasks that have been traditionally thought of as part of the product management function, such as product visioning, road mapping, and planning. However, the core of the product owner role is defined by some very specific responsibilities that are often more detailed than most product managers are used to, such as:

- Prioritizing the product backlog.

- Grooming user stories: preparing stories for a development Sprint, including fully explaining the business reason behind each story and contributing to the acceptance criteria.

- Collaborating regularly with the team and being available at all times to answer clarifying questions about any requirement and to inspect completed user stories.

- Participating in the Scrum planning and Scrum review meetings.

In commercial software development, the Scrum product owner role is often filled by a product manager or technical product manager but is more likely to be handled by a business analyst, a sales engineer, and other titles. For an in-house information technology project, the product owner might be a product manager but could also be a business analyst or a department head.

As teams have scaled Scrum in the enterprise to work on ever-larger development efforts, they often use a product owner hierarchy[14] (Figure 5-2). This hierarchy consists of one or more levels with a chief product owner at the top. The chief product owner commonly has a director or vice president-level title and would be responsible for overall product return on investment and success.[15] Each product owner is involved in overseeing the success of his or her specific product.

[13] Schwaber, K., & Sutherland, J. (2009). *Scrum Guide*. Retrieved from http://www.scrum.org.
[14] Pichler, R. (2010). *Agile Product Management with Scrum*. Boston, MA: Addison-Wesley.
[15] Schwaber, K. (2007). *The Enterprise and Scrum*. Redmond, WA: Microsoft Press.

Figure 5-2. Product Owner Hierarchy

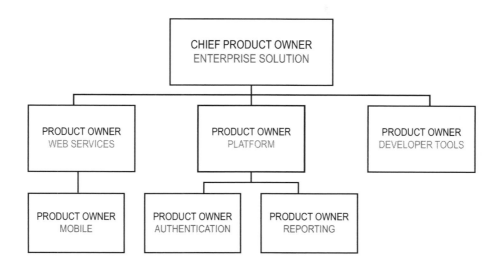

In organizations that do not use a product owner hierarchy, the Scrum product owner might collaborate with a product manager. In this situation, the product owner works closely with the development team and is focused at the iteration level, whereas the product manager focuses at the release and roadmap level.[16]

---

[16] Leffingwell, D. (2011). *Agile Software Requirements*. Boston, MA: Addison Wesley.

Chapter 6

Aligning ProdBOK with Other Existing Processes (and Why It Matters)

In this Body of Knowledge, the term "product management framework" (PMF) is defined as the process of managing the entire lifecycle of a product from conception, through development and production, to retirement. This PMF is a complete end-to-end structure for managing a successful product, and includes people, processes, data, business/organizational objectives, and, ultimately, customer satisfaction. The PMF is meant to focus not just on product deliverables but on the act of managing the product itself to achieve a desired result. Managing, in this context, is understanding what the goals are and putting a plan together to achieve those goals, while effectively dealing with change that may occur along the way. That goal, in relation to the PMF, encompasses customer satisfaction, organizational performance objectives, and overall market success throughout the life of the product. It's important to clearly define the PMF process because when it comes to product development, especially for new products, there are a number of business processes that *allude* to product management but actually focus on only a *portion* of the product lifecycle.

Product management, as modeled in this Body of Knowledge, naturally interacts with several other processes. It's vital that these processes work together efficiently to achieve the product's goals. Some of the more common processes and standards in the industry that are focused on management and delivery and are typically sources of confusion for a product manager are the Project Management Body of Knowledge, Business Analysis Body of Knowledge, and Agile Manifesto (Agile Software Development). It is important to understand these differing processes and bodies of knowledge to ensure appropriate alignment and increase the chances of achieving desired market results. A simple depiction of that relationship is captured in Figure 6-1.

Figure 6-1. Common Processes and Bodies of Knowledge That Operate within the Product Management Framework

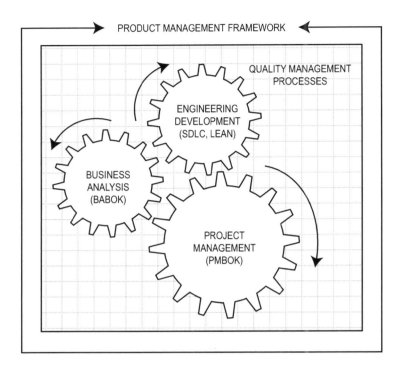

For optimum results, these processes must align. Without alignment, the gears in Figure 6-1 will grind and eventually stop, causing product and project failure. When put in the proper context, these processes can exist symbiotically, enabling product success. This is not to say that the PMF is simply a collection of other processes. On the contrary, the PMF has been designed to capture all the activities and deliverables a product manager and business leader need to manage a product line, from an undefined, "fuzzy" product idea all the way to maturation and retirement of the product after years in the marketplace. The PMF is where the supporting processes need to align and create value. The following sections will provide further context regarding these other types of processes and the value of aligning them with the PMF.

6.1 Strategy and Innovation Processes

6.1.1 Strategy

Strategy is about envisioning a desired outcome, charting an efficient course to achieve this objective, and aligning to that course of action as long as it makes sense to do so. Michael E. Porter, Harvard Business School professor, adds that,

"Competitive strategy is about being different. It means *deliberately* choosing a different set of activities to deliver a unique mix of values."[17]

Practically speaking, product managers split their time between developing and implementing product strategy and driving tactical execution. Many product managers use a set of strategy tools from Michael Porter's "Five Forces"[18] model to help evaluate market attractiveness and aid in decision making and planning. Those forces are:

1. **Entry.** How easy will it be to enter the market? New competitors are hampered by substantial barriers and might experience retaliation from existing competitors. For the entrant, some of the most common barriers are economies of scale, large capital requirements, limited access to distribution channels, and government regulations or subsidies.

2. **Threat of substitution.** Are there other products and services that can easily be substituted for the product under consideration? If so, and if there is little difference between products, customers can easily switch. Also, in the instance of rising prices, a consumer may decide to substitute another product.

3. **Bargaining power of buyers.** Do a small number of buyers impact a large portion of sales? Does one customer purchase a large percentage of the companies' products? Is switching between competitors relatively easy? These factors give buyers a great deal of power, particularly if the product is not extremely important to buyers or if they can do without it for a time.

4. **Bargaining power of suppliers.** Is there significant pressure from suppliers? If there are too few suppliers or it's not easy to switch suppliers, they can control volume and pricing, which can hamper a company's ability to function competitively.

5. **Rivalry among current competitors.** In crowded markets with little differentiation between products, competition will impact a company's ability to sustain profits and long-term growth.

To manage products effectively and deal with these five forces, Porter suggests that product managers use one of the three following strategies:

1. **Overall cost leadership.** Maintain the lowest cost in the market.

[17] Porter, M. E. (2006). What is Strategy. *Harvard Business Review*, 74(6).
[18] Porter, M. E. (1998). *Competitive Strategy: Techniques for Analyzing Industries and Competitors*. New York, NY: Free Press.

2. **Differentiation.** Deliver products that customers believe have a distinct or unique position in the market. This can be accomplished by combining several other factors, such as brand differentiation, unique features, warranties, or quality.

3. **Focus.** Focus on niche or limited segments to efficiently serve the needs of customers.

It is critical that product managers make clear, strategic choices in their product planning and development processes to avoid being "stuck in the middle" without clear price leadership, a clearly differentiated product, or a distinct focus.

6.1.2 Innovation

Innovation is the execution of a new or improved product, process, marketing method, or organizational method in business practices, workplace organization, or external relations.

The Oslo Manual[19] defines four types of innovation:

1. **Product innovation.** Introducing a good or service with characteristics or intended uses that are new or significantly improved, including significant improvements in performance or features, components and materials, incorporated software, user friendliness, or other functional characteristics.

2. **Process innovation.** Implementing a new or significantly improved production or delivery method. This includes significant changes in techniques, equipment, and/or software. The customer does not usually pay directly for this process, but the innovation may be required to deliver a product or service and to manage the relationships with the various stakeholders.

3. **Marketing innovation.** Applying a new marketing method involving significant changes in product design or packaging, product placement, product promotion, or pricing.

4. **Organizational innovation.** Executing new methods in the firm's business practices, workplace organization, or external relations.

It is important to point out that any of the types of innovation listed above can result in a *disruptive innovation*,[20] a term coined by Clayton Christensen. Disruptive refers to the innovation process that displaces entrenched products in established

[19] OECD. (2005). *The Measurement of Scientific and Technological Activities: Guidelines for Collecting and Interpreting Innovation Data: Oslo Manual (3rd ed.).* Oslo, Norway: OECD.
[20] Christensen, C. (1973). *The Innovator's Dilemma.* New York, NY: Harper Paperbacks.

markets to deliver dramatic value to stakeholders. An example of a disruptive innovation has been the emergence of digital media, which has replaced CDs in the music industry and is transforming the book industry.

Regardless of the industry, innovation is about change—in process and in thinking. And it's about producing outcomes that may be either radical or seemingly incremental but will bring about changes in processes, products, thinking, or business models within companies.

The product management lifecycle walks through the process of how products are managed in phases, from cradle to grave. Using this as the base process and adding an innovation funnel to evaluate, qualify, and prioritize ideas produces results. The approach focuses on gathering, categorizing, prioritizing, combining, and screening ideas, and on identifying viable options to implement these ideas.

Aligning the innovation and product management processes is essential. By aligning the process to the PMF, a product manager can integrate innovation activities into the workflow within an *existing* product management process. To gather ideas, product managers must use all of their available tools. The most successful and innovative companies use anthropological methods to discover unarticulated customer needs and gain penetrating customer insights. These needs must be well understood before any specific product can be built.

The entire process can be summarized in five phases:

1. **Staging.** The strategic innovation group is nominated, roles are identified, goals are determined, and a process is documented.

2. **Aligning.** This is critical. The innovation team and senior management align the focus and scope of the planned initiative.

3. **Exploring.** This is when the process is unleashed. Depending on the ideas generated and their scope, the team will discover new areas to begin the changes needed for innovation.

4. **Creating.** After capturing insights, the team begins to outline the business models or innovation changes that will take place.

5. **Mapping.** This road-mapping phase requires detailed timelines documenting when the ideas will be implemented.

6.2 Value Creation Processes

A value creation process[21] is the way the product manager and the project team organize around the work that needs to be completed. This process is when the team chooses the overall process to define market requirements, which are then concurrently broken down into functional specifications, design, development, and testing. Some of these deliverables may be created in phases or iterations. The plan could use a formal design phase or an evolution of the architecture and high-level design. Testing could be done as part of the process or saved for the end. The choice could be made to prototype for a while and then engineer the features, or implementation could be done by feature, observing how the architecture evolves.[22] Typically, engineers call these development lifecycles. However, from a product management perspective, the word "lifecycle" can be confusing. Therefore, it's best to name these processes based on what they do—create value for customers and organizations.

Historically, product managers have not been involved in choosing what value creation process is needed to deliver their product and features to market; rather, they typically leave it to the engineers or the quality department to decide. When the product manager does not choose, the value creation process can be filled with change, delays, and confusion as market demands and sales commitments force external constraints on a project that the broader development teams were not aware of, but the product manager expected all along. The way to change this behavior is for the product manager to better define the success criteria upfront and then understand the associated constraints or drivers (scope versus schedule versus cost). Said another way, a product manager should define upfront what would make the product a success based upon both market and organizational objectives. Once the success criteria are defined, the constraints on the product manager and the team can be understood. Only then can a risk- or business-based decision be made on what value creation process is right for the initiative.

A word of caution: this is not advising product managers to tell engineers how to do their job or software engineers how to code. On the contrary, the purpose is to understand the context of the process or processes that are being considered to deliver that value, and to have a collaborative team decide which process makes the most sense. Having the entire team better understand the context for the project and the end product can make all the difference. For example, the value creation process chosen for a product development environment would be different than that chosen for a manufacturing environment because the type of work and the constraints are different. Table 6-2 charts these differences and illustrates how choosing incorrectly could lead to failure.

[21] Geracie, G. (2010). *Business value creation: Collaborating with project management and business analysts to achieve sustainable market success.* Chicago, IL: Presentation at the Project Summit and Business Analyst World.

Table 6-1. Comparison of Manufacturing and Product Development Considerations

CONSIDERATION	PRODUCT DEVELOPMENT	MANUFACTURING
Availability of design requirements	Desired 100% upfront, but reality is that information arrives over the course of product development, requiring iteration/adjustment of design and/or rework.	Available 100% upfront (e.g., nut and bolt specifications).
Type of process	One-time process. Variability exists in the design process so that value can be added (the team adds value when they do something differently).	Repetitive manufacturing process.
Cost impact of change	Exponential. The later the change happens in the timeline, the larger the impact (i.e., exponential curve).	Linear. Change can happen anywhere along the timeline and have a linear impact.
Outputs	Designs "recipes" for complex products/solutions, valued ultimately in terms of impact on profit by the business, and in terms of valued functionality/utility by the customer. Value impacted by passage of time.	Tangible products (nuts and bolts). Inherent value relatively unaffected by time. The cost to produce each unit is the same as the one before and after it, so the cost is always the same.
Inventory	Design in process. Often, high value of inventory because cycle time for design in process turns is longer and number of turns is lower.	Work in process. Strategy is often to reduce work in process/inventory value through fast inventory turns.
Holding cost	Holding costs are high because of the low number of inventory turns and the increased risk of obsolescence as timelines lengthen. (Holding costs and design are very sensitive to time.)	Kept low by minimizing inventory volume through fast/multiple inventory turns annually.

Each value creation process optimizes for risk differently. There are three major kinds of value creation processes: serial, iterative, and iterative/incremental, which the software community typically calls "Agile."[23] However, care must be taken not to categorize all iterative/incremental processes as Agile. In software product development, Agile has become a catch-all for lifecycle descriptions—and consequently can be misused or applied improperly. Table 6-2 shows the different value creation processes and how a priority of constraints can help a product manager choose a process.

[22] Rothman, J. (2007). *Manage It! Your Guide to Modern, Pragmatic, Project Management.* Raleigh, NC; Dallas, TX: The Pragmatic Bookshelf.

[23] Rothman, J. (2007). *Manage It! Your Guide to Modern, Pragmatic, Project Management.* Raleigh, NC; Dallas, TX: The Pragmatic Bookshelf.

Table 6-2. Value Creation Processes

VALUE CREATION PROCESS TYPE	ENGINEERING OR DEVELOPMENT NAME FOR PROCESS	STRENGTHS & NECESSARY CONDITIONS FOR SUCCESS	PRIORITY OF CONSTRAINTS (WHAT IS THE MOST IMPORTANT DRIVER?)
Serial	Waterfall, Phase–gate	• Manages cost risk (if management uses the phase gates) • Known and agreed-upon requirements • Well understood system architecture • Well understood requirements that are stable and not in flux • Product development team is stable and dedicated properly to the initiative • Organization willing to accept risk of schedule delays due to defect identification and resolution that come much later in the process	1. Features set 2. Low defects 3. Time to release
Iterative	IBM Rational Unified Process (RUP), Spiral, evolutionary prototyping.	• Manages technical risk • Ever-evolving requirements	1. Features set 2. Low defects 3. Time to release
Iterative/Incremental	Lean, Agile (variations such as Scrum, Extreme Programming [XP])	• Manages both schedule and technical risk • Handles emergent requirements • Requires deep collaboration (easier to do with a co-located integrated team)	1. Time to release 2. Low defects 3. Feature set

The following sections will further explain the different types of value creation processes, providing the background needed to choose the appropriate one.

6.2.1 Serial Processes: Waterfall and Phase-Gate

In a serial value creation process, the product team moves through steps sequentially. Progress is seen as flowing steadily downward (like a waterfall) through the requirements, design, development, verification, and launch phases. The general idea is that the team first develops or obtains market requirements. Based on the market requirements, the team develops product requirements and performs analysis and design to determine the system, or "big picture." Once everyone agrees on the big picture, the team starts development. Once development is complete, the team integrates all the pieces and begins final testing. Although it isn't necessary for one phase to finish before the next phase begins, the one-phase-at-a-time mentality is common in the industry. The unmodified "Waterfall model" (Figure 6-2) shows progress flowing from top to bottom.

Figure 6-2. Serial (or Waterfall) Model

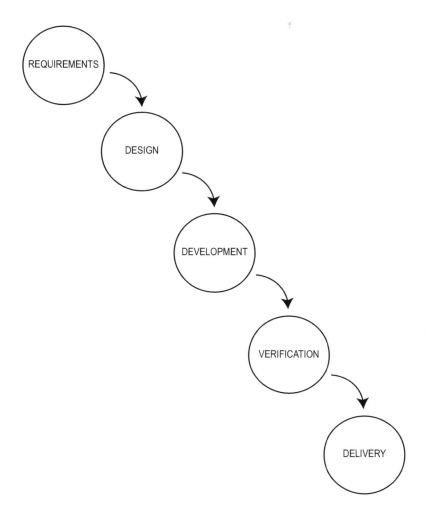

The serial, or Waterfall, process originated in the manufacturing and construction industries—highly structured physical environments in which after-the-fact changes are prohibitively costly, if not impossible. Serial processes can also be found in the medical device and pharmaceutical industries, where clear, orderly processes must be documented and followed, and clear traceability can be mapped to ensure quality and protect against external regulatory audits.

To be clear, a serial process is not a project management process. Instead, it is a product development process and should be considered a series of steps or techniques used to deliver product in a *serial* fashion. Typically, serial processes take longer because they are designed to be able to predict how long it will take to implement features, find and fix defects, integrate pieces of the system, or manage requirements changes—activities that are inherently unpredictable. Without a working crystal ball, it's impossible to forecast everything you need to know about the future. In a serial process, you have to allow extra time for tasks, like a final system test at the end of the project, to compensate for risks and problems you couldn't predict during the project.[24] It might make sense to allow for this extra time in development, depending on the product and situation.

A serial process can be advantageous from a quality perspective where external audits exist. Because it allows for clear lines of demarcation on the development process, it can show an external auditor that a clearly thought-out step-by-step process was followed before moving into the development phase. The serial process may be perceived as taking longer in development. But it may save time overall if it hastens the external auditing and approval processes. This process could be helpful in the medical device industry, for example, where FDA approval is required.

To arrive at product go/no-go decisions, a formal serial process known as phase-gate reviews can be instituted within an organization. The phase-gate process will typically review project deliverables and achievements during the relevant process phase and collectively determine whether to proceed to the next phase. Considerations such as strategic fit, technical feasibility, risk, market attractiveness, and competitive positioning are to be used consistently in decision making. The decision criteria represent the standards for management judgment and decision making and provide guidance in support of their assessment of content, quality, and consistency in decision making.

When a phase-gate review is complete, the participating team members recommend that the business owner take one of four possible steps: 1) continue to the next phase (go), 2) cancel the project (no go), 3) redirect the project based on strategic changes or gaps discussed during the review (rework), or 4) defer a decision (hold).

Phase-gate reviews are not the same as technical, architectural, or deliverable reviews, and will not replace them, as technical and other reviews should be conducted before phase-gate reviews.

During the phase-gate review process, decision makers ask a series of critical questions and examine key elements to move to the next gate. Here are some examples.

- Strategic alignment – the project and product fit the business strategy.

- Market of a minimum size exists and will still exist at time of launch.

- Technical feasibility is reasonably likely – risk areas have been identified and solutions are available that can be reasonably acquired by the project.

[24] Rothman, J. (2007). *Manage It! Your Guide to Modern, Pragmatic, Project Management.* Raleigh, NC; Dallas, TX: The Pragmatic Bookshelf.

- A product advantage or value proposition exists.

- A marketing plan exists to avoid building products or product capabilities that lack a "go to market" strategy and plan.

- An acceptable return on risk-weighted investment exists.

- Extent to which the new product offers unique benefits, meets customer needs better than competitive products, or provides superior value for the money invested exists. These estimates should arise from actual tests with customers. How were customers involved with evaluation of the product? What was their reaction? What criteria were used to select the best concept?

- Relative resources and experience of the team in projects of the scale, complexity, and technologies sufficient to support the development effort are available.

- Testing has been comprehensive and robust, ensuring a quality product.

- No "show-stopper" issues exist. If they do, can they be mitigated? And if so, what is the mitigation plan?

- All project and product risks have been communicated with appropriate mitigation and contingency plans.

- All parties have been communicated with, and all parties agree with the plan and the approach for execution.

Gate reviews are not intended to be informal discussions. They are critical business decision-making meetings used to optimize product/portfolio performance, scrutinize development investments, and increase the quality of development execution. Typically it's customary for all phase-gate review materials to be distributed at least one week before a gate review meeting to allow for adequate review and inquiries. This material should be sent from the project leader to the phase-gate committee members. The phase-gate committee members, at a minimum, should have the following cross-functional representatives:

- Product management

- Quality

- Manufacturing

- Sales

- Marketing

- Legal

- Engineering

- Operations

- Implementation

- Project management

During the meeting, the team will present the material and information to the phase-gate committee, demonstrating that the team has completed all necessary deliverables and work and is ready to move to the next phase.

6.2.2 Iterative

The basic idea behind the iterative process is to develop a system of repeated cycles (iterative) in smaller portions (incremental). With this process, the developer can take advantage of what was learned during the development of earlier versions. At each iteration, the team modifies the design and adds new functions. Most of the iterative processes do not require that pieces of the product be finished at the end of each iteration cycle. They also do not require concurrent testing and integration. The overall goal, from a product management perspective, is to get customer/ user feedback more quickly by creating and obtaining feedback on portions of the product sooner instead of waiting until the entire system is complete. The portion of the product being shown to a customer should highlight the problem and provide a solution that can be understood and implemented easily.[25]

To guide the iteration process, the product manager should create a project control list that contains a record of all tasks to be performed. This list should include such items as new features to be implemented and areas of the existing solution to be redesigned. During analysis, the product manager is constantly revising the control list. However, it is possible that the control list might also be managed by a business analyst or project manager in some organizations. The design and implementation of any iteration should be simple, straightforward, and modular, supporting redesign at that stage or as a task is added to the project control list.

The Rational Unified Process (RUP) is an iterative software development process framework created by the Rational Software Corporation, a division of IBM since 2003. RUP is not a single concrete prescriptive process, but rather an adaptable process intended to be tailored by the development organizations and software project teams that will select the elements of the process appropriate for their needs. RUP is based on a set of building blocks, or content elements, that describe what

---

[25] Rothman, J. (2007). *Manage it! Your Guide to Modern, Pragmatic, Project Management.* Raleigh, NC; Dallas, TX: The Pragmatic Bookshelf.

will be produced, the necessary skills required, and the step-by-step explanation describing how specific development goals will be achieved. The main building blocks, or content elements, are:

- Roles (who) – sets of related skills, competencies, and responsibilities.

- Work Products (what) – the results of a task, including all the documents and models produced while working through the process.

- Tasks (how) – a unit of work assigned to a role that provides a meaningful result.

6

Within each iteration, tasks are categorized into nine disciplines: six engineering disciplines (business modeling, requirements, analysis and design, implementation, test, and deployment) and three supporting disciplines (configuration and change management, project management, and environment).

The RUP process has four phases: inception, elaboration, construction, and transition. These phases allow the process to be presented at a high level, similar to a Waterfall-style project, although the key to the process lies in the iterations of development that lie within each of the phases. Also, each phase has one key objective and milestone at the end that denotes the objective.

In the inception phase, the product manager establishes a business case that includes the business context, success factors (expected revenue, market recognition, etc.), and a financial forecast. To complement the business case, the product manager also generates a basic use case model, project plan, initial risk assessment, and project description (the core project requirements, constraints, and key features). After these are completed, the project is checked by the stakeholders against the following criteria:

- Scope definition and cost/schedule estimates.

- Product requirements understanding as evidenced by the fidelity of the primary use cases.

- Credibility of the cost/schedule estimates, priorities, risks, and development process.

- Depth and breadth of any architectural prototype that was developed.

- Baseline establishment, to compare actual and planned expenditures.

If the project does not pass this milestone, it can either be canceled or reconsidered after being redesigned to better meet the criteria.

The elaboration phase is where the project starts to take shape. In this phase the team analyzes the problem domain and the architecture of the project takes its basic form. This phase must pass the milestone by meeting the following deliverables:

- An 80% complete use case model in which the use cases and the actors have been identified and most of the use case descriptions are developed. A description of the software architecture in a software system development process.

- An executable architecture that realizes architecturally significant use cases.

- Revised business case and risk lists.

- A development plan for the overall project.

- Prototypes that demonstrably mitigate each identified technical risk.

If the project cannot pass this milestone, there is still time for it to be canceled or redesigned. But after leaving this phase, the project transitions into a high-risk operation where changes are much more difficult and can be detrimental.

In the construction phase, the main focus is on developing components and other features of the system. This is the phase when the bulk of the coding takes place. In larger projects, several construction iterations may be developed in an effort to divide the use cases into manageable segments that produce demonstrable prototypes.

The activities of the transition phase include training the end users and support team and beta testing the system to validate it against the end users' expectations. The product is also checked against the quality level set in the inception phase.

6.2.3 Iterative/Incremental Processes—Agile, Scrum, Extreme Programming (XP), and Lean

The basic concept behind iterative/incremental-type processes is to develop a product through repeated cycles (iterative) and in small portions at a time (incremental), allowing the team to take advantage of what they learned while developing earlier parts or versions of the system.

The process starts by delivering a smaller subset of requirements. The team then iteratively enhances the product based on customer, stakeholder, and user feedback and evolves the features and functionality until the full system is implemented. Smaller, more frequent releases allow teams to deliver business value to the customer more frequently. This probe-and-learn process also allows the team to respond to environments where requirements are constantly changing.

When discussing iterative and incremental development, the terms *iteration* and *increment* should not be used synonymously. *Iteration* refers to the cyclic nature of a process in which activities are repeated in a structured manner. *Increment* refers to the quantifiable outcome of each iteration. Iterations can offer a development process of cyclical refinement, where the process improves upon what was already done. Incremental development takes it a step further, where the process yields progress against the overall product objectives of the next release or a new version of the product.

Agile is an umbrella term used to describe a number of development methodologies that share common principles associated with incremental/iterative processes and that correspond to the Manifesto for Agile Software Development.[26]

Agile methods focus on customer satisfaction and company goals, team collaboration, communication, frequent inspection, small and self-organizing teams, accountability, transparency, visual management, and continuous improvement. As mentioned in section 6.2, Agile can be used incorrectly to lump a number of different incremental or hybrid processes together that are not truly Agile. Some common Agile processes include Scrum, Extreme Programming (XP), and Feature-Driven Development. This text will first describe Agile from a product management perspective, then describe how it differs from other processes such as Lean or true incremental.

Agile approaches assume that change is pervasive and that a product manager's ability to correctly predict in detail how best to address customer needs is limited. Therefore, Agilists rely on the use of a probe-and-learn approach that incorporates frequent customer feedback. As a result, product managers working with well-run Agile teams enjoy greater visibility into the progress of their products, greater flexibility to adjust the product plan based on new information and emergent requirements, and extremely high quality when automated unit testing is fully implemented. Those who favor Agile feel that it gives product managers the option to release smaller increments of value more frequently and allows them to exercise this option if doing so provides competitive advantage or a better return on investment. Depending on how roles and responsibilities are split, working with an Agile team may require deeper collaboration and discipline. Agile practitioners believe the benefit of making this additional time commitment is fewer surprises, misalignments, miscommunications, and delays at the end of the development cycle.

[26] Beck, K., Beedle, M., van Bennekum, A., Cockburn, A., Cunningham, W., Fowler, M...Thomas, D. (2001). *The Manifesto for Agile Software Development*. Retrieved from http://agilemanifesto.org/.

The Agile Theory

Agile software methodologies are constructed differently than sequential methods such as those found in manufacturing. Manufacturing is suited to a defined process model: defined inputs yield defined outputs. Manufacturing excels at repeating the same steps to produce near identical items. Traditional software development methodologies like Waterfall attempt to map software development to a defined, sequential process (Figure 6-3).

Figure 6-3: Traditional Software Development Assumes a Defined Sequential Process

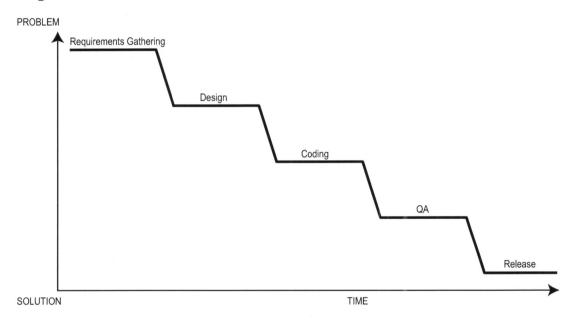

Agile methods assume writing new software is more like the non-linear path found in new product development than the predictable path of manufacturing. New product development requires research and creativity—both relatively unpredictable activities. New product development is thus considered an empirical process, with the team cycling between creating knowledge and identifying problems (Figure 6-3). The best way to manage an empirical process is through frequent inspection and adjustment.[27] Agilists believe that software development, including the product management step of gathering and validating requirements, is best suited to an empirical model.

[27] Schwaber, K., & Beedle, M. (2002). *Agile Software Development with Scrum*. Upper Saddle River, NJ: Prentice Hall. pp 24–25, 106–108.

Figure 6-4: Software Development Follows an Empirical Process

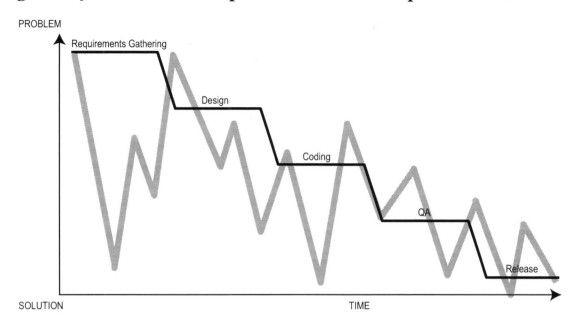

Requirements

Through the Agile process, the functional requirements are often written as user stories.

A common format for user stories is:

> As a <type of user>, I want to <do something>, so that I can derive <a benefit>.[28]

The user story captures the most important aspects of a requirement: who it is for, what they are trying to accomplish, why it matters to them. The user story also acts as a placeholder for a deeper conversation about the requirement. During this conversation details are added to the story. The user story is not a requirement specification in the traditional sense of the term. This supports Agilist's belief that face-to-face communication is the most effective way to create a shared understanding of a requirement between the development team and business stakeholders.

Estimating and Planning

Once an organization creates a vision for the product, the team develops a list of market and product requirements. The list is commonly prioritized by business value, risk, and dependencies. The prioritized list of requirements is typically

---

[28] Cohn, M. Retrieved from http://www.mountaingoatsoftware.com/topics/user-stories. To learn more on user stories, refer to Cohn, M. (2004). *User Stories Applied for Agile Software Development.* Boston, MA: Addison-Wesley.

called a product backlog. The development team estimates the relative effort of each requirement in the product backlog. The usual metric is a story point, but it can really be anything. Thus, a feature estimated at 10 story points is expected to take twice as long to develop as a feature estimated at 5 story points.[29]

After each iteration, the team counts how many story points it completed. This is the team's velocity and a measure of their throughput. The velocity can now be used to estimate how far through the product backlog the team will be at each iteration, as well as how many story points the team should commit to completing for the upcoming iteration.

By knowing how many story points of functionality are planned for a release, the product manager can track progress at each iteration and judge whether the release is on schedule by using a burndown chart (a graphical representation of work that is left to do versus time). Because each iteration produces working software, the product manager can see the actual progress and catch any miscommunications early in the process. Further, each iteration allows the product manager to adjust the plan based on the best available knowledge. For example, scope can be scaled back to ensure a release date will be met, new requirements can be added (Figure 6-7), and/or the requirements in the product backlog can be reprioritized, adjusted, replaced, or removed.

Figure 6-5. Agile Release Burndown Chart

This illustrates that the scope added in iteration three will require adjusting the number of iterations needed to complete the release and, ultimately, the release date.

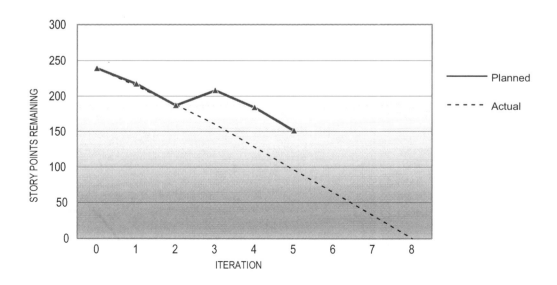

[29] Cohen, G. (2010). *Agile Excellence for Product Managers*. Cupertino, CA: Super Star Press.

Iterative Development

Agile teams develop software in iterations that generally range from one to four weeks. The iteration encompasses all phases of the development cycle, including product definition, analysis, design, code, and test. Each iteration produces a functional slice of the software that is usually tested and documented. At the end of each iteration, progress is reviewed based on the software created in the iteration, and the product backlog and the release burndown are updated.

As stated above, Agile teams prefer to develop software in functional slices. A functional slice cuts through all the layers of the product, from the interface to the logic and data tiers. A product team that spends a month creating the data tier, a month creating the logic tier, and then a month creating the interface would not be developing in an Agile fashion. Each iteration may not, however, produce rich, fully featured code. Early iterations might only produce a log-in screen or the ability to create a document but not edit or delete the document. Over time, with each successive iteration, more capability and polish is layered onto the product until it is ready to be released into the marketplace.

Visual Management

Often called information radiators, Agile emphasizes visual management so team members and management can see how projects are progressing and act quickly when needed. In addition to the burndown charts, many teams use physical or electronic product backlogs and task boards (Figure 6-6).

Figure 6-6. A Simple Task Board

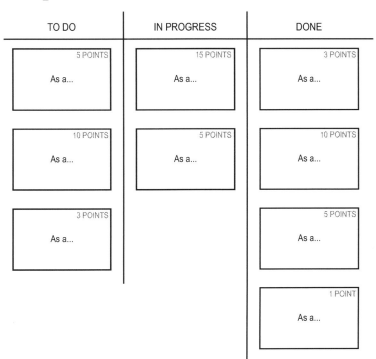

On the task board, the tasks start on the left. When a developer starts to work on a task, they add their initials to the task and move it to the "In progress" column. When the task is completed, they move it to the "Done" column. Boards may include additional columns such as Design, Testing, Sign-off, etc.

Although the task board's main purpose is to help the team self-manage the work, it also provides quick insight into the status of each requirement. The product manager knows which requirements are in queue, which are being worked on, and which have been completed. When a requirement shows up in the "Done" column, the product manager can quickly verify that it meets its intent and raise any issues.

Scrum

Scrum is an Agile process that was developed in the mid-1990s by Jeff Sutherland, Ken Schwaber, Mike Beedle, and others. It does not specify any development practices, but to make it work for them, teams have routinely integrated some XP practices like automated unit testing and continuous integration. A scrum team consists of the following:

- Scrum Master – Ensures scrum practice is followed and facilitates so the team can identify areas of improvement and remove roadblocks to its progress.

- Product Owner – Responsible for the success of the product. The product owner manages and prioritizes the requirements in the product backlog to maximize the value of the team's efforts.

- Team – Responsible for developing the product and doing it well. The team is composed of one or more developers and may include other roles (e.g., database administrators, user interactions engineers, quality assurance engineers) needed to build the product.

Teams contain between five and nine people. The team should be cross-functional and have all the necessary skills to transform the requirements on the product backlog into working software. With Scrum, when more than nine team members are needed, a new team is added instead of adding to the existing team. Teams smaller than five can also work. But because interpersonal communication tends to break down in teams larger than nine, it's wise to heed the upper limit.

Development occurs in iterations, which in Scrum are known as sprints. Sprints are defined as timeboxed and protected iterations that last no longer than 30 days.

Before the first sprint, a release planning meeting is held to set product goals and priorities for the release (which will likely require multiple sprints). Each sprint is structured around four types of meetings: planning, development, review, and retrospective:

- Planning – deciding what to build and creating requirements (the list of tasks needed to complete the user stories that the team has accepted into the sprint).

- Development – the actual coding and testing of the product. This is longest phase of the sprint and accounts for about 85% of the iteration.

- Review – demonstrating to the stakeholders what was built in the last sprint to get feedback for the next planning meeting (you need to know where you are to know what to build next).

- Retrospective – reflecting on what is working well and what could be improved.

Figure 6-7. Scrum Process Diagram

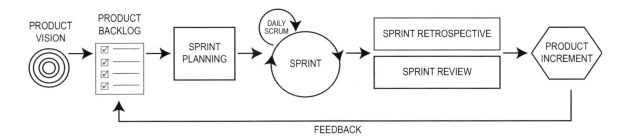

During the development phase, the team has a daily 15-minute stand-up meeting known as the Daily Scrum. During the Daily Scrum, team members share what they did since the last meeting, what they plan to do before the next meeting, and if anything is blocking their progress. The team also maintains a Sprint burndown chart in hours to track and plan their work. This is similar to the release burndown chart in Figure 6-7 except that it includes the task hours remaining within the iteration after each day.

Extreme Programming (XP)

Extreme Programming (XP) was developed by Kent Beck in 1996 while working on a payroll system at Chrysler. He describes XP as a "lightweight methodology for small-to-medium-sized teams developing software in the face of vague or rapidly changing requirements."[30] XP gets its name by taking common sense development principles to an extreme level. If code reviews are considered good practice, XP advises performing continual code review by programming in pairs. If testing helps produce bug-free code, XP advocates writing automated unit tests that run multiple times during the day and performing frequent end-user and functional tests. If refactoring helps improve code, XP dictates that developers always look for opportunities to do it. If integration testing helps uncover issues, XP followers complete software builds once or multiple times each day.

XP shares many similarities with Scrum, but does not have formal roles like the scrum master and product owner. XP does specify development practices covering testing, refactoring, continuous integration, pair programming, simple design, and coding standards. XP teams do not decompose stories into tasks during their planning phase. Thus, teams maintain a story point (rather than task hour) burndown chart during the iteration.

Lean Development

Lean methods derive from principles used in the integrated socio-technical Toyota Production System. James Womack, author of the book *Lean Thinking*, defines Lean as "creating ever more value for customers with ever fewer resources."[31] In addition to manufacturing, Lean has been applied to many other fields, including services, health care, and product development.

Similar to the Agile methods described in this section, Lean advocates a focus on the customer, collaboration, empowered teams, continuous improvement, and visual controls. Lean teams focus on the efficient flow of value through the system. In this way, Lean differs from other Agile methods. Lean does not use a time-boxed iteration to set the cadence of the development process.

Lean development focuses on fast, flexible flow, which looks to optimize value delivery by first minimizing queues. Queues are minimized by working in small batches. Small batches are managed by limiting the amount of work that may flow through the system at one time (also known as work in progress, or WIP). Because the development team is not spread across multiple projects or large blocks of

[30] Beck, K. (1999). *Extreme Programming Explained: Embrace Change.* Boston, MA: Addison-Wesley Professional.

[31] Womack, J. P. Retrieved from http://www.lean.org/common/display/?o=1366. To learn more, refer to Womack, J. P., & Hones, D. T. (2003). *Lean Thinking: Banish Waste and Create Wealth in Your Corporation.* New York, NY: Free Press.

work, this approach creates short cycle times. As cycle times shorten, the system approaches single piece flow – the ideal state where parts are manufactured one at a time and flow throughout the manufacturing and supply chain as a single unit.[32]

Lean addresses many of the challenges of traditional Waterfall development. One such issue is lengthy development times. Lean advocates believe that long development cycles occur because all work for a release must be fully defined or completed before passing it to the next phase. Waterfall encourages large batches of work, usually representing months of development, being managed through the system, which can create large queues at each stage. In an environment where requirements are changing rapidly, the typical serial/ Waterfall method may significantly reduce the product manager's ability to respond to new opportunities and information.[33] In these environments, Lean may be a process worth considering.

Lean also focuses the team on optimizing the whole system rather than areas in the system. Because it is expensive, many companies' plans are designed to ensure 100% utilization of engineering talent. Large batches of work are queued for the engineers. Because there is no slack in this system, any deviation from plan delays the project and all the projects behind it. As a result, release dates vary widely from plan. Further, feedback can be delayed in this system. A mistake in a requirement may not be caught until many months later during quality assurance. What would have been a quick fix if caught immediately can become a lengthy and involved process requiring meetings, document updates, code changes, and retesting.[34]

Lean teams employ a kanban[35,36] board rather than a task board. Task and kanban boards look similar, but where the task board is for tracking tasks, the kanban board is used to visualize flow through the system and enforce WIP limits. Likewise, Lean teams use a cumulative flow diagram instead of a burndown chart to track progress. The cumulative flow diagram highlights the relationship between WIP (how many items are being worked on at any one time), cycle time (how long it takes to complete an item once work is started on it), and throughput (how many items per week or unit time are completed).

---

[32] Reinersten, D. G. (2009). *The Principles of Product Development Flow: Second Generation Lean Product Development.* Redono Beach, CA: Celeritas Publishing.

[33] Ibid, p. 56–57.

[34] Ibid, p. 58.

[35] Kanban, Japanese for "visual cards," is a Toyota-created visual scheduling system that outlines what to produce, when to produce it, and how much to produce.

[36] Not to be confused with the Kanban Method, which also uses a kanban board. The Kanban Method is a Lean change management methodology developed by David Anderson and described in his 2010 book *Kanban: Successful Evolutionary Change for Your Technology Business.*

There are many more iterative and incremental processes than discussed in this brief treatment. Product managers should work with their teams to evaluate which method or methods would work best given the business culture, nature of the products, and the team's ability. Transitioning to Agile requires learning and practicing new skills to become proficient. Although training and coaching can shorten the learning curve and improve the chances for success, the team must decide whether the benefits outweigh the time needed for learning, practicing, and training. Additionally, the organization should consider whether the cost of transitioning to Agile for more mature products with a limited life expectancy justifies the cost.

Chapter 7

Product Management's Relationship with Other Disciplines

The product management process naturally interacts with several other processes. To the extent each of these is appropriately involved in the product management lifecycle, it's vital they all work together to ensure the optimum product management outcome. Although these relationships may come into play at specific times, core project management methods and processes are relied on throughout the entire product management lifecycle and often provide the execution platform necessary for bringing products to market. Section 7.2 describes these core methods and processes in more detail and shows how to effectively integrate them into the product management framework.

Program management and *portfolio management* are two management processes related to project management with unique attributes and value when applied to the product management framework. The interrelationships between project, program, and portfolio management are described in Sections 7.6 and 7.7.

7.1 A Closer Look at Project Management Methods and Their Application within the Product Management Framework

Project management is the discipline of planning, organizing, and managing resources to successfully complete specific project goals and objectives. Just as this ProdBOK introduces a framework, similar frameworks exist in the world of project management. Two of the more prominent frameworks are the Project Management Body of Knowledge (PMBOK®) Guide, developed by the Project Management Institute (PMI), and a methodology known as PRINCE2® (PRojects IN Controlled Environments), developed by the Office of Government Commerce, an independent office of Her Majesty's Treasury of the United Kingdom. Examining either of these frameworks is a useful way to understand the details of project management—its components' structure, methods, and processes that comprise the overall discipline of project management.

Within nearly any project management framework a number of individual methods and processes exist. The most common of these, core project management methods and processes, are identified and briefly described in section 7.2. Sections 7.3 through 7.5 identify ways that these methods and processes can be used or adapted to support the three major stages of successful product development: conception (the fuzzy front end), product development, and commercialization/operations.

The PMBOK Guide and PRINCE2 are commonly used to support project management efforts within an organization or to manage a project's lifecycle. These two documents address project management from different perspectives. Despite some differences in terminology, they have a common thread in terms of methods and processes. Project management methods and processes remain relatively constant. However, not every project will need to execute the full range of processes in each process group. By identifying the core methods and processes, regardless of the approach, a foundation for using project management effectively in the product management lifecycle can be established.

The type of project, product, and the culture of an organization will determine the type of process to be used, but the core process groups of initiating, planning, executing, controlling, and closing are common across many project management standards. Applying project management in the product management process can increase productivity, improve output quality, create efficient use of resources, and hasten time to market.

Project management is composed of a set of related processes that can be applied effectively to the product management lifecycle. Applying project management logically and at the appropriate levels of rigor within the product management lifecycle can produce very positive results and enhance a product manager's efforts. A well thought-out approach for using the tools and techniques of project management will help a product manager effectively use organizational resources and will add structure, standardization, and predictability to product development and enhancement projects.

According to PMBOK, PRINCE2, and other project management standards,[37] the project manager has overall project responsibility. To achieve success, the project manager should work closely with the project sponsor on staffing requirements and funding availability. The project manager is responsible for completing the project on time, within budget, and meeting any predefined requirements, including performance and quality.

[37] Some of these other standards include Association for Project Management (U.K.) and International Project Management Association, or American Society for the Advancement of Project Management, IPMA-USA's ICB and National Competence Baselines.

The project manager should be assigned as early as possible in the lifecycle—ideally at project inception—to establish project ownership and management responsibility and to begin to develop the project requirements. There is often an added benefit in assigning specific product domains to a project manager: it can allow the project manager to accrue additional knowledge about a particular product or group of products and increase both domain expertise and team efficiency during their involvement.

7.2 Core Project Management Methods and Processes

Project management, whether following PMBOK or PRINCE2, uses a common set of processes, tools, and techniques to achieve a project's objectives. This section briefly describes these methods and processes.

At the overall project level, methods and processes are subdivided into five high-level categories, or major process groups. The process groups are initiation, planning, execution, control, and closing. These processes are generally associated with the activities found in each phase of a project lifecycle. For example, regardless of the number of phases found within a project lifecycle, each phase is initiated, planned, executed, controlled, and closed. This application of the core project management processes provides a level of consistency throughout the project lifecycle.

7.2.1 Methods and Processes Used in Project Initiation

The term *initiation* generally refers to the activities associated with defining and approving a new project or determining whether a project should continue into the next phase/stage as a current phase is nearing completion. Typically, the core methods and processes include:

- Identify the project sponsor – Determine the source of funding for the project.

- Review business case – Review projected financial performance, project feasibility, and connection to business strategy.

- Develop project charter – Prepare a high-level document that describes the project, anticipated risks, key stakeholders, major milestones, constraints, and boundaries.

- Conduct a kick-off meeting – Provide the project team with information about the project and prepare to develop detailed plans.

- Establish project baselines – Baselines associated with project cost, schedule, time, and quality (performance) are used to measure the effectiveness of a project's execution. As a result of the unit's performance against these baselines, the project team may propose acceptable contingencies and buffers to ensure that change can be successfully managed within the overall constraints of the project.

- Approve the next phase plan – Initiation also refers to the decision to allow a project to continue into the next phase. Reviews are generally scheduled at or near the completion of a project phase. The review is an evaluation of project performance. Performance reviews include a comparison between actual results and approved baselines. Schedule variance, cost variance, scope changes, quality variances, risk, benefits realization, and other factors are considered to determine whether the organization should continue to support the project.

7.2.2 Methods and Processes Used in Project Planning

Project planning includes a set of processes that will detail how the project will be implemented and who will perform the activities. Project planning involves defining the scope of the project and the actions that must be taken to achieve the established objectives. Core planning processes typically include:

- Define the project scope – Creating a detailed description of the work that must be completed to produce the desired deliverable and developing a project scope statement or statement of work. This document provides a basis for more detailed planning.

- Implement a work breakdown structure – Breaking down the defined project scope of work into more detail, ensuring that the project is laid out clearly and completely. This provides the basis for determining project activity cost and duration estimates. It is also used to control changes to the project scope.

- Develop schedule – Placing project activities defined in the work breakdown structure in a logical sequence, determining resource requirements, estimating activity durations, identifying the project critical path, refining the schedule to meet requirements, and identifying where project slack exists.

- Determine project budget – Producing an estimated total cost for the project by determining the costs of each activity and aggregating all costs to create a baseline.

- Plan quality – The level of quality associated with the project will impact cost, schedule, and decisions about the type of resources that may be used. Quality (project performance) must be planned at the beginning. The deliverable associated with process is called the quality plan. This plan is based on project requirements and success criteria and describes how conformance to requirements will be validated and how product and project errors will be prevented.

- Plan communications – As projects are executed and results are reported, the project stakeholders require updated information about how the project is performing. Project communications planning generally includes:

  o Identifying and analyzing project stakeholders

  o Determining the information needs of each stakeholder

  o Deciding the methods to gather and distribute information

  o Establishing what information will be provided to the project stakeholders and the detail and frequency at which the information will be provided

- Deploy risk management – A process that parallels all other planning processes. Risk management is quantifying uncertainty. During project planning, the project team must consider the uncertainties associated with all facets of the project, such as:

  o Deciding the methods to gather and distribute information

  o Inaccuracies in estimating activity duration and costs

  o The culture(s) associated with delivering the project

  o Changes in organizational processes

  o External factors, such as the potential for regulatory changes

  o The use of internal versus external resources and the related impact on capital expenditures

  o The economy

Risk management includes identifying potential risk events, prioritizing risk events through detailed analysis, planning response strategies, and determining how to control risk during the entire project lifecycle.

7.2.3 Methods and Processes Used in Project Execution, Monitoring, and Control

Project execution, monitoring, and control are about making sure the project schedule and other baseline success measures, such as cost, scope, and quality, meet requirements. The core methods and processes of project execution and control include:

- Verifying the work completed – As work is completed and deliverables are produced, an assessment is performed to determine whether the work and the deliverable are acceptable.

- Managing change requests – A change control process is established during the detailed planning of the project. It is necessary to manage change to avoid adding work into the project plan, creating an unfavorable situation known as "scope creep." A change control process will help minimize the costs associated with change and keep the project team focused on objectives.

- Performing quality assurance reviews – Quality reviews or quality audits are performed periodically during the project lifecycle to identify performance areas that show variances or deviations from the original baselines established during initiation and planning. These audits and reviews are feedback mechanisms designed to help get projects back within acceptable performance parameters.

- Acquiring project resources – As the project plan is executed, the project manager and team will obtain the resources identified in the plan. Resources may include people, machines, tools, and equipment.

- Procuring goods and services – It is often necessary to obtain services and resources from external suppliers. Procurement may involve make-or-buy decisions, requests for proposals, and negotiations to determine terms and conditions of the contract.

- Managing variances – During plan execution, project metrics and work results are analyzed and deviations will be discovered on all but the most trivial projects. These deviations may be interpreted as favorable (e.g., ahead of schedule) or unfavorable (e.g., over budget). An excellent technique for measuring variance, although not commonly used, is earned value management. Earned value management compares planned and actual results to determine whether variances exist and the extent of their magnitude. Corrective actions are taken based on the variance analysis.

- Managing stakeholder expectations – The information needs of project stakeholders will vary depending on the stakeholder's interest in the project and their authority. During planning, the project manager and team generally develop a communications plan for disseminating mission-critical information to all of the appropriate stakeholders.

- Monitoring and managing risk – Project risk is present from the initiation of the project through completion. Risk management is a process that includes identifying potential risk events, identifying risk symptoms or triggers, prioritizing risks, determining the most effective response to a risk situation, and monitoring and controlling new risks that may develop. Risk control also addresses risks that have been mitigated but may reappear as a threat to the project. This is the phase when contingency plans and mitigation strategies are commonly used.

7.2.4 Methods and Processes Used in Project Closeout

Closeout processes bring the project or project phase to an organized and well-planned conclusion. The core methods and processes include:

- Conducting final project reviews – Once the project and all deliverables are complete, the project manager conducts a post-project review to analyze overall project performance and deliverables as well as the suppliers and contractors involved. Although it is common for the team to document lessons learned and identify areas for improvement at this time, it is preferable to document and identify these more frequently throughout the project phases and as processes are executed. This is advisable because if the team waits until closeout:

  o They might forget important information from early in the project.

  o The benefits of process improvement can be realized immediately rather than at the next project.

  o Key staff, who may have important project knowledge, may no longer be with the project during a closing phase.

- Closing all financial accounts – In some instances, projects will have an accounting system that identifies the source of funding and how charges are processed. At project completion, a final accounting is performed and the accounts associated with the project are closed to prevent additional charges to the accounts.

- Completing and closing all procurements – Many projects include contractors and subcontractors. Work is often outsourced and work orders are processed. Procurement also includes purchasing materials and paying accounts. At project completion, the project manager and team review all purchases, contracted services, work orders, and other procurement items, including contract terms and conditions, and arrange for termination according to organizational procedures.

7.3 Applying Project Management during the Conceive Stage ("Fuzzy Front End")

Project management can effectively be used in what is commonly referred to as the conception or ideation stage of a project – the "fuzzy front end" of the product management process. Project management is generally considered a regimented and logical process. If this regimented nature veers toward inflexibility, there could be problems if it is implemented incorrectly in the dynamic front-end of product management. Still, there are many advantages to using project management core processes early in the product management lifecycle.

In most organizations, product management is responsible for creating a new product or improving a product or service and bringing enhancements to market. There are two parallel paths involved in this process. The first involves idea generation, product design, detailed engineering, development, testing, and delivery or deployment. The second involves market research and marketing analysis. Each of these paths is important and can benefit from project management's structured approach. New product development and the product management process are critical to an organization's growth and are actually part of the high-level strategic processes of product lifecycle management. Stakeholder communication, frequent cross-discipline reviews, and major executive gate or milestone approvals of the project management process can improve the quality of the product, increase profitability, improve time to market, and increase the efficiency of organizational resource use.

The fuzzy front end is the often unorganized, sometimes messy starting point or kick-off period of the new product development process. It's the time when an organization develops ideas for new products, formulates a concept of the product or products to be developed, and decides whether to invest in further developing the idea.

During this time, when ideas are flowing and interpretations of designs, customer needs, and business needs vary, it may be difficult to use a set of defined tools and techniques. But without them, the fuzzy front end can become prolonged and extremely costly. In most organizations, there are limited resources, time, and money available; therefore, a process is needed to keep the team focused on generating a meaningful outcome. The fuzzy front end actually ends when an organization approves and begins formal development of the concept.

Typically, a project is arranged in phases. Each phase has specific activities, outcomes, and deliverables. Engaging project managers early in the lifecycle can help identify those critical activities, outcomes, and deliverables sooner and can maximize the effectiveness of the overall project and make delivery of the product to the customer more efficient.

Closely comparing the project lifecycle and the product management lifecycle reveals similarities and provides the opportunity to use project management techniques. Product development in the fuzzy front end requires iteration, adjustment of the design, and a continuous review of requirements. Requirements often change rapidly and some form of requirements control is necessary. There may also be periods of rework and in some cases a need to scrap the concept and begin again. It is necessary to plan for variability during the conceptualization and early design of the product.

Project management can be applied effectively during the fuzzy front end of the product management cycle by using the following techniques and processes:

1. Setting objectives – Determining or defining measureable success criteria, establishing objectives, and communicating strategic goals to improve the efficiency of the resources involved by providing information about how actions impact the whole business.

2. Scope management – At the fuzzy front end, ideas are being generated. Scope management may help manage idea generation or conceptualization by keeping the team focused on priorities and minimizing the potential to move beyond the defined problem or area of opportunity.

3. Risk management – Idea development and conceptualization can be hampered by rules and restrictions, but creativity without some elements of control could lead to disaster. Risk management can minimize waste, eliminate unsafe situations, and prevent actions that could endanger operations.

4. Status report process – Keeping all stakeholders involved and in sync with the team's activities and progress.

At the fuzzy front end, it may seem difficult to apply the core project management techniques. The unique environment of the fuzzy front end – where structure and discipline seem out of place — may make it difficult to apply tools and techniques. However, the people involved at this stage must realize that resources are not unlimited and there are specific strategic goals associated with managing and developing a product.

There is also tremendous value in having the project manager involved from the very beginning to ensure that the plan is realistic and that they have a complete understanding of the desired outcome. Organizations often assume that certain critical aspects of a project are well-known, but this is frequently not the case. These assumptions can slow the team's momentum as the late-arriving project manager has to come up the learning curve. A project manager who has been engaged from the very beginning can also help provide continuity of communication as the project shifts from conception to execution.

7.4 Applying Project Management during Product Development

Product development may have different definitions depending on the industry and the internal processes used by an organization. After the fuzzy front end, the product lifecycle includes the following phases: Plan, Develop, Qualify, Launch, Deliver, and Retire. Using project management processes during the Develop and Launch phases can significantly improve the probability of delivering a product that functions as planned and successfully introducing it into the marketplace. During the Develop phase, the product undergoes reviews, requirements verification, and changes introduced via new opportunities and shifts in market conditions or customer requests.

Project management methods and processes will help the product manager through this phase by ensuring that the planned tasks are completed and by establishing an approved process for managing change. As the product moves through the cycle, it will enter the project lifecycle and be subject to and benefit from the tools, techniques, and processes described earlier in this section.

Applying project management methods and processes is usually essential to the successful delivery of a new product.

During the Develop phase the following activities may be performed:

- Rapid prototyping

- Rough layouts and final prototyping

- Mechanical design

- Engineering design and assembly planning

- Planning for manufacturing product components

- Product assembly and testing

- Standards compliance

- Cost optimization

- Quality reviews

- Publishing product documents

- Contingency planning

Project management provides methods for managing each of these activities through the core process described in 7.2.

Another variable in product development efforts is the level of technological challenge, which is sometimes expressed in terms of the "probability of technical success." As the technological challenge grows, so does the level of uncertainty. Many of the principles described above apply here, with regard to the choice of project management methods and approaches. For example, on projects that require a substantial amount of breakthrough (also called discovery), it is common to recognize that several trials may be needed to accomplish the objective. In this case, developing a project schedule requires using some number of iterations to properly model the predicted reality.

7.4.1 Project Management Activities in the Develop Phase

Each phase of a project has a distinct set of activities and processes applied to ensure that it continues to move forward. Typical processes or activities performed during this phase include:

- Developing updates and status reports

- Conducting meetings and conference calls to review progress and identify issues

- Creating meeting minutes and other project documentation

- Implementing the change control process

- Managing project resources, including re-allocation

- Conducting project budget reviews and variance reporting

- Monitoring schedule and efficiency in the use of time

- Using an enterprise project management software application for project tracking

The Develop phase of the product management lifecycle provides the most natural environment to apply project management processes and methods. The team has defined the product, identified the resources, established a budget, and defined the requirements. There will be changes and issues, and new risks will emerge. Project management provides the governance that maintains the flow of work and the processes to determine project and product performance.

7.5 Project Management in Commercialization/Operations

Project management can also play a valuable role *after* product development— in product commercialization and in ongoing operations. The key to developing an appreciation for the useful role of project management in these two worlds is recognizing that many of the process elements found within those stages of the product management framework *can be configured as projects.*

7.5.1 Potential "Projects" Related to Product Commercialization

Product managers must properly prepare for the eventual launch of their product and for the significant number of activities that occur afterwards. Some of these activities are so large and complex they can legitimately be characterized as projects themselves. Some notable examples are:

- Tracking and measuring actual performance metrics related to the product(s)

- Creating a plan for managing the future supply chain

- Developing a plan that coordinates all aspects of a product launch

- Treating the implementation of the marketing mix as a project

- Building plans for addressing product-related service and warranty work

- Initial training of channel partners and sales staff

7.5.2 Potential "Projects" Related to Ongoing Operations

At times, product managers must ensure that the ongoing operations stage after product launch has been properly planned for, or that they have developed a long-term operational management plan and implemented it at the right time. As with product commercialization, many of these activities could be quite complex and could consequently be configured as projects. It is important to clarify that the project portion is the implementation of these activities, as opposed to any ongoing operation of each activity.

Examples may include:

- Building just-in-time or Lean manufacturing methodologies
- Implementing value-enhancing efforts, such as value engineering, value analysis, and value stream mapping
- Considering operational readiness as a project
- Working to optimize the supply chain
- Developing and implementing a maintenance plan for operational equipment
- Treating training of operations personnel (operators, maintenance staff, etc.) as a project
- Creating and implementing an inventory management system or process

7.6 How Program Management Relates to Product Management

Most organizations identify and manage *programs* as part of doing business. One type of program is a group of related projects coordinated to achieve benefits and control that could not arise from managing each project separately.

Programs occur frequently in product management. One common manifestation of a program is an entire collection of product-oriented projects. Here, the program is likely to be a combination of research and development, operational readiness, commercialization, and other related project efforts associated with one or more products. Many companies, for example, have been known to introduce a suite of products within a single, coordinated initiative — *a program*.

Among the larger challenges in successfully managing programs of this nature is effectively coordinating simultaneous individual projects. Duplication of effort, oversights, failure to manage interactions, and failure to leverage economies of scale are common challenges. In fact, such challenges are quite likely to occur in situations where multiple product managers and/or multiple business units are participating.

These problems can be effectively addressed for virtually any program by introducing these three elements related to the discipline of project management:

- Core project management methods and processes at the program level
- Sound program management practices
- Dedicated program management personnel

7.6.1 Core Project Management Methods and Processes at the Program Level

By applying the methods and processes detailed in Section 7.2, product managers can add structure, organization, and control to a collection of interrelated projects, often yielding a more successful program outcome.

- During *program planning*, project management methods and processes can be used to:

  o Identify project-to-project interactions (at the task level)

  o Develop the overall program schedule

  o Estimate the total program cost

  o Identify and assess program-level risks and uncertainties

- During *program execution*, core project management methods and processes can be used to:

  o Track overall program progress

  o Monitor and manage program risk and uncertainty

  o Communicate across projects

  o Share data and information across projects

  o Conduct program-level team meetings

  o Manage stakeholders

  o Report program status to senior management and key stakeholders

7.6.2 Sound Program Management Practices

Whereas classic project management methods focus on *individual initiatives*, program management tends to focus on managing the *interfaces* among multiple initiatives and *leveraging the common elements* between them. Some value-added benefits product managers can expect from applying program management methodologies are:

- A business focus (i.e., evaluation of profitability, economic rate of return, etc.)

- A strategic focus (i.e., satisfaction of organizational objectives and goals)

- Effective coordination across:

    o Products

    o Organizational boundaries

    o People

    o Functional responsibilities

    o Project activities

    o Program deliverables

- A consistent approach to project governance and oversight

- Prioritization and sequencing across projects

- Allocation and ongoing management of resources across projects

- The grouping and/or collaboration of similar work efforts across projects

7.6.3 Dedicated Project Management Personnel (Where Appropriate)

When considering all of the project and program management methods and processes described above, a critical question emerges: Who is going to be responsible for their effective implementation at the program level?

Although a product manager could be appointed to fill the role of program manager—and therefore be tasked with introducing project management—there are two significant challenges associated with that approach: project management competency and the "two-hat" syndrome.

Project management competency

Although some contend that "anybody can do project management," underestimating the value added by an individual with a high degree of project management knowledge and competency can have significant negative consequences to organizational product initiatives.

The two-hat syndrome

Trying to manage a project while acting as a technical expert or a market expert (in this case, a product manager) is viewed as one of the most challenging jobs in the world of projects. It requires individuals to continually divide their attention between their product management and project management duties. The risk of overload is considerable.

These challenges suggest that using a dedicated project management specialist should be strongly considered when managing product-oriented programs—even if that individual is not deeply knowledgeable of specific products. This often takes the form of a product manager working in concert with an individual who is highly competent at coordinating complex initiatives. The key to making this approach work is to clearly define the roles and responsibilities for each contributor as well as the reporting relationship.

In these situations, it's common for the project management specialist to be viewed as an on-demand resource, acting in a service and support role. It's widely viewed that a program manager who is involved very early in the *overall* program lifecycle is in a much better position to make high-quality program decisions than one who is assigned after many crucial program decisions have already been made.

Some of the specific benefits of using project management specialists are:

- Lack of personal, political, product, and technology bias
- Knowledge of the most appropriate management approach for given situations
- An appreciation of effects beyond the program boundaries (i.e., impacts on operations, engineering, legal, etc.)
- Keeping the development process focused and moving forward
- Focusing on the achievement of product objectives and outcomes

7.7 How Project Portfolio Management Relates to Product Management

Within product management, using a portfolio management approach to coordinate the various interactions and interrelationships of products and product lines is common. A similar—if not somewhat overlapping—practice exists in project management.

Because both techniques involve coordinating a collection of projects, there are many similarities between program management (previously described in Section 7.6) and project portfolio management. Perhaps the greatest similarity comes in the ways core project management methods and processes may be applied.

But there are some critical differences between the two management types. For example, although program management focuses on coordination across projects that are often interrelated, project portfolio management focuses on selecting and prioritizing a collection of projects that may not necessarily be related.

And while program management often focuses on the ultimate fulfillment of high-level, targeted, deliverable-oriented objectives, portfolio management typically focuses on pursuing a number of project initiatives that, collectively, will fulfill an organization's long-term strategic and operational goals and objectives. The impact, effectiveness, and success of a project portfolio is frequently tied to—and expressed via—evaluations, judgments, and metrics related to strategic intent, strategic goals, key value drivers, key performance indicators, and so forth. The primary mission of project portfolio management is to identify, select, and execute the specific combination of projects expected to have the greatest positive financial and strategic impact on the organization while balancing the associated risks and leading to the highest organizational likelihood of success.

Not surprisingly, the greatest interaction between project portfolio management and product management occurs in situations where the portfolio includes many product-oriented projects—specifically, portfolios that focus on a product line or a family of functionally related products.

To better understand how product managers can optimize the application of an overall portfolio management approach, it's useful to consider in greater detail the critical objectives of the portfolio management approach in general. The key objectives of portfolio management are:

- Pursue only those projects necessary to fulfill organizational goals
- Ensure a strong link between company strategy and projects

- Enable the portfolio owner to get the best "bang for the buck"

- Develop a big picture view and promote broad understanding of the volume of project work—both in-process and planned

- Facilitate a diversified and balanced approach to projects. Some common dimensions of balance are:

  o Markets served (diversified)

  o Geographic regions served (diversified)

  o Goal horizon (long term vs. short term)

  o Risk (business, technical, financial, corporate image, etc.)

  o Application of technology

  o Resource utilization

  o Project size (money, time, quantity of resources)

  o Competitive advantage

  o Government mandate

  o Predicted return on investment

When considering the role of project management in portfolio management and in support of product initiatives, questions ordinarily surface, including: When should project management be brought into the cycle and how?

Sections 7.2 through 7.4 outlined where and how project management can be effectively applied within the product management framework. However, the kinds of activities needed to support successful achievement of portfolio management product objectives—such as those identified in the bulleted list above—often take place before initiating development of any specific product (and therefore, before initiating any project cycle). This period is often named for its main functional objective—portfolio development.

During portfolio development, candidate projects exist and the organization is actively assessing in which ones to invest. As a result, the role of project management in the process is sometimes underappreciated and, at times, completely discounted. There are, however, a number of value-added benefits to be realized by including project management specialists during portfolio development. Their role is typically advisory, and can yield some important inputs throughout the portfolio development process, such as:

- Enabling the portfolio owner to get the best "bang for the buck"

- Recognizing alternative methods and approaches for solving a problem, addressing a need, or exploiting an opportunity

- Pinpointing any appropriate and available technologies

- Estimating resource requirements for a potential project effort

- Identifying the functional groups that should participate in a given study

- Coordinating a study or an analysis of alternatives

- Helping to prepare project business cases

- Identifying projects most aligned with business objectives

- Determining the most efficient combination of projects, relative to the available skill set, to deliver maximum value

As with program managers, product managers who either lead or participate in portfolio management activities are likely to benefit by involving their project management colleagues in the process.

7.8 Business Analysis

Business analysis is a set of activities, tools, and techniques an analyst uses with stakeholders to understand the structure, policies, processes, and operations of an organization. Business analysts use these activities, tools, and techniques to analyze needs and recommend solutions to help an organization achieve its goals. When coupled with a product manager, the business analyst (BA) can be a skilled partner who helps facilitate, communicate, analyze, and recommend business solutions.

Business analysis has become more prominent since the late 1980s, which has created a focus on formalizing the BA as a key facilitator of business change within organizations. This increased focus has been driven by a demand for faster marketplace responsiveness, more sophisticated product offerings, a higher reliance on information technology (IT) applications, outsourcing trends, and increasingly stringent regulatory requirements.

As organizations evolve to meet these challenges, they are working to improve their business analysis capabilities. BAs that are properly trained and have the appropriate capabilities and experience can help define solutions, communicate with stakeholders, analyze problems and information, and elicit requirements (commonly referred to as product features). Last but not least, the BA is well known for being an interpreter between business stakeholders and IT teams.

Additionally, BAs are now playing key roles in helping specify the "business behavior" that enables product offerings. This business behavior is a level above the actual technical design and implementation capabilities we often think of as IT software applications. The design of business behavior is intensely focused on realizing the intent of a product's goals while balancing organizational and technology constraints and trade-offs.

Within complex organizations where multiple and diverse strategies, capabilities, stakeholders, and customer audiences are a reality, having a capable business analyst on board to help with product development initiatives can minimize risk while increasing the probability of an initiative's success.

7.8.1 Business Analysis Governing Organization and Body of Knowledge

In October 2003, the International Institute of Business Analysis (IIBA®) was formed to maintain standards for the practice of business analysis. Since its formation, IIBA has become the leading association in the world of business analysis.

In collaboration with industry experts, the IIBA authored the Business Analysis Body of Knowledge (BABOK®). The BABOK is a collection of knowledge that reflects generally accepted practices in business analysis. Similar to the PMI's PMBOK and the ProdBOK, the BABOK gives organizations an understanding of where business analysis activities and techniques can be leveraged in their businesses.

7.8.2 Product Management and Business Analyst

Although not all organizations use BAs in their product management and product development efforts, those that do often find that BAs play a valuable role. Brainstorming, capturing the voice of the customer, analyzing requirements, and scrutinizing business behavior are a number of activities where the BA brings value to the product management lifecycle. Numerous opportunities exist in this lifecycle where the product manager can work closely with one or more BAs to collaborate on deliverables and milestones and achieve product-related goals. By engaging BAs early in the lifecycle and during planning activities, product managers can determine where business analysis activities and techniques can be incorporated to maximize effectiveness.

The following section introduces three elements that can help the product manager understand when and how to leverage business analysis throughout the product management lifecycle:

1) BA skills and knowledge

2) Scenarios for leveraging business analysis

3) The role of the BA in product design

7.8.3 Business Analysis Skills and Knowledge

Product managers have numerous challenges when envisioning, planning for, designing, and launching products. These challenges include:

- Competing for the attention of essential resources (i.e., key resources from different functional areas)

- Meeting the expectations of multiple stakeholders (varying sponsors and customer segments)

- Organizing large amounts of disparate requirements (i.e., conflicting and ambiguous requirements)

- Alternative approaches to achieve product goals (multiple solutions to a problem with various trade-offs)

- Leveraging existing organizational and platform capabilities (using existing processes and infrastructure and fitting into organizational product roadmaps)

- Organizational and technology constraints (siloed functional areas and complex legacy processes and systems)

By leveraging the BA's skill and knowledge at key points in the lifecycle, product managers can mitigate some of the risks often associated with product management and development. Below, a number of these skill and knowledge areas are summarized.

Communication and Facilitation Skills

Guides discussions between various product stakeholders to increase clarity and understanding of product features and requirements, areas of responsibilities, and expected outcomes, values, and priorities. BAs with these skills:

- Help stakeholders effectively articulate their views

- Support negotiations between parties

- Document the minutes and results of meetings

- Help keep meetings focused and organized

- Identify and document important issues

- Encourage stakeholders to reach win/win outcomes

- Identify potential alternative design solutions

Business and Functional Subject Matter Expertise

Has knowledge of business practices, business concepts, and their relationships along with business acumen and the language of the business. BAs with these skills:

- Understand solutions that have proven effective in similar circumstances

- Are familiar with industry or functional area operations, processes, and practices related to organization structures, job functions, and work activities

- Have background working with relevant regulatory and compliance frameworks

- Possess knowledge of major competitors and partners for the organization

- Hold knowledge of major customer segments and similar products

Organizational Knowledge

Understands the formal and informal aspects of the organization, including structures governing personnel, processes, and decision making. BAs with these skills:

- Recognize and can navigate the relationships between business units and key stakeholders

- Are able to identify the necessary subject matter experts in the organization

- Comprehend the IT software applications and their relationship to supporting the business

- Have insight into the informal lines of communication and authority

- Are sensitive to the internal politics that govern or influence decision making

- Understand the organization's terminology

- Are familiar with the products or services offered by the organization

Analytical and Abstract Thinking Skills

Can apply analytical and abstract thinking to analyze problems, propose design solutions, and comprehend how personnel, processes, and technology within an organization interact as a holistic system. BAs with these skills:

- Understand organizational behaviors and their impacts that result from interacting components of the business

- Comprehend and can assess how external forces can affect the business

- Are able to assess how changes to a component of the business affects the whole business

- Understand how the business will adapt to external pressures and changes

- Can apply new ideas to resolve problems

- Are capable of thinking creatively to generate new ideas and concepts

- Are familiar with how existing ideas and concepts can be leveraged in new ways

The Effective Application of Business Analysis Techniques

Use industry-standard techniques that help analyze, communicate, facilitate, and transform the business. BAs with these skills:

- Understand when and how to apply the appropriate technique for a situation

- Effectively use notation and semantics that communicate accurately and are easily understood by all the stakeholders

- Ensure integration and traceability between analytical artifacts to preserve intent and the voice of the customer

- Can specify and model business behavior through the use of business analysis artifacts

7.8.4 Scenarios for Leveraging Business Analysis

There are numerous situations throughout the product management lifecycle in which business analysis and the use of a BA is instrumental in achieving desired outcomes. A brief tour of these follows.

Facilitating Brainstorming and Idea Generation

Using appropriate facilitation and elicitation techniques to focus stakeholder meetings on developing creative alternatives.

Setting Goals and Measures

Providing a structured approach to communicate, align, and decompose goals, tactics, and associated metrics.

Engaging and Eliciting Stakeholder Business Needs

Eliciting stakeholders through a range of elicitation and analysis techniques to define scope and identify product requirements.

"As-is" and "To-be" Process Modeling and Analysis

Describing the current product assets and comparing them with the goals, performing gap analyses, and facilitating implementation planning to support products.

Estimating

Analyzing components, circumstances, and characteristics to achieve product goals and features; estimating effort, duration, cost, and benefits.

Identifying and Analyzing Capabilities

Identifying capabilities within the organization for enabling product offerings and analyzing organizational capabilities for aligning product strategies (short-term goals and longer-term roadmap considerations) and product features.

Designing Business Workflow and Rules Interactions

Specifying the business behavior (process workflow) to support product features and enforce organization policies and product-specific rules.

Assisting with Procedure and Training Development

Developing process-, role-, and application-related documentation with information on developing procedures and training material.

Considering Alternatives and Trade-Offs

Analyzing, creating, and presenting alternative solutions and trade-offs for stakeholders to consider.

Validating That the Selected Solution Meets Requirements

Ensuring, through reviews, simulations, and by providing inputs to testing, that solutions support product features and usage scenarios.

7.8.5 The Role of the Business Analyst in Product Design

One of the most highly valued contributions a BA can bring to the product management lifecycle is helping to identify a competitive advantage through the design of a new product. BAs can play a crucial role in product design as marketplace factors place increased emphasis on innovation and speedy product introductions. Defining how to successfully launch a product in today's complex organizations is no small task. Siloed departments, legacy systems, and poorly understood processes are often obstacles that the product manager has to overcome. The reality is that almost all products at virtually all organizations are supported by technology of some kind. Technology is no longer just a way of more efficiently supporting a product—it's now an essential part of delivering differentiation to realize a competitive advantage in the marketplace.

Change in the travel industry over the last 10 years is a good example of this. Online reservations are no longer a side business—they are part of the core travel industry business. Delivering superior automation solutions has been a key battlefield in this industry. Although the focus initially was on using the Internet as a new channel, the battle has now moved to providing automated ways to create packages, finding fare combinations that reflect different objectives, providing loyalty-based offerings, and delivering promotional offerings that provide differentiation.

Ensuring that a product delivers differentiation and is a success requires more than providing engineers with a bulleted list of desired product features. Most often, a product's features are enabled through a set of interactions between processes, rules or policies, data, and IT applications. These interactions need to be carefully designed to ensure that the product supports multiple customer usage and exception scenarios. By analyzing product usage scenarios and recommending operational business behavior to support these scenarios, the BA helps technology engineers create a solution that meets a product's usability goals. In this role, the BA supports the design of the product by helping shape features into a cohesively designed solution that meets the intent of a product's strategy.

An example of how a BA can help ensure the best product design can be found in this story of a hotel marketing campaign. With only a few weeks' notice, a hotel franchise wants to roll out a new marketing campaign for the Super Bowl that promotes longer stays by offering guests a third night free when booking a two-night stay. In helping design a solution to support the new campaign, the BA would consider the importance of timing and communicate the trade-offs in implementing a quick solution versus the flexibility in features that may be desired in the future.

Although BAs can play a valuable role in designing how a product should work, IT departments create and maintain software applications that enable a product. It is helpful to view IT as the product "production facility." IT delivers the hardware and software platforms to execute the product designs that a product manager and BA specify through product design and business analysis. This separation of product design and technical engineering helps the product manager, with the BA's assistance, ensure there is always a clear focus on meeting the product goals.

This concept of separating product design and technical engineering can be further illustrated by the design and manufacture of commercial aircraft. An aircraft is made up of millions of parts. During design, the parts and the way they fit together to form a system are identified. Based on the effort that went into the design, the aircraft is expected to behave a certain way. It would be unacceptable for the aircraft manufacturer to decide that an equivalent behavior could be achieved by combining and eliminating certain parts. The expectation is that the aircraft product design indicates the exact set of parts that will make up the aircraft when it is assembled, and it is the product designer's role to ensure that the aircraft as a whole performs correctly. Using business analysis activities and techniques, we can see this same product design role being played by a BA in support of the product manager's goals.

7.9 User Experience and Product Management

The relationship between product managers and user experience professionals typically begins in the Conceive phase of the product management lifecycle and concludes at the end of the Develop phase. However, a strong case can be made that user design should continue to play an active role throughout a product's lifecycle.

Product managers and user experience professionals share a common interest in creating as much value for a product's end users as possible and doing it in ways that are intuitive. This makes these two groups ideally suited to partner throughout discreet projects or across a product's lifespan. This partnership enables user experience professionals to leverage their knowledge of solid design principles, requisite skills, and an understanding of how to apply the right amount of process to help the product manager create value for the customer and the organization.

7.9.1 A Closer Look at User Experience

User experience can be defined as a person's perceptions and responses that result from the use or anticipated use of a product, system, or service. User experience includes all of a person's physical and psychological responses that occur before, during, and after use. It encompasses all aspects of the end user's interaction with an organization's products. These aspects include interfaces, graphics, industrial design, physical interaction, architectural structures, messaging, and related documentation.

Universal Design Principles

A working group of architects, product designers, engineers, and environmental design researchers from the Center for Universal Design at North Carolina State University[38] collaborated to establish the following seven principles to guide a wide range of design disciplines, including environments, products, and communications:

- Equitable use
- Flexibility of use
- Simple and intuitive use
- Perceptible information
- Tolerance for error
- Low physical effort
- Size and space for approach and use

The principles, described below, may be applied to evaluate existing designs, to guide the design process, and to educate both designers and consumers about the characteristics of more usable products and environments.

Equitable Use: The design is useful and marketable to people with diverse abilities, which includes providing the same means of use for all users—identical whenever possible and equivalent — when not – and making provisions for privacy, security, and safety equally available to all users. A good example is a rocker switch commonly used for turning on and off room lighting—nearly everyone can operate the switch because the large rocker is easy to locate and activate with minimal force and manual dexterity.

Flexibility of Use: The design accommodates a wide range of individual preferences and abilities, including accommodating right- or left-handed access

[38] North Carolina State University, Center for Universal Design, www.design.ncsu.edu/cud.

and use. Examples include hand mixers with swivel cords to accommodate use with either hand.

Simple and Intuitive Use: Use of the design is easy to understand, regardless of the user's experience, knowledge, language skills, or current concentration level. Guidelines include eliminating unnecessary complexity and providing effective prompts and feedback during and after the task. An intuitive door handle design, for example, provides visual cues indicating where to grab the handle. A door with poor visual cues (low affordance) leaves people either pushing when they should pull or vice versa.

Perceptible Information: The design communicates necessary information effectively to the user, regardless of ambient conditions or the user's sensory abilities. Guidelines include using different modes—like pictorial, verbal, and tactile—and maximizing "legibility" of essential information. An example is a crosswalk system that provides a pictorial "walk/don't walk" display, verbally announces "walk," and provides buttons that are pressed to activate the system.

Tolerance for Error: The design minimizes hazards and the adverse consequences of accidental or unintended actions. Guidelines provide warnings of hazards and errors and fail-safe features. Handrails, for example, separate the in and out traffic lanes in a space, serving as safety and way-finding features that assist in traffic flow and organization.

Low Physical Effort: The design can be used efficiently and comfortably and with a minimum of fatigue. Guidelines allow end users to maintain a neutral body position, use reasonable operating forces, and minimize repetitive actions. Ergonomic keyboards are a classic example as are desks that can be raised for standing and lowered for sitting.

Size and Space for Approach and Use: Appropriate size and space is provided for approach, reach, manipulation, and use, regardless of the user's body size, posture, or mobility. Guidelines provide a clear line of sight to important elements for anyone seated or standing and adequate space for use of assistive devices or personal assistance. An example is an adaptable base cabinet with doors that slide into the cabinet or are quickly removable, providing knee space for a seated cook or wheelchair.

These principles are not intended to constitute all criteria for good design, only universally usable design. Other important factors such as the goals and needs of the user, aesthetics, cost, safety, gender, and cultural appropriateness must also be considered when designing.

Design Standards for Computer-Based Interactive Systems

The International Organization for Standardization (ISO) established the industry standard for the ergonomics of human-computer interaction (ISO 9241). There are two parts to this standard, 9241-110 and 9241-210.

ISO 9241-110:2006 defines ergonomic design principles and provides a framework for the analysis, design, and evaluation of interactive systems for designers of user interface development tools and style guides. It also provides guidelines for user interface designers, who will apply the standards during the development process; developers, who will apply the guidance during design and implementation of system functionality; buyers, who will reference it during product procurement; and evaluators, who must ensure that products meet its recommendations. To learn more about ISO 9241-110:2006, visit www.iso.org/iso/home/store/catalogue_tc/catalogue_detail.htm?csnumber=38009.

ISO 9241-210:2010 provides requirements and recommendations for human-centered design principles and activities throughout the lifecycle of computer-based interactive systems. It's intended to be used by those managing design processes, and is concerned with how hardware and software components of interactive systems can enhance human-system interaction. To learn more about ISO 9241-210:2010, visit www.iso.org/iso/home/store/catalogue_ics/catalogue_detail_ics.htm?csnumber=52075.

User Experience Skills and Knowledge

User experience standards lay the foundation for superior design. However, to effectively implement these standards, user experience professionals must have an array of skills. According to *The Invisible Computer,*[39] user experience is not a single discipline but a combination of several skills. And they're rarely found in the same person. These skills include:

- **User research:** The ability to observe potential users in their normal settings to better determine user needs. Training for this discipline is most apt to come from anthropology and sociology, where the skills of careful, systematic observation and effective interviewing are taught.

- **Behavioral design:** The ability to create a cohesive conceptual model for the product that is consistent and easy to learn and understand. Behavioral design must mesh the task requirements with the skills, knowledge, and capabilities of the intended users. Skills in behavioral design usually come from cognitive science and experimental psychology,

[39] Norman, D. (1999). The Invisible Computer: Why Good Products Can Fail, the Personal Computer Is So Complex, and Information Appliances Are the Solution. Cambridge, MA: The MIT Press.

especially from programs in human-computer interaction. Having a strong understanding of design concepts is also extremely important in creating good behavioral design.

- **Model building and interaction design:** The ability to rapidly build product mock-ups—simulated systems that can be tested. Here the skills typically come from computer programming, electrical and mechanical engineering, and model building of the sort usually taught in schools of architecture and industrial design.

- **Usability engineering:** The ability to create test scripts, facilitate studies with the end users (e.g. consumers, business people, etc.), and analyze data. Designers with this skill set understand the pitfalls of experimental tests and can effectively conduct usability studies that provide meaningful feedback for the project at hand. User testing of prototypes allows for fast-paced iteration of designs to better meet the users' needs, whereas other types of studies provide feedback on existing products and services. Most usability studies can be conducted rapidly or at a more laid-back pace. The difference in speed can affect the quality of the study and the depth of the analysis. Recruiting participants for these studies can be done very quickly as well, or more time can be taken to examine the candidates and find the best possible fit. It's important to distinguish between user research and usability engineering. User research focuses on up-front envisioning methods while usability engineering emphasizes testing and other evaluation methods that typically occur much later in the project.

- **Graphic design:** Focuses on visual communication. Graphic design is a creative process that combines words, symbols, and images to create a visual representation of ideas and messages. Skills in graphic design usually come from the visual communication or communication design fields.

- **Industrial design:** The ability to develop solutions for problems of form, usability, and physical ergonomics. Industrial design is the process of combining applied art and applied science to improve the aesthetics, ergonomics, functionality, and usability of a product. Skills for this discipline typically result from an education in industrial design, product design, engineering, or manufacturing.

- **Technical writing:** The ability to present useful information that is clear and easy to understand for the intended audience. Technical writing requires an understanding of the audience and the activities the user wants to accomplish, and the skills to translate often idiosyncratic and complex design into something that makes sense. These skills are most frequently taught in instructional design programs.

The User-Centered Design Process

With a strong understanding of the principles of design and the necessary skills to achieve the stated product objective, designers rely heavily on process to use these attributes to reach the product's design goals and objectives.

User-centered design (UCD) is a process in which at each stage of a product's design, designers pay extensive attention to the needs, wants, and limitations of end users. UCD can be characterized as a multi-stage problem-solving process that not only requires designers to analyze and predict, based on ergonomic design principles and how people are likely to use a product, but also to test the validity of their assumptions with regards to human behavior in real-world tests with actual end users. Such testing is necessary because it's often difficult for a product's designers to understand intuitively who a first-time user of their design is and what each user's learning curve may be.

The chief difference between UCD and other product design philosophies is that UCD tries to optimize the product around how customers can, want, or need to use it, rather than forcing them to change their behavior to accommodate the product.

There are six key principles to ensure that a design is user-centered:

1. The design is based upon an explicit understanding of users, tasks, and environments.

2. Users are involved throughout the design and development.

3. The design is driven and refined by user-centered evaluation.

4. The process is iterative.

5. The design addresses the *whole* user experience.

6. The design team includes multidisciplinary skills and perspectives.

UCD answers questions about end users and their tasks and goals, and then uses the findings to make decisions about development and design. UCD of a web site, for example, seeks to answer the following questions:

- Who uses the site?

- What are the users' tasks and goals?

- How experienced are the users with the site and others like it?

- What functions do the users need from the site?

- What information might the users need, and in what form do they need it?

- How do users think the web site should work?

- What is a normal environment for using the web site? What is an extreme environment?

- Is the user multitasking?

- Does the interface utilize different input modes such as touch, speech, gestures, or orientation?

Depending on an organization's philosophy and constraints, a product manager may do some or all of these activities, work with user experience professionals in or outside the department that perform these activities, or be responsible for working with outside contractors or agencies that perform these activities for them.

7.9.2 Product Management and User Experience

Whereas product management is focused on the market and the customers' business needs, user experience focuses *on the end user's interactions with the products and services.*

For enterprise solutions, the customer is usually someone in executive management interested in finding the best way to bring efficiency to an operation, whereas the actual user is typically a company employee more interested in completing their daily assignments as easily and effectively as possible. The economic buyer is looking at the overall workflow of the organization and how specific solutions might improve it, whereas the user's needs tend to emphasize the solution's ease of use. For this reason, product management and user experience personnel *must work together* to understand the market, customer, and users' needs, and to design and develop product solutions that meet these needs.

User experience (UX) resources are often highly valued and therefore quite scarce. In fact, company size often impacts how much user experience expertise is readily accessible. As a result, an organization may take one, or perhaps a combination, of the following approaches:

- In smaller organizations, product managers may perform user experience activities, or

- The user experience professional may be required to act as a product management proxy until the organization can add a product manager.

- Product managers may seek to employ an internal user experience professional or hire an external company.

- If the company is of sufficient scale, user experience may be another department or function that works with the product managers.

Regardless of the organizational approach, product managers and user experience professionals typically interact during the activities described below.

Identifying Problems and Quantifying Opportunities

User experience and product management team members frequently work together to better understand the market, customers, and the customers' end users. As part of this process, they conduct qualitative research primarily with the end users. The work can also include reviewing the target market segmentation and demographic data to help establish the design direction. They interview stakeholders, customers, and observe and interview users to gain insight into the product domain and user population and to determine the interactive experience. Product management may provide high-level market information to inform user experience team members of the type of research methods needed.

Product management and UX professionals develop requirements called use cases. A use case is a single example of use—a user interaction with the solution— that is well-defined and meaningful from the user's perspective. Use cases:

- define the tasks and expected outcomes,

- provide a concise medium for modeling user requirements,

- are a powerful task-based model for understanding user needs and guiding user interaction design, and

- guide the design of communicating objects to satisfy functional requirements for engineering.

UX professionals may also create other deliverables to support the development effort such as *personas* that describe the archetype user and *mental models* that act as a gap analysis showing the needs of the user compared with what is being offered.

Writing Requirements and Validating Solutions

User experience assists product management in validating solutions. User experience professionals develop, conduct, and analyze surveys, interviews, and/or observations. The data from these studies help identify problems and opportunities that are realized in the requirements.

Prototypes are developed to elicit feedback from customers to validate that the identified solutions meet their business needs. Models or wireframes are used to elicit feedback on conceptual user interactions. Models and wireframes are basic visual guides used to suggest the layout and placement of fundamental design elements in the interaction design. They provide a visual reference for the structure of the solution, define the positioning of global and secondary levels of the information hierarchy, and maintain design consistency throughout the solution. It can be easier for an individual to respond to a model or wireframe than to be asked about a concept verbally.

Writing the requirements and validating the solutions is an iterative process. When new insights into validating the solutions appear, the requirements must be updated. Updated requirements require more validation. This process continues until the requirements are adequately validated.

Analyzing Requirements and Designing the Solution

User experience, as part of or under the guidance of product management, conducts an analysis of the market, technology, and competition, in terms of the user goals and interaction design, early in the solution lifecycle to determine the design direction of the user interaction. A person or team conducts user research, observations, surveys, focus groups, competitive reviews, and other activities to better understand the market, customer, and end-user problems that are being solved in terms of the user experience and interface design.

The person or team develops storyboards, flow diagrams, wireframes, prototypes, and other artifacts to validate the workflow for the solution. Prototypes are iterated with customers and their end users to be sure the solution continues to solve their business problems.

Insight from the design analysis can cause some revisions and/or refinement to the initial requirements.

Writing the Specification and Building the Solution

Product management writes market and product requirements, and UX writes interaction specifications of the user behavior and interaction design. Wireframes, models, and other prototypes must be evaluated with the customers' end users for effectiveness, efficiency, and satisfaction before final specification.

User interaction specifications should be completed before development. For an iterative development process, evaluations and specifications should be completed "just in time"—an iteration or two before they're needed. The interaction specification, along with product management's other requirements, should communicate to engineers the intended target audience for the solution and what problems will be solved for the market, customers, and end users.

Engineers build the solution based on the requirements and specifications provided by product management and UX. UX may work with engineers on the user interaction design clarification. Sometimes technology issues require revisions to the interaction design, in which case UX and engineers work together to determine the best approach for each case. Engineers test and fix "bugs" in the final phases of development or end of iteration. UX reviews the interaction design and may request changes to ensure that the design developed meets the needs of the end user. These change requests can be informal or formal, depending on the size of the team and the organization's development process.

Further evaluation may be conducted in user acceptance testing, beta testing, and/or when the solution is in production. Participants may be observed, surveyed, interviewed, monitored in social media, etc. to better understand their interactions with the experience. Findings from these evaluations may be applied to the next release of the solution.

The relationship between user experience and product management is central to ensuring that the products brought to market not only generate value for the customer and the organization, but that the final product is intuitive and user-friendly. Effective collaboration between these two professions increases the likelihood that the product has the greatest chance to succeed.

7

SECTION 2:
The Product Management Lifecycle Framework

This section describes the stages and phases of the product management lifecycle. While the product management lifecycle is represented as a linear and phased model, the actual implementation of the various components is subject to localization based upon practitioner needs and should not be viewed as a prescriptive step-by-step process. The intent is to provide the reader with a comprehensive view of the various tasks and activities that are typically undertaken during the product management lifecycle phase so practitioners can make the best decisions on the actual utilization of the various elements described in this section. Factors such as company growth stage, product development methodology selection, available resources, culture, and organizational structure influence how product management is practiced.

Chapter 8

Introduction to the Product Management Lifecycle Framework and Process Groups

8.1 The Advantages of Implementing a Standard Product Management Lifecycle Framework

Adopting a standard product management lifecycle framework is important because it provides a common way to describe and communicate with parties in the profession and with counterparts outside the profession. Lacking a common way to describe the profession and its core foundational elements increases complexity and inefficiency. By adopting a standardized product management lifecycle framework, the profession improves efficiency and simplifies communication, to the benefit of all parties.

8.2 A Common Lexicon

The product management lifecycle framework establishes a common lexicon for describing the information, activities, practices, and deliverables required to bring products to market. It also presents core foundational principles that enable effective management of a product throughout the entire product management lifecycle.

Some of the benefits of having a common lexicon are:

- Makes product management more relevant and effective by defining the boundaries of the profession and how its professionals interact with key functional partners in delivering value

- Provides a universal, standardized framework for managing products throughout their lifecycles

- Empowers product teams to develop mutual and well-understood commitments at each stage of a product's evolution and increases the clarity of communications

- Enables product teams to execute more effectively at each phase of the product management lifecycle

- Establishes a platform for developing a common set of tools to help product teams bring quality products to market

8.3 The Product Management Lifecycle Framework

The product management lifecycle framework represents the passage of time and illustrates the universal nature of product management as products move through their various life stages, beginning in new product development or acquisition and continuing until final market withdrawal. Taken in its entirety, the product management lifecycle illustrates a complete "cradle-to-grave" perspective of a product's existence.

As depicted in Figure 8-1, once the product has been developed or acquired, it moves into commercialization, manufacturing, and operations stages where it's introduced, grows to maturity, and declines, eventually leading to withdrawal from the market.

Figure 8-1. The Stages of the Product Management Lifecycle

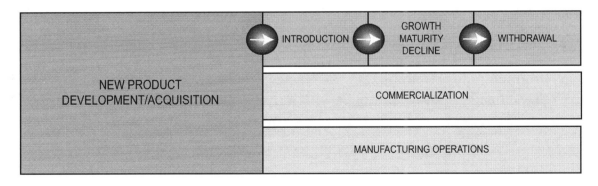

A new product also evolves through a number of common, standard, and predictable *phases* during its lifecycle. The standard phases are labeled as simple, universal verbs describing the major activity of each phase (Figure 8-2):

Figure 8-2. The Seven Phases of the Product Management Lifecycle

At the conclusion of each phase is a decision point (represented by triangles in Figure 8-2) that indicates the transition from one phase of the product management lifecycle to the next. Decision points are milestones that represent critical business decision-making junctures used to optimize performance, scrutinize product development investments, and increase the quality of execution.

The criteria used in decision points reflect standards and criteria established by senior management to assess risk and effectively manage investments. The outcome of each review is a recommendation by the product team to the executive sponsor or steering committee to:

1. Continue to the next stage (Go)

2. Cancel the project (No-Go)

3. Redirect the effort based on strategic changes or gaps discussed during the review (Rework)

4. Defer a decision (Hold)

These reviews are not the same as technical, architectural, or deliverable reviews and shouldn't replace them; technical and other reviews are conducted *before* decision point reviews.

Some questions that should be examined at the various decision points are:

- Do the project and product fit the business strategy (strategic alignment)?

- Does a market of a minimum size exist, and will it still exist at launch time?

- Is there first-hand customer data illustrating that the new product has unique benefits, that it meets customer needs better than competitive products, or that it provides superior value?

- Is technical feasibility reasonably likely? Have risk areas been identified and are solutions available that can be reasonably acquired?

- Has a product value proposition been developed?

- What is the "go-to-market" strategy and plan?

- Is an acceptable return on risk-weighted investment available?

- Do resources with related experience exist to construct a team that has the scale, complexity, and technologies needed to support the development effort?

- Has testing been comprehensive and robust, ensuring a quality product?

- Do any "show-stopper" issues exist? If so, can they be mitigated, and is there a mitigation plan?

- Have all project and product risks been communicated and do they have appropriate mitigation and contingency plans?

- Have all parties been informed of and agree with the execution plan and approach?

Figure 8-3. The Combined Stages and Phases of the Product Management Lifecycle

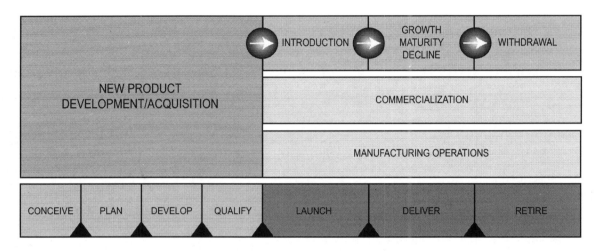

Source: The Association of International Product Marketing and Management (AIPMM)

When combined, the stages, phases, and decision points compose the entire product management lifecycle framework that all products follow.

8.4 Defining Roles within the Product Management Lifecycle Framework

To discuss the actual process groups, further exploration of the cross-functional aspect of the product management role is needed. Product managers are tasked with singular responsibility throughout the entire product lifecycle for the products they represent. However, they rely heavily on collaboration with other functional parties across the organization to achieve their objectives. Product managers can't do it alone.

Organizations allocate cross-functional responsibilities differently based on need, company growth stage, and the available skills on the team. Therefore, it's essential to provide an effective tool for defining these critical product responsibilities within an organization. Titles and roles can be highly variable, so knowing who is doing what improves the overall flow and is important to a product manager's success.

One of the best ways to gain role clarity is to use a RACI matrix.[40] A RACI matrix defines the parties that will be **R**esponsible, **A**ccountable, **C**onsulted, or **I**nformed as the product migrates through the product management lifecycle. By defining who is doing what and their interdependencies, product managers improve the likelihood of success and their ability to effectively deliver value cross-functionally at each process phase.

Four Key Roles:

- **Responsible** parties do the needed work for a specific deliverable or task. Usually only one person is responsible for a specific activity.

- **Accountable** parties are ultimately accountable for the correct completion of the deliverable or task. Only one accountable party signs off on the finished task.

- **Consulted** parties' opinions are sought when developing a task or deliverable. These parties are sometimes called subject matter experts. This is meant to be two-way communication.

- **Informed** parties are kept up to speed on the progress of a deliverable or task. This is usually one-way communication.

Table 8-1 illustrates how having clarity on the roles and relationships of the members of the extended product team can increase efficiency. Although this example only illustrates a small subset of the extended product team and the breadth of activities, it shows how the roles can be clearly defined.

Table 8-1. Abbreviated RACI Matrix – Technology Industry Example

STRATEGY	PRODUCT MANAGER	BUSINESS ANALYST	PROJECT MANAGER	ENGINEER	QUALITY ASSURANCE
Business plan	Responsible/ Accountable	Consulted			
Business analysis	Accountable	Responsible	Informed		Informed
High-level feasibility study	Consulted	Consulted	Informed		Informed
High-level solution proposal	Consulted	Consulted	Informed		Informed
Product decision matrix	Responsible/ Accountable	Consulted			
High-level feature matrix	Accountable	Responsible	Responsible	Consulted	Consulted
Rolling 12-month roadmap	Responsible/ Accountable	Informed	Informed	Informed	Informed

[40] Jacka, J. M., & Keller, P. J. (2009). *Business process mapping: Improving customer satisfaction* (2nd ed.). Hoboken, NJ: John Wiley and Sons Inc.

Role clarity is essential for increasing the effectiveness of the product manager and the cross-functional team across the product management lifecycle. To maximize efficiency, everyone on the team, including the executive sponsor, must understand their role and their dependencies.

8.5 Mapping a Product's Production Process

Once the organization understands the various stages and phases of the product management lifecycle and the role of the parties involved in value creation activities, it's possible to construct the operational flow for the product.

To stay in sync with the product team, a product manager must understand the process being used to develop *and* support the product. Product managers should start by gaining clarity on *their* role and the deliverables they're responsible for, then strive to understand the entire product process. Understanding the cross-functional product activities—information, people, and processes—increases execution efficiency and effectiveness. Figure 8-4 illustrates the entire process, the roles involved, the degree of involvement, and what deliverables are expected at each phase of the lifecycle.

Figure 8-4. Product Production Process Example[41]

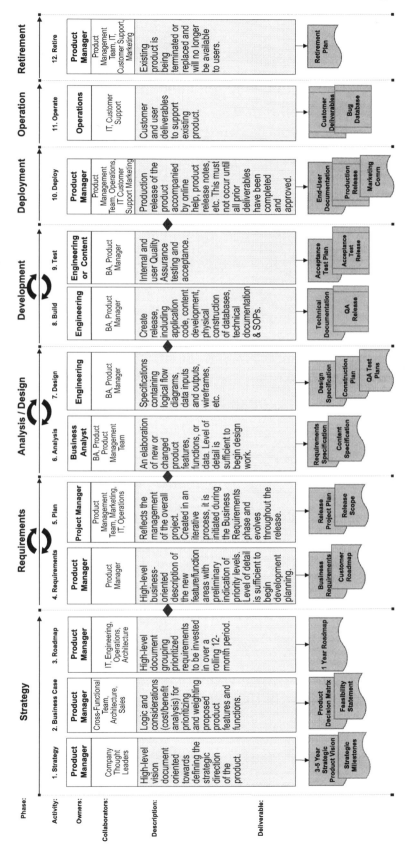

8

41 Geracie, G. (2010). *Take Charge Product Management*. Chicago, IL: Actuation Press.

The completed process map shows everyone involved in the production process (roles, linkages, and deliverables). Outlining the process clarifies the hand-offs and increases overall efficiency.

The basics of the product management lifecycle, including its stages, phases, and decision points; the RACI matrix and its usefulness in bringing clarity to the product team's roles; and how all this information comes together in an operational roadmap for products have been covered above. Next, an examination of the underlying process groups and their inputs and outputs will be conducted.

8.6 Product Management Processes for a Product

To optimize a product's success and meet its objectives, product managers must thoughtfully use knowledge, skills, tools, techniques, and collaborative teamwork. Each process inherently contains a series of inputs and outputs to attain the desired results.

To achieve success, product managers must:

- Understand the product management lifecycle, including the individual stages and phases that comprise the process in its entirety.

- Choose appropriate process groups to most efficiently achieve the overall product objectives.

- Follow a defined approach to adapt and localize the standard processes to meet organizational objectives.

- Recognize that strong product management processes rely upon contributions from stakeholders from adjoining professions to achieve the desired result.

This body of knowledge documents the information needed to manage a product across all the phases of the product management lifecycle. These phases include Conceive, Plan, Develop, Qualify, Launch, Deliver, and Retire. Additionally, these processes apply universally to all goods and services and across various industries. The processes represented reflect general agreement that the use of these processes is likely to increase the chances of success for the product and the product manager.

However, the fact that these processes are universal doesn't mean that the knowledge, skills, and processes described should *always* be applied to every product. Product managers, working closely with their teams, must determine which processes are appropriate for their circumstances; a certain degree of localization is to be expected.

Product managers need to carefully contemplate each process and the related inputs and outputs. The material in this section is intended to establish a process framework that product managers must consider as they manage their product. Additionally, the processes in this body of knowledge are largely interrelated—they are interconnected and tied directly to the product management lifecycle.

Because product management is a leadership role, success is often tied to a product manager's ability to work closely with team members to achieve a common objective. It is therefore a cross-functional undertaking. This integration requires that each product, and the supporting processes, be appropriately aligned with the processes of the contributing functions in order to optimize results and achieve organizational objectives. These processes can fail when the contributing functions do not adequately perform at a level that ensures success. In many cases, product managers will work closely with their counterparts in project management to ensure that each party meets the process and deliverable obligations.

This section overviews the product management lifecycle and outlines the specific processes related to each phase. These phases have their own process groups that, in their entirety, compose the product management lifecycle. Each process group will specifically define the process steps for each of the seven phases.

Although these product management processes are presented here as discrete elements with clearly defined interfaces, this is not always the case in the real world. In actual practice, these processes often overlap and relate to each other in ways that are not identified here.

8

Chapter 9

The Fundamentals

9.1 Levels of Product

Marketing professor Philip Kotler established the concept that there are five levels of product that constitute a customer value hierarchy[42] (Figure 9-1).

Figure 9-1. Kotler's Five Levels of Product

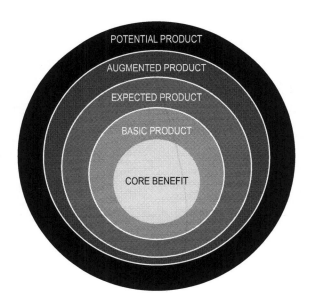

The first and most fundamental level is the *core benefit*. Customers don't seek to buy products, they seek out benefits that satisfy needs or wants. The next level is the *basic product* that is comprised of the actual product or service purchased. The basic product is comprised of a set of attributes or features that define and differentiate it from other products.

[42] Kotler, P., & Keller, K. (2011). *Marketing management* (14th ed.). Upper Saddle River, NJ: Prentice Hall.

The third level is the *expected product* and defines a higher level of expectation the customer has from the product and the company selling it. This level includes delivering the core benefit but also aligning it to other expected parameters, such as speed, quality, and support. The fourth level is the *augmented product*, which takes the product beyond its expected level. These items might be included for no extra charge, such as free shipping or fresh flowers in the customer's hotel room, or they may be available as an extra charge, such as an extended warranty or in-home installation.

The fifth level is the *potential product* and describes what the product can be at some point in the future. This level can be achieved through customization or personalization, such as adding content or applications to the product, or through ongoing extensions of the product features over time.

There are several ways to add value to a product beyond the basics and differentiate it from the competition. However, the other product levels will not matter if the core benefit is not delivered. The customer will likely reject the product if it does not contain the core benefit the customer is seeking.

9.2 Product Lifecycle

The product lifecycle is a general concept that drives product strategy planning. It is a visual representation of sales versus time.[43] Figure 9-2 illustrates the classic S-curve shape of the lifecycle. Over time, the curve passes through four different phases, much like a biological lifecycle: Introduction, Growth, Maturity, and Decline.

Figure 9-2. Product Lifecycle

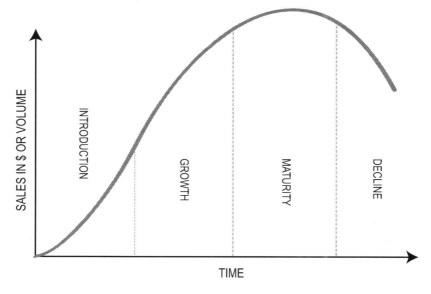

[43] Kotler, P., & Keller, K. (2011). *Marketing management* (14th ed.). Upper Saddle River, NJ: Prentice Hall.

In the Introduction phase, sales start at zero and slowly ramp up as marketing activities begin to create awareness and early adopters try the product. A successful product develops momentum and the sales rate accelerates through the Growth phase. Then sales growth begins to slow as the market starts to saturate and sales flatten in the Maturity phase. Finally, sales growth begins to fall in the Decline phase and the product is eventually discontinued.

The actual shape and time frame of this curve can vary dramatically by market, industry, and product, so Figure 9-2 is a general representation. Some products may have very rapid growth and equally rapid decline with no middle stage, such as in fashion or fads. In most cases, the Maturity phase is long, relative to the initial Introduction and Growth phases. The majority of products in most companies are in the Maturity phase.

From a strategy perspective, it's necessary to pinpoint where products are on the product lifecycle continuum because each phase incorporates unique characteristics about the customers and the state of competition. There is also a general view of how profits are flowing from the sales at each phase, indicating how investments need to be planned.

The product lifecycle can also be applied to markets or, more specifically, product categories. An entire industry can go through this lifecycle representation and eventually be discontinued, as has been the case for typewriters, eight-track tapes, floppy disks, and encyclopedias.

9.3 Market Segmentation

A *market*, as defined in economic terms, is where buyers and sellers conduct transactions, and where the dynamics of supply and demand operate. From a marketing perspective, a market consists of groups of current or potential customers who have specific unmet needs that could be met by goods or services. For example, there's the automotive market where customers have demonstrated the need for and desire to purchase automobiles as a form of personal transportation to easily get from one place to another.

Within this broad definition of a market, there are typically many different sub-markets that begin to organize customers into smaller, more specialized groups based on some unique characteristics or needs. These sub-markets are called *market segments*. For example, the automotive market can be divided into the car and truck segments, with buyers for each requiring different solutions to address different needs. Each of these broad segments can be further refined into many different segments resulting from customer needs around the automobile price ranges, size of the vehicles, fuel costs, etc. These needs can be met by varying the *marketing mix*—product, price, promotion, and place—or in the case of service deliveries, the extended marketing mix of people, process, and physical evidence.

Market segmentation can be obtained by grouping customers by specific attributes. For consumer markets, some common attributes are:

- Demographic — gender, age, race, ethnicity

- Socioeconomic — income, education, occupation, neighborhood

- Psychographic — personality, values, attitudes, interests, lifestyles

- Behavioral — product purchase patterns and usage, brand affinity

- Geographic — location-specific by city, state, region, or country

For business markets, common attributes include:

- Industry/Firmographic — size, product categories, classification by Standard Industrial Classification, verticals, geography

- Behavioral — what they purchase, what they produce, how they produce

- Needs-Based — what they want or need, drivers for their actions

- Customer Tiering — potential fit, alignment of firm-to-company strategy, lifetime value

Segmentation is accomplished through market research, either primary or secondary. *Primary research* is going directly to the actual or potential customers in order to gain information or data; it includes surveys, interviews, and observations. *Secondary research* uses indirect methods from other sources, such as published reports, public or commercial databases, websites, and agencies.

The data obtained can then be analyzed for groupings or trends among various different sets of attributes to create meaningful segmentation models for a specific company. Understanding specific characteristics of a market segment and the relevant issues or needs that customers have within this segment is at the core of successful product strategy. The primary goal is to identify the gaps that exist in current solutions relative to identified market needs, and develop a better solution along some axis that the segment values.

9.4 Innovation Types

Innovation is the concept of bringing a new idea into the world and is the primary driver of new products and markets. Innovation can occur at multiple levels in a company, including core technology, products and services, platforms, processes, and the company's business model (how it operates and makes profit). It can also occur across a spectrum from incremental to disruptive.

Incremental innovation is a small advancement beyond what already exists. On a scale of measured improvement, incremental innovation raises an attribute by some linear increment, such as 10%. This improvement can be in performance, cost, speed, quality, etc. In a product or service, it can include new features that incrementally add functionality or improve user experience. Most products that have ongoing sustaining development activity are implementing incremental innovation.

Radical innovations are large changes to the existing landscape and can add a larger linear improvement, such as 10 times improvement. It can also be a non-linear change that redefines the attributes of a product, such as adding the mobility element to traditional wired phone service as with the introduction of the mobile phone. Other terms used to describe this type of innovation are discontinuous, breakthrough, or transformational.

Disruptive innovations are different from the more common types of incremental and radical innovations. According to Clayton Christensen, disruptive innovations create value along a different dimension from existing offerings, subsequently "disrupting" the incumbent companies, businesses, and markets. Christensen states that radical innovations are different from disruptive innovations since radical innovations improve value along the existing value dimension of existing products.[44]

Radical innovations can create new markets for the company and spawn a significant period of revenue and profit growth. It also is an area of extreme high risk, with the majority of projects failing. For example, venture capitalists expect only one out of every ten investments in startup companies to provide a significant return, but that one can be so large it offsets all of the other losses.

Radical innovations also have a unique adoption process in the marketplace versus proven products, characterized by different profiles of the adopters at different points in the product lifecycle. Within the Introduction and Growth phases are sub-phases overlaid on a bell curve for different groups of customers adopting the

[44] Christensen, C. (1997). *The Innovator's Dilemma*. New York, NY: HarperBusiness.

innovation over time. Figure 9-3 illustrates the diffusion of innovation bell curve against the normal product lifecycle curve.

Figure 9-3. Diffusion of Innovation Bell Curve

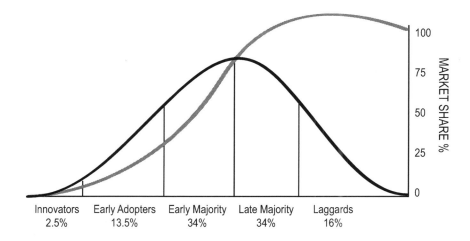

This concept was originally presented by Everett Rogers in *Diffusion of Innovations*[45] and by Geoffrey Moore in *Crossing the Chasm*.[46] Moore added a discontinuity in the adoption cycle between the Early Adopters and Early Majority, known as the "chasm" due to the large behavioral difference between the two profiles.

Moore also introduced the notion of the *whole* product required to bridge this gap, which is related to Kotler's expected level of product. The concept suggests that Early Adopters are willing to take a partial product that delivers the core benefit and are willing to sacrifice certain attributes or other commonly associated expectations in order to be first in obtaining the product. They are very forgiving of missing attributes and may even complete the product themselves.

The Early Majority, on the other hand, have a higher expectation and thus the whole product needs to provide all of the expected levels of performance, quality, services, and components to make it fully usable "out of the box." In summary, the expected product attributes vary along the adoption curve for radical innovations.

Between the minimal level of innovation and the disruptive innovation that creates entirely new industries, there can be different increments of innovation that can be pursued depending on the environment for any given company. Investments in pure research, technology improvements, and process methodologies all yield different perspectives on how to view and pursue innovation.

[45] Rogers, E. (2003). *Diffusion of Innovations* (5th ed.). New York, NY: Free Press.
[46] Moore, G. (2002). *Crossing the Chasm.* New York, NY: HarperCollins.

One concept that is relatively common in higher levels of innovation is *ideation*, or the generation of new ideas. Ideation is a structured method of creating new ideas that goes beyond brainstorming. Some core elements that make up ideation include:

- A formal event, such as a two-day workshop at some location

- A diversified set of participants who can bring different perspectives to the discussion

- A focused set of objectives or problems to solve

- Pre-work in order for the participants to properly prepare and analyze the situation before arriving

- An experienced facilitator to lead and optimize the activities

- Documentation with follow-on activities and assignments

9.5 Levels of Strategy

Business strategy can be described as analytical thinking and the commitment of resources to action and innovation. This strategy includes making decisions today about an uncertain future and taking the right risks while exploring opportunities. From the perspective of product management, strategy occurs at several levels of the organization.

The highest level of strategy is at the company level. The goal of corporate strategy is to define which markets the company competes in and how it will leverage company assets and capabilities to achieve success in these markets. This goal is easiest to visualize in a larger global corporation with multiple divisions and product lines. A market is defined as a relatively homogeneous set of members who share general characteristics, have generally similar needs, and are reachable as a group. The company strategy can also include what categories of products it will provide to address these markets, and there may be multiple categories addressing the same market for different needs.

The company strategy will also include how it intends to address these markets, and how it might leverage its major strategic assets and capabilities, and in what proportions. These assets can include its brands, distribution, manufacturing, product development, unique processes, and intellectual property. The company strategy is typically reviewed and updated on an annual basis aligned around the budgeting process, but it can also be more dynamic and aligned to monitoring and responding to changes in the market or deviations from current plans.

For example, a consumer products company could define its current company strategy as focusing on growth in specific emerging international consumer markets through adapting its products to local needs or entering adjacent product categories. Other company strategies could include investing in a new growth category while maintaining or decreasing investment in its current mature categories. An example of this is Proctor and Gamble's decision to pursue a targeted strategy of 40/20/10. This strategy entails focusing on its 40 biggest category/country combinations, its 20 largest innovations, and its 10 most lucrative developing markets.

The next tier of strategy is at the product level. Product strategy ranges from the overarching product portfolio strategy to the individual products or product components. Startup organizations may have only one product and one product strategy, whereas large and complex organizations will likely not only have individual product strategies but a portfolio strategy that aligns the various individual product strategies toward a common goal or objective.

Product strategy is focused on market segments, their needs, and the specific solutions to those needs. The solutions to these different needs are the goods and services offered by a company.

Depending on the size of the company, this hierarchical breakdown could be at a product category, product line, or individual product level. There can be many different product strategies in a company driven by different market segments, and there can be hierarchical reporting up to a broad category.

A category encompasses a large, generic set of products, such as household goods. Product lines are narrower offerings of similar products that may provide smaller variations in the offer, such as different options, complementary functions, or accessories.

A simple view of how to visualize a high-level set of strategy options is through the Ansoff Matrix shown in Figure 9-4.[47]

---

[47] Ansoff, I. (1957). Strategies for Diversification. *Harvard Business Review*, 35 (5), 113–124.

Figure 9-4. Ansoff Matrix

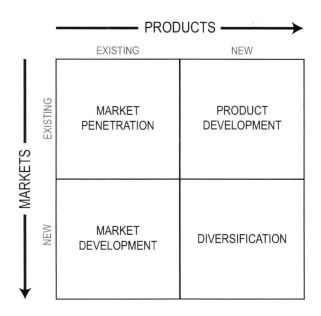

This grid plots Markets on one axis and Products on the other. If the focus is on the current market with current products, then the strategy is one of *market penetration*—obtaining growth by selling products to more customers in existing markets or getting existing customers to use more of an organization's existing products. If a decision is made to expand horizontally into new products, then the focus is a *product development* strategy requiring investment in building new solutions. If there is a need to expand vertically into new markets or market segments, then the focus is on *market development*, adapting products to the new market and focusing on distribution and marketing activities. Expanding in both directions creates a *diversification strategy* of both new products into new markets, with associated investments in several activities. An overall product strategy can have elements of each of the Ansoff trajectories with different priorities and resource allocations directed appropriately.

Diversification strategy involves the most risk for a company because it has the most unknowns and least amount of current knowledge and leverage it can apply. If the market is already proven with current companies supplying products, then the risk can be mitigated through an acquisition strategy of one of the existing players. If the market is unproven or in an emergent state, then the risk involved is similar to a startup organization. In this case, a customer development process that involves incremental product, market, and business model development may be required.

The product management function should lead the development of product strategy. Individual product managers have responsibility for single products, multiple products, or product lines. For large system-level products with a high degree of complexity, a product manager may own only a small set of capabilities or features and must coordinate with other product managers or teams to architect the overall strategies.

Directors or vice presidents typically own a portfolio or full set of products, a category, a product line, or a large product, and will generally own the overall portfolio or product strategy across their span of control.

9.6 A Closer Look at Product Portfolio Management

Product portfolio management is a strategic process that runs in parallel with the company and individual product strategies. It serves the function of optimizing the overall value of the products being delivered by the company relative to investment.

Product portfolio management is sometimes confused with *project* portfolio management. However, project portfolio management focuses upon projects, programs, and other related work and is not focused on nurturing the overall health and value of the products in a company's portfolio.

Product portfolio management involves managing overlapping product lifecycles to ensure that the overall investment for both the short- and long-term profits is maximized. As new ideas for solutions emerge in the organization, they're often assessed by a committee or team for attractiveness for the business to pursue. For large companies, the number of new ideas to assess and track can be quite robust and the portfolio management activity can be complex. For smaller companies, the process can be more straightforward, but still difficult to manage.

The balance of a product portfolio is important to take into account with a diversified view to address both planned and unpredictable outcomes, much like a diversified personal investment portfolio. This diversification attempts to balance current products with new products, current markets with new markets, short-term versus future revenue, and low-risk versus high-risk ventures.

The product portfolio also needs to be aligned to support the strategic objectives of the overall business. The portfolio management process is the link between corporate strategy and product strategy. Finally, portfolio management helps to maintain the appropriate flow of product-related projects into the organization so as not to overload or starve available resources but to optimize their utilization.

9.6.1 Portfolio Analysis

Product managers rely on product portfolio analysis tools, such as the Boston Consulting Group (BCG) Growth-Share matrix and the GE-McKinsey matrix to analyze the market, customer needs, and product lines in order to decide which products should be retired. These tools are illustrated in figures 17-1 and 17-4.

These tools are often used in conjunction with competitive and market analysis to ensure that the decisions made by the product manager are aligned with the market forces that can affect product outcomes. This helps ensure that product decisions take advantage of favorable changes in market forces in order to increase the likelihood of success.

The BCG Growth-Share matrix is a two-by-two matrix that helps classify products into four types: Stars, Cash Cows, Question Marks, and Dogs. The GE-McKinsey matrix is similar to the BCG matrix. It's a three-by-three matrix that compares different products based on Competitive Position and Industry Attractiveness. This matrix allows the product manager to compare competitive position, industry attractiveness, market size, and market share for different product offerings.

Products that are classified as having low competitive position and low industry attractiveness, low competitive position and medium industry attractiveness, and medium competitive position and low industry attractiveness are candidates for retirement.

Industry Attractiveness is estimated by analyzing the market size, the market growth rate, the market profitability, the competitive intensity, the overall risk of returns in the industry, the entry barriers, the pricing trends, opportunity to differentiate, demand variability, segmentation, distribution channels, and technological development.

Competitive Position is estimated by analyzing factors such as strength of assets and competencies, market share, market share growth potential, brand strength, customer loyalty, relative cost structure, relative profitability, distribution strength, production capacity, record of innovation, management strength, and access to financial and other investment resources.

These tools are often used along with SWOT, PEST, or TIME analysis to help establish the context of how external factors impact product decisions and outcomes.

- SWOT analysis identifies an organization's Strengths and Weaknesses and market trends that create Opportunities and Threats within an industry.

- PEST analysis identifies Political, Economic, Socio-cultural, and Technological factors that impact an organization's industry.

- TIME analysis is an alternative method that identifies Technology, Industry, Market, and External events and trends that impact an organization's product outcomes.

Chapter 10

The Conceive Phase

10.1 Setting the Stage

The Conceive phase begins the journey through the full product management lifecycle. This phase is often called the "fuzzy front end" of product development because it's not a linear process starting at point A and arriving at point B. This process is in contrast to how the other phases typically operate with specific objectives, milestones, deliverables, and timelines. The front end of the process is much more unpredictable and may involve retracing steps, changing directions, and potentially making no measurable forward progress for some period of time.

The product manager should approach the Conceive phase as more of a research activity than a delivery activity. The following discussion of the Conceive phase will be centered on specific questions that need to be answered at different points in the process.

The Conceive phase is split into two sub-phases or activities that can occur sequentially or independently as two separate processes. The first activity, Concept Identification, concerns finding new market opportunities that may be addressed by a product delivered through the organization. The second activity, Concept Investigation, explores and analyzes a specific product concept for viability and attractiveness to pursue it.

Before diving into the questions and activities of the Conceive phase, it's important to understand some high-level concepts that will help frame the overall phase.

10.2 Product Concept Identification

Concept Identification is a sub-category of the Conceive phase and entails performing an overall situation analysis for external and internal environments, creating and prioritizing strategy options, and selecting a product concept as a supporting initiative.

The situation process used for external and internal assessments is commonly called a *SWOT Analysis*, which identifies Strengths, Weaknesses, Opportunities, and Threats. SWOT Analysis is depicted in figure 17-5.

10.2.1 External Assessment

The heart of a successful portfolio or product strategy lies in understanding what's going on in the market that will create opportunities and threats. The market is external to the company and is in a state of constant change. For some industries, this rate of change is relatively slow with the flow of products, competitors, and overall market dynamics quite stable for years. In other industries, especially high-tech and software, the situation is more volatile as an entire product lifecycle can be less than one year.

The external assessment attempts to understand several different trends that can affect your business, including:

- Market view – changing market growth, emerging markets, and demographic, geographic, behavioral, and psychographic trends

- Competitor view – new entrants, strengthening or weakening of competitors' products, reputation, key customers, locality, and financing

- Technology view – advances, obsolescence, adoption, and declining costs and availability

- Partner view – changes in distribution channels, suppliers, and value chains

- Environmental view – changes in regulations or laws, financial markets, and political or geo-political impacts

It is also necessary to attempt to identify which trends have the largest potential impact. This requires looking further down the road. Some impacts are obvious, such as a new competitor entering the market with an attractive offering that is gaining attention and warranting a response. Many are less obvious, such as trends or new products outside the product's specific industry, but with an analogous impact or use that may threaten the entire industry. For example, the Internet, along with innovative companies leveraging it, has brought significant challenges to several industries, including retailing, publishing, and communications, and will certainly impact many more.

Besides understanding the broad market trends that have potential impact for products, a company must also have a keen understanding of its current and potential customer needs. The most common process of collecting this information is known as Voice of the Customer (VOC). This method seeks to go beyond simply asking customers what they want and need. It attempts to understand the customers' underlying goals and then identify gaps in current solutions for achieving those goals. This can lead to both incremental and radical innovations.

The VOC process can involve many different types of market research, ranging from surveys and interviews to detailed studies of how customers perform current activities. Many insights can be gained by simply mapping out a process flow of how customers currently perform tasks to achieve their end goal and identifying bottlenecks or needs that are ripe for new innovations.

An example is the Apple iTunes® service.[48] Whereas the introduction of the iPod® music player had several new innovations that enhanced the user experience over previous music players, most potential customers did not have a library of digital music to put on it. The early adopters of the product converted their often large CD music libraries to digital file format. For most people this was a headache. The introduction of the iTunes online music store enabled customers to easily purchase new songs and immediately listen to them. Sales of the iPod skyrocketed after the barrier to adoption was addressed.

Many tools and services now exist for implementing VOC activities. A strong VOC program requires an ongoing process involving multiple functions and levels within a company. The final result is to gain a deep understanding of current limitations in the marketplace that can ultimately create new product opportunities. It may also reveal behavioral changes occurring within customers that could present threats to existing products.

The largest challenge for most organizations is managing the volume of potential information. Finding a place to store it, making it easily accessible and searchable, and keeping it up to date is a tall order. Those who make strategic product decisions need to be able to consume this information. Managing this information is an ongoing process fundamental to every product manager's role.

General questions that need to be asked on a regular basis to gain or maintain an understanding of the external influences include:

- What external trends or events are occurring that could create new market opportunities or present a threat to the current business? What is the timing, growth, and size of the trend?

---

[48] iTunes and iPod are registered trademarks of Apple Inc.

- What emerging needs are being identified through VOC research? What patterns are recurring within market segments that could create new opportunities or threats?

- What importance and priority should be assigned to each finding? Which ones will create the most impact for the business?

Table 10-1. External Assessment: Inputs and Outputs

INPUTS	OUTPUTS
• Primary and secondary market research • Monitoring industry and relevant news and publications • Voice-of-the-Customer research	• Aggregated research findings • Prioritized external findings

10.2.2 Opportunity and Threat Identification

Once thought has been given to trends occurring in the market, the next step is to identify how they may impact the company in both positive and negative ways. Trends or patterns that have a positive impact can lead to the identification of specific opportunities that may allow pursuit of new initiatives. Trends or patterns that have a negative impact can lead to the identification of specific threats to the current business that need to be avoided or minimized in the future. In some cases, both opportunities and threats can result from the same driver.

For example, a large demographic trend in the United States is the aging and retirement of a large percentage of the population known as the Baby Boomers. There are several associated trends that will impact various industries, including higher demand for healthcare, retirement facilities, travel and recreation options, health and fitness offerings, leisure and entertainment options, retirement planning services, adult education, and more. A company in any of these categories could envision broad needs and foresee ways that they may be able to capitalize on the trends. Even companies outside the categories could entertain entering one of these markets.

There are also potential negative consequences to existing categories. Those that may experience lower demand could be sports equipment, single family housing, and larger automobiles and trucks. Companies in these categories could foresee how the need and demand for their products many diminish over time.

At this point, the major objective is not to jump to solve the opportunity or threat, but to acknowledge it and understand it in as much detail as possible. What specifically is the opportunity? Are there sub-segments or sub-categories of the market that may have distinctly different impacts? For example, within the healthcare or travel categories discussed above, there are dozens of sub-categories that will be impacted in varying ways.

How big is the expected change and over what time frame? In our example, the full impact of the changes may occur over several years due to the wide age distribution of the Baby Boomer generation, and the corresponding decline will be fairly predictable. For other types of market trends, especially technology or regulation changes, the impact may be felt more quickly in specific industries.

The high-level questions to be answered during this identification activity include:

- What specific opportunities result from the external assessment? What market problems or needs emerge relevant to the business?

- How big is each opportunity? What is the potential?

- What specific threats result from the external assessment? What changes are occurring that can negatively affect the current or planned business?

- How big is each threat? What is the impact if the threats are not addressed?

Table 10-2. Opportunity and Threat Identification: Inputs and Outputs

INPUTS	OUTPUTS
• Prioritized external drivers	• Identified opportunities and threats and estimated size of the impacts

10.2.3 Internal Assessment

The internal assessment identifies strengths that can be leveraged to address the external opportunities and threats. Capitalizing on these strengths will increase the likelihood of success. This assessment also identifies weaknesses that might limit the ability to address threats and that will need to be minimized in pursuing product initiatives.

Like the external assessment, the internal assessment includes several different views, including:

- Competitiveness view – includes market share, market coverage, growth trajectory, brand strength, diversity of offering, completeness of offering, loyalty, and barriers to switching

- Product view – product capabilities and gaps, price, quality, product line breadth and depth, costs, and profitability

- Competencies view – processes, intellectual property, knowledge, core and distinctive, flexibility, culture, and leadership; may be at a company or group level versus product

- Resources view – people, capital, assets, financing, materials, and economies of scale; may be at a company or group level versus product

- Partner view – capabilities of suppliers and channels, capacity, speed, exclusivity, and breadth (these may be at a company or group level versus product)

Some of these views are more relevant at a company or group level and play into a high-level company or product category level and are therefore inherited by lower level product line or individual product strategies.

Like the external assessment, gathering this amount and variety of information requires some effort. Some data will be obtained from outside sources, such as overall industry statistics to help you determine your relative market share or develop category forecasts. Estimating competitor performance and market share from public sources or through top-down/bottom-up estimates is also required.

At the product level, high-level competitive analysis is needed to identify major capabilities and solutions provided to the marketplace to help identify any gaps in the current product line. An internal product audit may also help to consolidate information about costs, profitability, quality issues, changes in sales trends to specific segments, or continued requests for specific functionality.

A side effect of performing the internal assessment will be uncovering additional opportunities and threats. These will be the result of gaps found in the product or organization as potential overall threats to maintaining business, or gaps in the competitor offerings that may present additional opportunities.

When considering opportunities and threats discovered in the external assessment and this internal assessment, the questions to be asked include:

- What strengths does the company possess that can be leveraged to address this opportunity or threat?

- What weaknesses does the company possess that must be overcome in order to address this opportunity or threat?

- What weaknesses does the company possess that could be minimized by addressing this opportunity or threat with a strength?

Table 10-3. Internal Assessment: Inputs and Outputs

INPUTS	OUTPUTS
• Industry and segment market and financial statistics • Customer visits and surveys • Internal product audit strengths and weaknesses • Competitive analysis • Internal capabilities audit	• Additional opportunities and threats added to prioritized list • Consolidated list of relevant strengths and weaknesses

10.2.4 Product Strategy Options

The overall situation analysis achieved through external and internal assessment is a good start to understand the current status of the product, but it's not the stopping point from a strategy development perspective; it's only the beginning.

It would be a mistake for the thought process to end here without defining specific strategy options to pursue to capitalize on the opportunities or neutralize the threats. The next step is to develop specific initiatives or projects that could address each of the opportunities and threats. This analysis leverages strengths to maximize opportunities for success and recognize specifically where weaknesses may have an impact or be impacted.

For example, an exercise equipment company making home-based equipment has identified the Baby Boomer aging populations as an opportunity for wanting to stay fit while getting older. The company has identified that the equipment needs to have lower impact on joints, be less strenuous to use, and provide options for entertainment or fun while exercising. Some specific strategy options to achieve these goals are:

- Modify existing exercise equipment to address these needs

- Create a new line or brand of equipment specifically targeted at this segment

- Rebrand an external company's equipment to test the market first before diving in with new development projects

To decide on the most attractive option, the product manager needs to consider what the strengths and weaknesses are for each. For example, does the company have the right existing products to be able to meet the need through adaptation? Are resources available for creating a whole new line of products? Does the company have the skill sets needed to develop products with these new requirements? Are the right distribution channels in place to address the market available, even with rebranded products?

Not all strategy options have to be product-based. There is a full toolkit of options to work with, including other elements of the marketing mix such as price, promotions, and place (i.e., distribution channel). There are also non-marketing elements that wrap around the product, such as support and maintenance, ordering and payment processes, and partner or third-party offerings that can be leveraged.

Developing strategy options that leverage strengths and minimize weaknesses can be an intense exercise and take several iterations. However, this is at the core of identifying and assessing the options to make the best choices. It is a true team exercise that can also be executed as a formal ideation event. It also provides an assessment of how to leverage as many company and current product strengths as possible.

Product strengths should be leveraged as much as possible, and relevant weaknesses have different levels of impact. Some weaknesses will be areas that need to be addressed for maximum success. Others will prohibit action on specific initiatives and will need corrective action for any progress. Action is particularly critical if there are major weaknesses related to addressing a large external threat, which is often the case when a disruptive innovation enters the market and incumbents are unable to respond due to inherent limitations in their existing business model. At a product level, this situation could exist when a competitor offers major new functionality that cannot be easily countered due to existing product architecture. In both of these situations, a new weakness has been created by competition that requires specific action and investment to counter the threat.

The questions to be answered for developing strategy options include:

- What initiatives can the company pursue that will leverage their strengths to capitalize on the identified opportunities?

- What initiatives can the company pursue that will leverage their strengths to minimize the likelihood and impact of the identified threats?

- What initiatives can the company pursue to minimize their weaknesses that prevent or diminish capitalizing on the identified opportunities?

- What initiatives can the company pursue to minimize the weaknesses that increase the likelihood and impact of the identified threats?

The next step is to prioritize this list of potential strategy options. The objective is to identify the strongest initiatives that address promising opportunities and critical threats. Opportunity initiatives that leverage several strengths while also minimizing or reducing weaknesses will likely drive the highest success potential. Threat initiatives that remedy weaknesses that are significant contributors to the threat present the highest defensive position. Depending on the perceived urgency of the threat, these initiatives may become the top priority.

Table 10-4. Product Strategy Options: Inputs and Outputs

INPUTS	OUTPUTS
• External assessment • Internal assessment	• Prioritized strategy options

10.2.5 Create the Product Concept

Top strategy initiatives provide a high-level approach for addressing product opportunities and threats in the marketplace. These initiatives will be at the same level as in the original analysis, such as product category, product line, or individual product.

For example, initiatives generated at the product category level could involve expanding a product line for the existing market to increase penetration, or adapting an existing product line to enter a new market segment. For an individual product, an initiative could be adding major functionality to a software product to upsell existing customers or lowering the cost of a manufactured product to become more competitive. For each of these initiatives, there may be multiple tactical possibilities to pursue.

To proceed further into the Conceive phase, the product manager needs to look at the strategy options and pick one to focus on. For this transition, the product manager needs to take off the macro lenses and begin focusing on the specifics of one possible project, as if through a microscope, to assess its high-level viability for success.

A retirement investment portfolio can illustrate this transition. Depending on the person's age, earnings, and temperament for risk, there are methods for deriving an investment strategy consisting of an allocated mix of stocks and bonds across different types of investments—large or small cap, income- or growth-generating, etc. This allocation would be analogous to the prioritized set of strategy initiatives developed up to this point. Now it's time to identify and assess the actual investments that could be made across all of the possible stocks, bonds, and funds available within the framework of the investment strategy.

In the case of product management, the team looks into the *possibilities* of one project. If there are several product ideas to pursue, the product management team needs to perform a high-level assessment of each one, and then compare them against selection criteria. This resultant single project is called the Product Concept, which identifies a specific market need and conceptual solution to solve it.

10

At this stage in the process, the team needs to answer some fundamental questions as an initial screen to decide if they want to proceed with further investigation. The Product Concept can be a lightweight document that answers the following or similar questions:

- What market problem needs to be solved?

- Who specifically has the problem? What buyers and users?

- How big is the opportunity for the company who solves it?

- What is the market window for this opportunity?

- What is the competitive situation for this solution?

- What are the main features of the solution and key success factors?

- What are the company's key differentiators?

- How should this solution go to market?

- How can business success be measured with this solution?

Note that much of the information needed may already exist as a result of the situation analysis and development of the strategy initiatives. This document just pulls that information into a single location and adds more structure and depth to the conversation. The team can also add other means of describing the concept, such as mockups or diagrams, to help explain the solution in more detail.

It is possible that a product concept can originate outside the formal top-down approach used in this discussion and arrive in an ad-hoc way through normal day-to-day activities, such as a customer visit. In this case, some focused background research will be necessary to answer all of the questions. Regardless of how and where the idea starts, the product concept begins the initial step of assessment as a potential project for resources to be assigned to investigate further.

The product concept can be generalized to a broad set of proposed projects within the domain of product. It can be for a new product, a major upgrade to a product, or for an upcoming feature release, as in the case of software. It can also center on enhancements outside of functionality that increase the overall perceived value of the product to the customer, such as cost, quality, user experience, and support. It is not uncommon to utilize these enhancements as other levers available for increasing value and differentiation in the market.

Table 10-5. Create the Product Concept: Inputs and Outputs

INPUTS	OUTPUTS
• Prioritized strategy initiatives • Voice-of-the-Customer research • Focused market research	• Product concept

10.2.6 Product Concept Approval

The product manager now has one or more product concepts to consider moving forward to undergo a rigorous and detailed investigation. What the product team actually has are ideas that can now be applied to an initial screen to determine if the team should proceed.

A natural part of the overall product management lifecycle is to provide some management decision points between each phase. As an idea moves from Conceive to Plan and then onto Develop, Qualify, and Launch, there are business objectives and measurements to apply to ensure the product concept is on track. This process implies that at any point, the product concept may fall below the needed threshold to continue and can be stopped (Figure 2-6).

Figure 10-1. Only the Strongest Product Concepts Survive Through to the Launch Phase

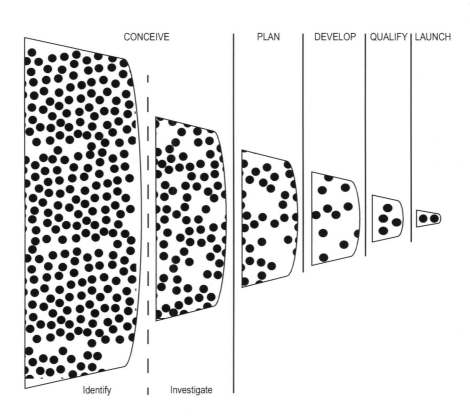

145

In the early Conceive phase, there are many ideas, usually too many. The product manager needs to prune this list into something more manageable. The more promising opportunities progress to the Investigate sub-phase and only the most promising will exit to the next phase: Plan. This process continues until Launch, when only a few viable projects remain.

In many companies, the picture looks more like a pipe than funnel starting at the Plan phase, so that any product concept that enters at this point is assumed to be a candidate for launch and gets a free pass all the way through all of the gates. This accounts for many products being introduced into the market that really never should have been.

The goal at this point in the Identify sub-phase of Conceive is to assess which ideas are the most promising and which to continue with a deeper look. Because there is not yet much information about the product concepts to go on, each one must be analyzed at a more subjective level.

The product manager can develop a prioritization matrix that allows the scoring and weighting of each of the potential opportunities on a similar scale across a number of different factors. This matrix can be developed using any criteria that make sense for the specific objectives of a company or strategy. Here are some possible questions to help determine the criteria:

- What is the market attractiveness (growth and size of market)?

- What is the competitive attractiveness (few players, fragmented, or dominant players)?

- What is the timing for entering the market (too late, now, soon, future)?

- How much market value is provided by the conceptual solution?

- How much differentiation is provided by the conceptual solution?

- How large is the potential gain for the company?

- How well-aligned strategically is the concept to company objectives?

The move from the Identify sub-phase to the Investigate sub-phase could be a formal gate review in the overall portfolio management process, or it can be an informal decision point that is approved by a functional manager or core product team. The goal is to screen out less attractive opportunities as quickly as possible to focus resources on the strongest concepts, reducing overall risk for the portfolio and the organization.

Table 10-6. Product Concept Approval: Inputs and Outputs

INPUTS	OUTPUTS
• Candidate product concepts • Assessment and scoring criteria	• Approved product concept

10.3 Product Concept Investigation

Now that a specific solution concept has been chosen, the goal is to flesh it out with more substance. The intent is to apply the right amount of resource and time commitment such that the market, technical, and business assessment can validate that the effort *should* proceed.

The amount of resources to achieve this sub-phase can vary significantly depending on the size of the investment, risk being considered, and the organizational culture. In a rapid cycle organization considering a smaller incremental opportunity, the effort and output of this analysis can be very lightweight. For an organization considering a major strategic investment, the resources and time spent in this analysis can be significant.

In many organizations, once a product has hit this entry point into the product management lifecycle, the concept is considered "ordained" as an official product. A less risky approach at this juncture would be to consider the product concept as *a hypothesis*, and that it has to prove itself in business terms to move forward. A company with this attitude will more likely find the failure points and appropriately kill the project, or adapt the concept to overcome the weaknesses and build a stronger foundation from the beginning.

The Investigation sub-phase will be segmented into the following high-level activities:

- Establish Cross-Function Product Concept Team – Form the team that will do the work.

- Product Charter – Define the purpose of the product, its success parameters, and what the expected outcomes are.

- Market Investigation – Gain a greater level of understanding of the target market, the customer, the market problem, and the competitive solutions. Document written market requirements.

- Solution Investigation – Identify alternative product solutions and generate high-level estimates of the effort required for each candidate solution and the costs to deliver each in the form of high-level estimates. Assess the

10

solution trade-offs and select the best candidate to pursue, including buy, build, or partner analysis. Document the initial product requirements of candidate solution.

- Market Feedback – In parallel with the above activities, obtain market feedback that the requirements are captured correctly and, as much as possible, gather feedback on the candidate solution.

- Product and Marketing Strategy – Develop the high-level product vision and strategy to achieve it. Identify the initial overall go-to-market strategy for how the product will be launched to the market.

- Business Case – Roll up the anticipated revenue forecast and overall business cost and return for pursuing this opportunity and the associated risks.

The process is not necessarily linear, which contributes to the idea of this still being the fuzzy front end. The activities may proceed in more of a spiral or ad-hoc fashion as new information is uncovered, assumptions validated or disproved, and initial estimates determined that don't support a successful outcome. These discoveries are better to uncover upfront with low investment of time and resources than in later phases when changing direction will be increasingly more difficult and costly.

10.3.1 Document Naming Conventions

Within the Conceive and Plan phases of the product management lifecycle, there are a number of commonly used documents that are similar in their intent and scope, but carry different names. This is especially the situation with regards to how the requirements for a product or service are specified. It is not the intent of this guide to be prescriptive towards a single convention. We have instead split out various pieces of information into different conceptual representations to help simplify the discussions. This guide uses the terms Market Requirements Document (MRD) and Product Requirements Document (PRD) as placeholders for the many different forms of requirements documents in actual use. The MRD is intended to refer to market segment-specific definitions of needs and has more focus on describing the market problem, gap, or need to be addressed. The MRD may originate in a marketing or product management organization and the PRD in a technical organization. The PRD is intended to refer to product-specific definitions of the conceptual or planned product and thus is more focused on the solution to be delivered. It is also not uncommon for a single document to fill both roles, though this can become unwieldy and unfocused for a larger product.

In addition to the specific requirements for a product, each of these documents can contain additional information about how the product will be delivered. In the case of the MRD, the marketing strategy for how the product will be positioned, distributed, and communicated can also be included. In this discussion, this has been split out to a separate Marketing Strategy Document. In the case of the PRD, the development plan for major milestones, resources required, estimated costs, and overall project plan can also be included.

Other common names for the MRD are Business Requirements Document and Customer Requirements Document. Other common names for the PRD are Functional Requirements Document, Functional Requirements Specification, Functional Specification, and Software Requirements Specification.

The physical implementation of these various documents can also vary widely, from text documents to spreadsheets to intranet wikis to requirements management software. The format is not as important as the capture of the right information at the right level of detail to support the planning and development of the product for a given organization.

The goal in organizing the documents in this fashion is to provide containers for the specific information that is discussed, with consideration for the primary audience. These documents communicate a large breadth and depth of potential information and need to be organized into manageable chunks.

10.3.2 Establish a Cross-Functional Product Concept Team

The establishment of a cross-functional team is the first step toward getting a product concept refined and fleshed out. The team needs to be cross-functional due to the number and variety of tasks that need to be performed. It requires product management as the central business driver of the effort with support from others in the organization as key contributors. Typical involvement includes marketing, engineering, design, manufacturing/operations, and support. The team also often includes additional involvement from sales, research and development, information technology, finance, and external partners or vendors.

Building a cross-functional team and assembling team members into an effective unit is one of the central tasks of a product manager. Product managers act as the team leader. This is a natural position for the product manager as their role is to know the customer need, communicate vision and strategy, and optimize results by creating and sustaining value throughout the *entire* product management lifecycle. Product managers and product owners are the only parties that stay with the product from its conception to ultimate retirement.[49] This commitment to the product over the entire product management lifecycle represents a best practice for product managers and owners.

Successful cross-functional team leadership requires support and thoughtful engagement from the senior leadership team in addition to allocation of appropriate resources. The product manager must articulate a clear purpose and ensure that the goals of the team are well defined and effectively articulated to all the team members.

Once the team is identified, ideally the project manager and/or product manager should create a project charter. Charters are documents that define the purpose of the team, how it will work, and what the expected outcomes are. It is a guiding document that the team and its sponsors create at the beginning of the effort to make sure that all the cross-functional team members are clear on the objective.

A project charter answers a series of important questions about the team's mission and objectives. Once drafted, it's then shared with the product team. Team members ask questions at the first team meeting and offer suggestions in order to clarify the mission. The final decision regarding any requested revisions to the charter is made by whoever has created the team. This is likely to be the team leader or sponsor. An alternative approach to developing the charter centers on bringing the team together to draft the charter as a group in order to create stronger buy-in.

The charter document answers several key questions:

- Who is on the team and what is each individual's role?

- What is the purpose of this team?

- What are we trying to achieve?

- How will success be defined?

- Who is the sponsor?

- What deadlines have been set for this effort?

- What financial resources are allocated to the team?

- How often is the team expected to meet?

The required approval for the charter can vary depending on the organization and effort expected from this phase. For a lightweight analysis, the team can self-approve and for larger projects a formal sponsor approval may be required.

---

[49] Actuation Consulting and Enterprise Agility. (2012). *The Study of Product Team Performance, 2012.* Chicago, IL: Actuation Press.

Table 10-7. Product Concept Team: Inputs and Outputs

INPUTS	OUTPUTS
• Identified product concept candidate • Allocated resources	• Assembled project team • Approved Conceive phase project

10.3.3 Market Investigation

The purpose of the market investigation activities is to understand the overall needs of the market segment and the market gap that's being addressed by the product concept. How the product concept got identified in the first place will dictate how much effort and what focus is required for the market investigation.

For example, if during the market assessment the team identified opportunities to expand into a new market with its high-level concept, then a significant amount of new research may be required to investigate and understand the market segments, buyers, and users in much greater detail. On the other extreme, if the product concept is an extension of an existing product in the current market, then there may already be a wealth of information and further research may be minimal except for specific usage scenarios. If the product concept originated through VOC activities that involved in-depth analysis of user activities, then the market investigation may be more focused on understanding competitive solutions better and why the gap exists.

The primary output of the market investigation will be some form of market requirements that describe the market gap in enough detail to enable a thorough investigation of possible solution implementations. It will also begin to drive portions of the marketing strategy that are discussed in later sections.

The overall questions to be answered in the market investigation are:

- What attributes of the target market(s), including sizing and growth?

- Who are the buyer and user groups in each market segment, and what are their major goals and characteristics?

- What are the scenarios where the market gaps are exhibited? What are the desired scenarios for customers to achieve their goals?

- What is the full set of needs a solution must address to close the gap and be competitive in the market and with what relative priorities?

The process and resources used to acquire this information can also vary widely by company and even by project. It could involve directly talking to customers through VOC activities or it can involve customer proxies: expert or market-facing specialists who have experience with customers who can provide input on their behalf. These resources are often internal, such as sales people, sales support, customer support, and product marketers, or they can be external resources such as consultants, partners, and vendors with relevant market knowledge.

The process can also be largely executed by the product manager or with the help of other team members with more specialized skills in these areas. These can include market researchers, product marketing, business analysts, user experience professionals, and technical staff. It is common in some organizations to approach this as a team activity and leverage the different perspectives obtained from all of the team members in aggregate. Different skill sets will view the situation through different lenses, and some unique insights may be gleaned through a conversation spanning these cross-functional viewpoints.

Understand the Target Market

A first step in understanding the market gap is to identify in more detail the target market attributes and specifically *who the customer* is who will buy and use the product. As discussed in the Market Segmentation discussion earlier in this section, this is the time to define the key attributes and characteristics of the target market. The product team may have already obtained this information from market research or may have to do additional research. The team must also identify the size of the overall market, current state of penetration, and growth potential.

A common sizing approach for the market segment is to do it in steps. The first step is to estimate the Total Available Market (TAM), also called Total Addressable Market. This is an estimate of the maximum revenue number or total customers available to all competitors in the segment for all competing solutions. Next, the team must determine how much of this market can be accessed. This is called the Serviceable Available Market (SAM), or Served Available Market.

Many factors influence this analysis. If the market is highly penetrated by competitors, then the opportunity will likely be a small niche not addressed by the competition. The growth potential of the segment may also be limited in this scenario. If the market is emerging and there are no competitors with a large share of the TAM, then the opportunity may be large, assuming the product has the right solution to jumpstart the growth phase of product lifecycle. Product managers also need to consider how much of the market can be reached. If the TAM is global, but the sales channel reach is geographically limited, then the SAM should reflect this limitation. Once the target market is clearly defined, then the customer needs to be identified.

The *buyer* is defined as the person who is paying for the product. Buyers are motivated by getting the expected value out of the product compared to the perceived cost. Therefore, the buyer is the target for the overall product value proposition. The buyer is also a target for the sales process. Understanding how the buyer seeks information, makes decisions, and purchases the product will influence the entire go-to-market strategy. If entering a new market, new sales channels may need to be developed to reach them.

The *user* is defined as the person who will directly use or interact with the product's functionality or capabilities. The user is motivated by accomplishing a specific task or a goal. There can also be multiple users of a more complex product performing different tasks. There can also be different levels of users from an experience or expertise perspective, such that they will use the product to accomplish a similar end goal but may want to do it in different ways. Therefore, the user is the target of the product functionality and overall user experience.

Buyer and user information is obtained through market research and interviews, and then organized into similar buyer and user groups with similar characteristics. A common method of organizing the different profiles is through the use of personas.

Personas are representations of the similar groups that are personified such that they are given characteristics of an individual in order to bring them to life. The information conveyed by a persona includes demographic, psychographic, and behavioral information relevant to the market segment product. They are also often given real names and imaginary photographs to make them more tangible. The overall goals are to have a common frame of reference for all of the people on the project, to understand for whom they are developing the solution, and to use the information to help them make decisions along the way. Personas can be valuable tools throughout the product management lifecycle.

Buyer personas represent specific groups of buyers that the sales channels are likely to encounter, such as a department manager and purchasing manager for a business product. These personas will help drive the development of the important components of the value proposition in addition to the messaging and sales materials to communicate it.

User personas represent specific groups of users who will use the product in different ways or have different expectations of it. An example could be a group administrator who installs and sets up a software product for the end users versus the end user who uses it for the job on a daily basis. These personas will help drive decisions and prioritization for product capabilities and functionality, and specific design decisions impacting usability, such as look and feel.

Table 10-8. Understand the Target Market: Inputs and Outputs

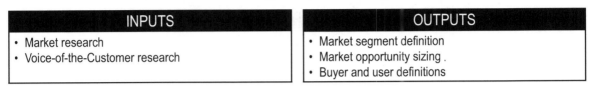

INPUTS	OUTPUTS
• Market research • Voice-of-the-Customer research	• Market segment definition • Market opportunity sizing . • Buyer and user definitions

Illustrate the Market Problem

One of the most important tasks for product management is capturing the market problem in a broad context so that the rest of the team can fully understand the situation. Very often, only a small part of the problem or need is captured without information that could be useful in developing a complete and possibly innovative solution.

Problem scenarios are one method for describing the market problem to be solved. They are an easy way of describing a typical situation that a persona encounters. They can also illustrate the desired or conceptual solution with the new product being used. For this discussion, problem scenarios will be included in the MRD, and solution scenarios illustrating the conceptual solution will be included the PRD. These latter scenarios are more commonly called *Use Cases* or *User Stories*, especially for software products.

Scenarios can take several forms, depending on the type of product being developed and the level of detail needed to capture the information. One common format is a simple story consisting of a few paragraphs or bulleted steps in a sequence. The intent of a scenario is to capture some key elements, including the persona(s) involved, a setting for when the problem is occurring, the overall goal the persona wants to achieve, common steps the persona performs, and major decisions the persona makes that can affect the flow.

Other methods for illustrating usage scenarios can be *storyboards* that combine both illustrations and story steps, or flow diagrams that show major activities and decision points graphically. The overall objective is to describe, in a simple and comprehensive way, the challenge the persona has in achieving its high-level goal with existing solutions in the market.

Often it's just the complexity or number of steps required to achieve the goal that is creating the opportunity for a new solution. Many successful products have resulted from simplifying the task flow or organization of information, enabling the persona to achieve its goal more easily. Also note that the persona, either the user or buyer, may not have explicitly asked for the simplification, since he or she may not have known a better way might exist. This is called a *latent need*.

The best product companies understand this concept and drive innovative solutions that expand the possibilities by capturing both latent and identified needs. Scenarios are a way of capturing the persona's world so that the internal team can utilize it to more effectively envision latent needs and innovative solutions.

Table 10-9. Illustrate the Market Problem: Inputs and Outputs

INPUTS	OUTPUTS
• Identified market gap	• User problem illustrations

Analyze the Competition

In addition to identifying and understanding the market gap that exists in buyers achieving their goals in a more effective way, it's important to also understand the alternative offerings in the market.

The goal is to understand why, in spite of potential offerings in the market, the gap isn't being addressed. It could be that the competitors' offerings have the wrong feature sets, incomplete end-to-end or poor user experience, are too complex, are priced too high, etc. Or perhaps the solutions were intended to address a different problem for a different segment and were not really intended to focus on this particular gap as a complete solution. It may be concluded that the competition is addressing the gap, but the majority of users are not choosing those solutions. This scenario should cause the product management team to think deeply about the real problem and potentially reconsider entering the market with their current concept.

The competitive assessment performed as part of the product concept in the previous section was focused at a higher level of company-to-company competition, though it could have also been at product level if the information had already been researched. In this section, specific product-to-product capabilities will be compared.

The best way to perform a competitive analysis is to first identify all of the major competitors that appear to be targeting the potential market segment with a similar or alternative solution. For the industry and solution, this may be easy with just a handful of known competitors. In other cases, there may be dozens of potential competitors, so it will take some pre-assessment of those who have the strongest market offerings. The next best alternative for users should be considered and it may be none of the current competitors. Home, grown solutions may actually offer the strongest competition and is very often the case in early stage markets where nobody has yet created the right solution for the majority of users.

The next step is to identify the key capabilities of the solutions being offered to the market and attempt to rate how well the capabilities are delivered and if they meet the market need. This is not always easy or straightforward. Ideally, obtain competitor's products and then use them. This technique provides the greatest insight into their capabilities and user experience, but is not always possible if they are not available in the open marketplace through third parties. Reviewing competitor products may also highlight some features that the product management team didn't consider. A competitive analysis example is shown in figure 17-8.

The easiest method to obtain product information is to find literature or peruse websites, which may identify what the competitor's feature sets are, but may not identify how well they are implemented. In some cases, you may be able to obtain third party reviews, such as through trade magazines, bloggers, or independent review services that publish results. For many products, these reviews are not available and the product manager may have incomplete information about the competition. Additional actions can be taken to fill in the void such as user interviews, scouring online forums, or even hiring secret shoppers.

The product manager should also include information beyond product capabilities to include the full end-to-end experience of the buyer and users, such as ease of purchasing, delivery, installation, paying, support, and maintenance.

As the product team begins to collect the results, they can build a matrix of features and capabilities with competitors' ratings, and how well their solution competes. An example of effective content and presentation would be Consumer Reports®, who publish comparative matrices of hundreds of types of products.[50]

Product managers should note that more features do not always correspond to a better product and often dilute the core value proposition. It is potentially better to be superior along key attributes of the solution rather than trying to offer a full complement of average features. It is tempting to think that a product can be strong across a full spectrum of capabilities, but few companies have this depth or the resources to compete effectively in this manner.

Not all features in a product have the same level of importance. Some are fundamental capabilities required to provide the core benefit of the product. Others have varying levels from "somewhat important" to "not important at all" for certain users, and competitors may have included them to appease an important customer

[50] Consumer Reports is a registered trademark of Consumers Union of United States.

or simply because other competitors included it. These are *not* good reasons. The product team should make every capability earn its way onto their feature list.

Market importance can also drive prioritization across the features. If the product team is short on resources or time to complete all of the desired features, then the unimportant features should be removed.

The product team should also assess "how well" or "how complete" a feature is implemented by the competition. Just because a feature is included doesn't mean it's implemented well or completely by a competitor. Attempt to get more granular in identifying how well the competitors execute on the capability. Create levels of criteria that would describe a well-executed feature versus mediocre or poor. These could be along the lines of performance, completeness, and quality. There may be opportunities to surpass the competition in execution, especially for those features that have been marked as important to the segment. This enables the product manager to fine-tune the allocation of resources to the capabilities providing the biggest impact.

This assessment can span as few as a dozen high-level features for a simple product, or dozens for a more complex product. It is often useful to group them by category for easier reading and to stay at a relatively high level because it's easy to get bogged down and lose sight of the major value the product is offering by going too deep into minor feature variations.

Table 10-10. Analyze the Competition: Inputs and Outputs

INPUTS	OUTPUTS
• Competitive research	• Competitive feature analysis

Document the Market Requirements

The major objective of market investigation activities is to understand the overall market needs to be satisfied by the product concept, and to document those needs in the form of market requirements. Refining the definition of "customers" into buyer and user personas is one part of that effort, as are the problem scenarios that help create context around the problem. The major effort is in specific details about capabilities, including any constraints and quality levels that need to be attained to meet customer expectations for the total solution.

Due to the broad differences in products across industries, the specific detail required can be very different. One common categorization between different types of requirements is functional requirements versus non-functional requirements.

Functional requirements are used for products that have some amount of interactivity with the user; the specific high-level functions the user can perform. For example, a simple blender could have capabilities of turning the unit on and off, as well as selecting one of three different blending speeds to blend to different consistencies of the mixture. An advanced blender could have functionality for setting any possible speed range from a minimum to a maximum, a means for timing the duration of the blending, and a means of feedback that measures the specific viscosity or other parameter of the mixture.

Non-functional requirements describe qualities and constraints placed on a product. Qualities can include usability, performance, reliability, compatibility, and a whole list of possible capabilities of a system. These specify "how well" a system needs to perform for specific measurements. Constraints can include "how much" a system needs to support and can include items like operating environment, certifications, compliance, physical attributes, documentation, and reporting requirements.

The MRD creates an overall view of what is needed in the marketplace to address the gap. It should be focused on the problem to be solved *and not the solution* to be created, but as discussed earlier, can also lead into the definition of the conceptual solution that will be addressed in the PRD in subsequent sections.

Special emphasis should be placed on each of the market requirements having a measurable assessment of success. For example, performance requirements terms such as fast, high-performance, or highly scalable are subjective terms and should be avoided. *All of the requirements need a specific measurable parameter* from the market's perspective that would define whether the solution meets the criteria. For example, a high-performance requirement could be specified in terms of a minimum number of transactions per second of a certain type or if the product can perform the entire sequence of activities within a minimum period of time. The result should be measurable and have a definitive pass or fail result against the requirement.

Prioritization is also a key part of the requirements process. Individual requirements or groups of requirements can be prioritized to indicate their relative importance from the market perspective. Common methods include "High, Medium, and Low" or "Must Have, Important, and Optional" designators. Alternatively, organizations can develop more sophisticated decision matrices that weight various desired criteria in a fashion that is meaningful to the organization. These criteria can include relative business value, competitive advantage, estimated cost of development, linkage to product strategy, and financial criteria to name a few. Creating a rank-ordered list of features is another approach, so that the most important ones appear on top and lesser ones on the bottom.

This helps later discussions about solution options, including cost and schedule impact, and there is nearly always a trade-off of capabilities against these parameters. It is neither useful nor realistic to indicate all identified capabilities as being a high priority of market need. The true value of any specific solution is highly dependent on identifying the few key attributes that drive the overall core benefit as the "must haves" and leaving other capabilities or their level of implementation as negotiable with lower priorities. Oftentimes, the major prioritization discussions are not about the major features, but smaller second- or third-level features within these larger groups that may be used by only a portion of the targeted user segment.

A Closer Look at the Minimum Viable Product Concept

An extreme example of this prioritization is the concept of Minimum Viable Product (MVP). The MVP is truly the very minimum set of functionality that the organization can put into the market with the specific intent of testing whether it correctly identified the problem and core benefit. This concept could contain a single major path through a problem scenario with no decisions or alternatives for the user. The MVP can represent a minimum test devised to validate that the market need was correctly identified and the product concept addresses the core need. You may be able to achieve this through mockups or simple prototypes as will be discussed in the solution investigation below.

In the actual delivery from a solution perspective, the MVP is an incremental version of an eventual fuller vision that contains just the very core capabilities targeted at early adopters. The goal would be rapid market feedback coupled with an equally rapid ability to evolve and adapt the product to get it right before investing into capabilities for a broader market. The initial prioritization needs to be extremely aggressive in paring down the delivered solution to bare bones in order to get to market as fast as possible to obtain feedback that the market need has been correctly identified and core benefit is being delivered.

10

The overall contents of the MRD should include:

- Definition of the market segment, specifically the buyers and users of the envisioned product.

- Detailed definition and illustration of the market problem to be solved.

- List of market requirements covering various aspects of the required functionality and associated qualities and constraints placed on the solution. All requirements should be measurable and have quantitative success measures and emphasize the whole product or solution from the customer's perspective.

- Prioritization of the market requirements against the perceived market importance.

Table 10-11. Document Market Requirements: Inputs and Outputs

INPUTS	OUTPUTS
• Market segment definition • Buyer and user definition • Market problem illustration • Competitive analysis	• Market requirements document (MRD) • Prioritized requirements

10.3.4 Solution Investigation

Up until this point in the Product Concept Investigation, the focus was on identifying and detailing market needs that may have emerged from a variety of different research methods. It is now time to define how to address the need.

This is a natural transition point in the process from defining *what* is needed in the market to *how* the need will be addressed. There is also typically a shift in the primary owner of the activities from product management to the development team, but this does not always have to be the case.

The most important idea to realize at this point is the possible existence of an unlimited number of potential solutions, each with specific trade-offs. There is not a single "right" solution to any customer need. The solution domain is a multidimensional space in which there are many different solutions. Each potential solution has strengths along some dimensions while having weaknesses along others. One dimension may be price, as the cost to create a superior product can be expensive in terms of unit cost and cost to create and deliver. Another may be complexity of use in that an attempt to do everything well can make a product complicated. Finally, the ability to deliver the perfect solution to the market in the needed time frame may not be achievable with the resources available.

So the major effort of the solution investigation is to explore the possible implementation options, including the cost and time to deliver each.

Identify Solution Candidates

There may already be some ideas for candidate solutions based on the different levels of discussions that have occurred. The scope of the product concept may also be relatively narrow, such as adapting an existing product for a new market or expanding a product line with similar-type products. In these situations, a fairly small field of candidates may already have been thought through, and so this activity may be complete or relatively small.

In other situations, there might not be a candidate list. This could be the case if the development team has not yet been involved in the discussion to provide input on potential solutions. It may also be the case where the concept is new for the company and many different approaches could be used.

In the earlier discussion regarding types of innovation, the process of ideation was defined as a form of structured idea brainstorming. In much of the literature, ideation around solution candidates is the prime target of the activity, especially for new product solutions. The defined market requirements illustrate the market problem to be solved, and the MRD contains specifics on the types of functionality needed, as well as the constraints and qualities the solution needs to provide. This provides a framework to focus the brainstorming activities.

One method for implementing solution ideation is through structured workshops where a group of people are brought together specifically for brainstorming. These are sometimes called Joint Application Design or Development sessions. The sessions can include participants from several functions, and even include external customers and partners.

Another method is working with customers to jointly come up with solutions, which can be especially useful if lead users are identified. Lead users are thought-leading customers who are already creating adaptations of the product or other solutions to better solve their needs and are leaping ahead of most other customers. A major benefit of identifying these customers is that they provide immediate market feedback that helps the product manager to mold the solution and make priority trade-offs.

Another method gaining popularity is the concept of open innovation, where a particular problem is presented to an open community of customers or partners, and where a competitive environment exists for proposing solutions. The best

10

ideas are then rewarded through some payment mechanism or outsourced to the partner to develop under contract.

Regardless of which methods are used for the solution ideation process, a useful activity across any of them is the development of *solution scenarios* that help paint the picture of the user activities that would result with each candidate solution. Analogous to the problem scenarios illustrating the market problem, the solution scenarios illustrate how the solution makes it easier to achieve the goal. This can also directly identify where the value is being created for the customer.

The exercise equipment example discussed previously to modify existing home-based equipment to better accommodate the needs of aging Baby Boomers led to major requirements, including the need for the equipment to have lower impact on joints, to be less strenuous to use, and to provide options for entertainment or fun while exercising. Our ideation process would involve brainstorming modifications that could be made to accommodate each of these requirements while also attempting to quantify how well it solves the particular need. Some ideas could rank high on achieving one of the requirements, but rank low or even negatively against the other requirements.

The items on this completed list could be ranked comparatively against each other based on the total value created, which would provide an initial list of prioritized solution candidates to investigate further. Then the product management team could analyze these solutions relative to other alternatives to determine if they provide significant value to this specific segment versus the existing equipment or offer something better than what is already in the market. If not, they may need to step back and consider other approaches.

Value identification is a key step in coming up with real measurable benefits from the solution, such as savings in time, reduction in complexity, and savings of real cost. These benefits are fundamental drivers of the solution value proposition. Different solution candidates may provide vastly different results when viewed from the perspective of measurable benefits. This scenario view can also immediately eliminate any further investigation into most of the solutions, based simply on the comparison of relative benefits.

It is easy to overestimate the value created from a market perspective for a solution candidate. This overestimation happens due to internal biases for cool technologies, pet ideas from executives, ideas originated from important customers, and internal politics. Diligence is required to gather market information and maintain an *objective market-centric view* which provides the best vantage to create real value.

Table 10-12. Identify Solution Candidates: Inputs and Outputs

INPUTS	OUTPUTS
• Market requirements document (MRD)	• Solution candidates (prioritized)

Study Feasibility and Alternatives

The list of prioritized solution candidates provides the basis for further study to identify if the solution is truly viable. There are many perspectives to consider, but the major questions to be answered are:

- Is the solution technically viable? Can the company develop and produce it?

- What is the effort, time, and cost to deliver it? Are there multiple options?

- What are the major risks in delivering it? Can they be mitigated?

A *feasibility study* examines the proposed effort to help ensure that any product development undertaken will provide a fully functional product on a technical, financial, and operational level. The study typically includes an alternatives analysis, which offers workable alternatives for the system design and development. When the feasibility study and *alternatives analysis* are combined, the resulting comprehensive view of the proposed product makes the risks easier to assess.

The detail includes an analysis of the objectives, functional requirements and design concepts, the effectiveness of integrating automated systems to efficiently and economically improve the program operations, and an evaluation of alternative approaches you can use for the product to achieve its objectives.

As indicated earlier, the primary activities during this phase are likely driven by the development team or from specific design and architecture functions with collaboration from product management. The effort and duration of the analysis can vary dramatically, depending on the amount of new development work that is required versus what can be leveraged from existing products and expertise.

The analysis is also driven from company culture and how much information is required to make a decision before moving to the next phase. Some organizations are more comfortable in moving forward with unknowns that they are confident they will figure out along the way. These organizations should also be more comfortable cancelling a project that runs into problems. Other organizations are much more risk averse and need to try to discover every potential pothole they could stumble on because once development starts, cancelling the project is problematic.

Once the development team identifies feasible technical solutions and has an idea of the full scope of the envisioned solution, the next step is to generate cost and timeline estimates. The cost estimates include both the estimated unit cost of materials and labor to produce or deliver individual products to customers, plus the development costs to create the product in the next phases of the product management lifecycle. The development costs include the internal resources required and estimated durations, plus major equipment, materials, and other external vendor costs. At this point in the process, the estimates are quite high-level or rough-order-of-magnitude (ROM) estimates.

The estimated timeline is derived from the overall estimated effort and logical flow of high-level activities. It also is at a ROM level and expressed in terms of months or quarters for the project to deliver to some milestone, and often contains ranges or confidence level of the estimates. End date ranges can be approximated if a start date is assumed.

If there are multiple options in the solution implementation, especially driving large potential variations in unit cost, development cost, or timeline, then all of the options and trade-offs can be presented for consideration in the eventual decision process. It is often best to explore alternatives at this stage to anticipate the inevitable request for how it could be done faster and cheaper.

Finally, the team should identify any significant risks for the development of the product. These risks can be in the solution implementation itself, in the expertise of available resources, the known unavailability of needed resources, or the new processes and learning required.

A useful technique for assessing the overall importance of risks is to assess both the likelihood of risks occurring on the product and the impact to the project. A risk that has a high likelihood of occurring and has a major impact to the product or project should be considered a red flag with significant effort put into how to reduce or mitigate it.

For products that have an incremental or evolutionary delivery, such as technology and software products, this may also be an opportunity to start thinking about phasing of specific capabilities of the product. This phasing could be driven from the priorities of requirements in the MRD or it could be that some capabilities will take longer than others due to complexity or effort required. This phased view of product deliverables would be the preliminary thoughts around the future product roadmap.

The formality of the deliverables from these activities can vary from a short study write-up summarizing the feasibility, estimates, and risks, to a formal document or presentation supported by spreadsheets and other more detailed materials.

Experience Design Research

A company needs to have a deep, detailed knowledge of its customers' needs before it can design solutions. A company can build upon prior knowledge and experience to design and develop better products and services. Each new generation of solutions improves based upon market and customer feedback.

Sometimes when a company addresses a market need, the solution may completely eliminate existing workflows, activities, and tasks with a better process. Customers may know only "their" way of doing things while the solution provider may have a broader perspective across many customers' processes and a deeper understanding of the capabilities of a newly available technology.

Listening to customers' suggestions may simply lead to incremental improvement instead of disruptive or truly innovative market solutions that are normally derived from latent or unknown customer needs. It is by direct observation of the existing solution that the team may see how the customers actually interact with the products and services in their own work environment. Many things are never verbally communicated because the user is unconsciously doing them or they do not see them as important to mention.

It is also important for product managers to consider the strengths and weaknesses of the competitors' solutions and how the various customers' goals, process workflows, activities, and tasks are similar and different. Innovative thinking can often be aided by looking at solutions that have been developed in other markets and adapting them.

Experience design research supports the requirements work necessary to understand the people who interact with the product. The research can be part of a larger segmentation exercise to select a specific sub-segment of end users to initially target, as opposed to the larger segment. This exercise is often done to reduce the scope of the initial version by targeting early adopters within the target segment who may be more tolerant of missing functionality or interactions. This output can be fed back to update the MRD and also to the business case for market sizing and forecasts.

User research can be accomplished in a number of ways. Some of the most commonly used mechanisms include surveys, focus groups, interviews, and ethnographic studies. The objective is to understand the needs and goals of the target audience in order to develop the reference personas used in the requirements process and to understand in detail how they accomplish their goals currently without the proposed solution. This could be with respect to a competitive offering or by using alternative methods. The insights obtained can enable innovations in the product that accomplish the user's goals in new and better ways.

Information Architects, Business Anthropologists, or Usability Specialists develop, conduct, and analyze surveys, interviews, and observations. The data from these studies help identify problems and opportunities that are realized in the requirements.

Prototyping

One common method used in the feasibility study is prototyping. A *prototype* is an early sample or limited implementation of the product concept. Prototypes can serve a number of purposes, including:

- To align the team – helpful to get everyone on the same page and to avoid misinterpretation of ideas

- To work through a design – for designers and developers, a way to experiment with different design solutions and understand the design trade-offs

- To sell an idea internally – helpful to demonstrate the design solution to internal stake holders like senior management, other designers, or the engineering team

- To assess technical feasibility – Can engineering do it? What resources are available? Is it worth the effort?

- To present an idea externally – obtain market feedback or begin advance selling of a solution

In order to achieve these different objectives, prototypes typically fall into distinct categories as follows:

- **Proof of Concept** – Often uses existing materials, parts, and components to prove the new idea works or not. Can be for a full product or just critical parts to validate the overall concept is viable, such as the technical feasibility of specific functionality. Also called a Breadboard for electronic products.

- **Mock Up** – A rough implementation using crude materials such as cardboard, foam, paper, or wood to illustrate the concept in three-dimensional (3D) form. For software products, this can range from simple paper illustrations to software-based illustrations of screen flow. Also called a low fidelity prototype.

- **Model** – A form built for aesthetic appearance only. Usually built by hand for physical products to illustrate size, weight, and overall visual characteristics.

- **Virtual Prototype** – 3D Computer-Aided Design (CAD) rendering often providing the ability to visualize a physical product on a computer screen. For software products, can be an exact representation of the screens built from visual design tools. Also called high-fidelity prototypes or simulations.

- **Rapid Prototype** – A group of techniques used to quickly fabricate a scale model of a part or assembly using 3D CAD data, such as through a 3D printer; another form of model. For software products, it could be a visually accurate system using rapid programming tools or languages, but not intended for production release.

- **Working Prototype** – A functioning item but may not be fully operational, designed and engineered for manufacturability, or have the final appearance required. Useful for demonstrating to others or to obtain feedback.

- **Pre-Production Prototype** – A fully functional implementation that is still in the testing or validation stages prior to formal release. Often used for beta testing. For software, can be actual working code at varying degrees of progress.

Table 10-13. Study Feasibility and Alternatives: Inputs and Outputs

INPUTS	OUTPUTS
• Solution candidates (prioritized)	• Alternative/ feasibility study • Prototypes • Preliminary development plan • Cost and time estimates • Risk assessment • Preliminary product roadmap

Document the Initial Product Requirements

Now that the team has some direction as to the specific solution it proposes to deliver, it should be documented. Much like the MRD, the variations in how this documentation is accomplished can vary widely. While more detailed work is required during the Plan phase, this initial version documents the high-level view of features and architecture of the envisioned solution. While the MRD was focused on "what" is needed in the marketplace, the PRD is focused on "how" the need will be satisfied. The overall goal of the PRD is a response to the market needs identified in the MRD and answers the following questions:

- What are the overall goals and approach of the solution?

- What high-level functionality will be included in the delivered solution?

- What high-level constraints and qualities are driving the solution?

The focus of the PRD is on the functionality provided by the product and other system level qualities, often called the non-functional requirements. For software products, the major emphasis will be on the functionality to be provided, with the non-functional requirements defining the qualities and constraints for the system as a whole. For hardware products, including embedded software systems, much of the emphasis will be in defining the physical attributes and the operating constraints. For services, the emphasis is on procedural or workflow changes along with any necessary changes to environmental, architectural, or material changes such as interaction with new technology.

The level of detail required at this point is driven from the needs of the organization, but the intent in this discussion is to keep it at a high level for the initial version. This deliverable will be expanded in the Plan phase should this product concept get approved and exit the Conceive phase. For products that have ongoing development cycles, such as software, the PRD can also begin to narrow down what will be delivered in the initial release.

The PRD should include the major goals to be achieved by the product as described in the MRD and overall approach being taken to address the product needs. The intent is to provide context and an introduction to the overall solution before diving into specifics. Depending on the type of product, this high-level view can be illustrated in a number of ways, including:

- Block diagram of specific subsystems or groupings of functionality or activities

- Context diagram that illustrates the solution and other external systems with which the solution interfaces

- Drawing or mockup that illustrates the major physical aspects

If several alternatives were considered in the feasibility phase, the PRD should discuss the chosen approach and key aspects of the proposed solution, with reasoning as to why the approach was selected. This may help in subsequent phases of the project when additional team members join, to reduce relapses into discussions that have already occurred.

The description of the functionality can vary depending on the product type, but a good starting point would be to re-purpose high-level *solution scenarios*, or stories, developed earlier to illustrate how the user will use the product. This is the complement of the problem scenarios identified in the MRD, which illustrated the gap that existed for the user in achieving some goal.

The solution scenario in the PRD illustrates the set of activities the user performs using the solution. Another common way to describe these two scenarios is the "as-is" process for the problem scenario, meaning how the current activities are performed today, versus the "to-be" or "proposed" process for the solution scenario. These are also commonly documented as flow or activity diagrams.

The description of the functionality should also go deeper than just a story and should begin to focus on discrete sets of functionality that emerge from the usage scenario. One common approach in software is through Use Cases, which provide a step-by-step list of activities performed by an end user or external system (as an actor interacting with the system) and the system responses.

Another common technique is through *functional requirements* that have the form "The system shall (or must) <do something>." These can be derived from Use Cases or they can replace Use Cases.

Both the functional requirements and Use Cases can be complemented with graphical representations of documentation, including flow charts, work flow diagrams, data flow diagrams, and other forms of modeling as required. For software systems, it's also common to include some level of definition for the user interface, such as the high-level mockups or prototypes developed in the feasibility study.

A Note on Agile Product Development

Agile methodologies rely upon two key aspects of the Agile Manifesto to drive the requirements process. These are 1) individuals and interactions over processes and tools, and 2) working software over comprehensive documentation.

To that end, Agile organizations do not produce a formal PRD to define the product and the details of requirements are created "just-in-time" to support the Plan and Develop Phases. This is where the major deviation from the traditional serial or Waterfall methodology occurs.

The substitute for the PRD is typically a short product vision write-up discussing the overall product goals for the initial release with a high-level description of the solution coupled with a product backlog comprised of prioritized user stories.

A user story has the form "As a <persona>, I want <to accomplish something> so that <a benefit is realized>." For the initial start, the user stories are typically at a very high level, called epics, and evolve to a number of more granular user stories. These lower levels can be developed further in the Plan phase.

As a user story is readied for the development team, more detail is added by the product owner in the form of acceptance criteria that define testable success criteria for the user story. Other forms of documentation, including use cases and graphical documentation, can also accompany a user story to help define complex operations.

Non-functional requirements commonly have the form "system shall (or must) be <requirement>." As discussed in the MRD, these types of requirements especially need to be measurable and testable. For this high-level view, the non-functional requirements should focus on the overall solution qualities that have the greatest impact on product cost, development effort and time, and major risks. This list will evolve in later iterations of the PRD in the Plan phase.

An issue to be aware of is there are different levels of "how" for the solution definition. One is at an abstract level of requirements that indicate some capability the solution will provide, and the other is the specific implementation level where decisions need to be made as part of the design process.

These will be refined with additional qualities and constraints in the Plan phase followed by the actual "implementation how" or design decisions in the Develop phase. The latter would include the actual choice of switches used, their location placement on the product, and the specifics of how they operate.

Another issue is to address who is responsible for the PRD. As discussed earlier, the MRD typically originates in the marketing or product management organization and the PRD from the development organization.

Regardless, product management should always be responsible for the MRD. The situation can be less clear for the PRD, but in general the PRD should originate from the development team in collaboration with product management. In some cases, product management may be called upon to develop the PRD, and if this occurs, their focus should be limited to the high-level view.

As subsequent iterations of the PRD go deeper into refining the solution, the product and overall process will be better served by the addition of more solution-focused team members. These include business analysts, requirements managers, technical program managers, system architects, and user experience professionals. This enables product management to maintain appropriate levels of focus on the market needs and other deliverables, including product and market strategy as well as the business case.

Table 10-14. Document Initial Product Requirements: Inputs and Outputs

INPUTS	OUTPUTS
• Market requirements document (MRD) • Alternative/ feasibility study	• Preliminary product requirements document (PRD)

Obtain Market Feedback

In parallel with the feasibility and PRD activities above, it's also the best time to obtain quick market feedback on the solutions to validate that the team has correctly identified the market need and is creating a valuable solution. The longer the team waits to get specific market feedback, the higher the risk of increased wasted investment in time and resources. As discussed earlier, every solution idea at this point should be considered a hypothesis until market feedback can validate the idea as having potential.

The mockups or prototypes developed as part of the feasibility study can also be used in conversations with potential users or specific versions can be created for this activity. The goal is to allow the user to get an early approximation to the solution under consideration, including any implementation specifics that have been incorporated into the demonstration. They then can provide feedback on their level of satisfaction in using it to close the gap identified in earlier conversations.

Several outcomes can occur in these conversations. The ideal outcome is they are excited by what they see so far and can't wait for the company to bring it to market. More often, they like some things but not everything, or the limitations of the mockup prevent them from conducting a realistic experiment. What the product team is trying to identify is that they are at least directionally on the right path, and there may be some amount of iteration required to refine it. The more they can check off that they have identified the right problem and have some portion of a workable solution, the further along they are in moving the hypothesis to something more substantial.

The conversation can also reveal that the solution does not get the positive feedback that was expected. The user may find that the solution requires too many changes that feel unnatural or creates new issues or problems for them or just isn't any better than the current solution. It may be that the user is not the right target or is not an early adopter or does not feel the pain of the problem as deeply as others, and thus does not see the potential in the product. However, if the same feedback occurs across multiple users, then it is likely there is a solution issue or the market need was overestimated.

It is far better to have this realization now, with relatively low investment in resources and time, than to find it out months or quarters down the road after a failed product has been launched. The product team can continue to try alternative solution concepts to get past this point or they may decide that they have enough feedback to abort the project. While it can be difficult, it is important to be objective with the results and try to put egos and politics aside. *Market results are a critical measure of product success.* Obtain results early and often over the product management lifecycle to maximize chances of success.

Table 10-15. Obtain Market Feedback: Inputs and Outputs

INPUTS	OUTPUTS
• Market requirements • Preliminary product requirements • Feasibility models, concepts, prototypes	• Updated market requirements • Updated preliminary product requirements • Updated prototypes, working model • Market feedback assessment

Assess Operational Impacts

In addition to identifying the scope of effort, time, and risks associated with the development of the product, a high-level assessment needs to be performed for operational departments to identify any major impacts. It is easy to get lost in the creation of the solution capabilities and miss the big picture of building, operating, distributing, and supporting the solution.

The questions to be answered by this assessment are:

- Does the solution require major changes to the ways other products are currently built, operated, distributed, or supported?

- What are the estimated costs and resources required to address the impacts?

- What are the major risks associated with the impacts? Can they be mitigated?

Gathering this input usually requires participants from other cross-functional departments to understand the scope of the solution being created and to assess how they might be impacted. The results can vary from no impact to significant changes in processes and supporting systems. The latter can potentially create additional projects that rival the size of the solution development and have a significant impact on the overall business case.

Table 10-16. Assess Operational Impacts: Inputs and Outputs

INPUTS	OUTPUTS
• Market requirements • Product requirements • Prototypes	• High-level operational impacts

10.3.5 Develop the Product and Marketing Strategy

Until this point, most of the activities have focused on research and analysis to obtain as much information as possible about the market situation, market needs, solution alternatives and feasibilities, solution costs and timelines, and market feedback on the proposed concept. Assuming the product concept continues to show viability and value to both the market and the company, it's time for the product manager to solidify the overall strategy for the product and how it will be brought to market.

The high-level questions to be answered and added into the documentation include:

- What is the high-level vision of the product in terms of the target market, the high-level benefits that will be delivered, and the general strategy of delivery?

- What is the initial value proposition and positioning being targeted for the product?

- What are the initial thoughts on how the product will be launched and sold?

- What are the specific objectives to be achieved and in what time frames?

- What are the major product and market risks and how are they addressed?

- What are the key resources and programs necessary to support success?

Some of the information already exists from the activities to date and now can be consolidated into central locations for clarity and ease of use. The formal documentation of the strategies can be accomplished in several different forms, from being distributed in the MRD and PRD to separate specific documents addressing the questions. This distribution will be driven by the company's own processes, by which function or group needs the information and in what form, and the size and scope of the initiative. The overall framework for each question will be discussed here and can be localized as needed by the product management team.

Set Product Vision and Strategy

The *product vision* encompasses the general idea of what the product does for whom and with what high-level benefits. The intent is to keep the efforts focused in a consistent direction over the life of the product or at least the foreseeable future. For products that do not have an upgrade cycle, the initial value proposition will likely be its ongoing product vision. For products and services that evolve with ongoing updates and development activities, the product vision helps to maintain a common overriding theme that all future development will respect.

The product vision is not a list of features or capabilities. It describes what the product does for a specific target market in terms of benefits. For example, a product encourages healthy exercise in the home for an aging population and is gentle on the joints, fun to use, and affordable. Much can be interpreted from this vision that can be implemented through a variety of features, while also putting boundaries around it and implying what the product is not. The vision is enduring over the product lifecycle.

The product vision can also put stakes in the ground relative to competition that will force the product team to constantly stay ahead of their competitors by finding ways to make their product a market leader.

The initial *product strategy* describes, in general terms, how to achieve this product vision. Its intent is to provide the high-level context for the set of activities to be pursued in the Plan phase and beyond. For example, "our entry into this market will be through a newly branded product line that utilizes our existing products as a platform, but with specific adaptations addressing the unique requirements of this market."

The product strategy can also lay out a phased timeline or series of steps that are planned. This may be necessary to acknowledge that the product team does not have the necessary resources or the foundation in place to deliver all that they ultimately need, yet they want to deliver components of the product strategy. This approach can help break the overarching strategy into manageable and easy-to-understand pieces.

In addition to the focus on the strategy for the development of the product, additional thought should be put into any partner or ecosystem needs that should be addressed. The concept of the *whole product* comes into play here. Is the product team dependent on external third parties for complementary products or services that are needed to really deliver the envisioned value? For example, does the product depend on third party content, such as media, information, or data? Is the content already available or does it need to be created or aggregated? How would a customer acquire it and is it affordable? Is this product solving only a small part of a customer's problem and the rest is out of the product team's control? Does the product strategy address the gap?

Like the product vision, the product strategy does not constrain the innovations that could be developed by being overly specific, and it clearly defines the paths not to be taken. Unlike the product vision, the product strategy can vary over time as the product management team achieves milestones and decides the next major move based on the results and future market dynamics.

Providing an inspiring product vision can go a long way toward enabling the team to think in creative and innovative ways. Providing a solid product strategy will help focus activities, establish a direct link between the product and the company strategy, and clearly identify to everyone involved the high-level steps currently taken to achieve the vision.

Table 10-17. Set Product Vision and Strategy: Inputs and Outputs

INPUTS	OUTPUTS
• Target market • Market needs • Solution benefits • Feasibility study • Market feedback • Competitive differentiation/positioning	• Product vision • Product strategy

Set Preliminary Value Proposition and Positioning

The *value proposition* is a statement of the value the customer will receive by using the product. Value can be thought of as the difference between a customer's perceived costs versus his or her perceived benefits received.

The cost side of the equation includes not only the purchase price and any ongoing costs, but also the time and effort expended to purchase and use, plus any emotional, psychological, or social costs incurred.

The benefits side of the equation includes not only the direct benefits of achieving a goal, but also indirect or more intangible benefits along the other dimensions. The perceived benefit side needs to be higher than the cost side to provide significant value.

The value proposition is the "promise" to the customer of what they can expect from the product. Some products can provide a measurable improvement in something, such as 20% faster or cheaper than other existing solutions. Other products provide a more subjective value, such as being convenient or fashionable. Some of the most successful products are able to capture value that is both measurable *and* subjective. An example for the home exercise product line could be "30 minutes of use per day, in the convenience of your own home, helps you lose or maintain weight, improve mobility, and raise your energy levels."

The value proposition should focus on the primary benefits at this point and does not need to be in "market-ready" form, such as what would appear in an advertisement. The wording and the key elements will evolve over time as the product team finds out what resonates best with potential customers for the actual messaging. It may also evolve due to changes in the actual implementation of the product. Its purpose is to capture the value in a concise statement so that it can be succinctly communicated to the team.

If developing this statement is challenging, it may indicate that the actual customer value delivered is not high, which is why the exercise is so important from the beginning.

The *positioning* defines the product's unique advantage versus competition. It isn't just how the product is different from the competition, but also *why the difference matters* to the customer. The starting point here is to define the reference point for the competition. If the product team is developing something new to the marketplace, then the competition is the existing situation from the customer's perspective. If there are several existing competitors, then it's often useful to group them into similar categories and identify the unique advantage versus each different group. The product management team can also pick a single "target" competitor who becomes their benchmark for defining their advantage relative to them.

In defining positioning, it's tempting to focus on one or two specific capabilities as the advantage. However, similar to the discussion about value proposition, the question is: what unique *value* does the product deliver versus the competition? This will be at a higher level than features or capabilities. It is also tempting to rely on advantages outside of the product, such as strong brand name or distribution. While this might help enable the product's success, more will be achieved if the team finds real advantages in the product offering, and compounds the advantage with unique company or partner strengths.

Positioning for the exercise equipment example could be "while other equipment providers offer one-size-fits-all solutions for everyone, we provide specialized equipment to seniors that is easy to adjust, and easy to move and store, with a focus on safety to avoid injury."

It is also useful to combine the value proposition and positioning into a succinct overall statement. This is sometimes called an *elevator pitch*, a quick but comprehensive statement of the product's intrinsic value.

Identifying the true value the product provides to the market and why it's better than alternatives is at the heart of a successful product. It will drive development priorities, timing decisions, and overall product messaging throughout the product management lifecycle. While it will likely continue to evolve, it's imperative that the team establish the value early in the process. Too often, these elements are considered to be the marketing message that is created after the product is built. Unfortunately, if the value and differentiation are not identified in the concept phase and used to guide the product requirements and design, no amount of after-the-fact marketing is going to overcome this weakness.

Table 10-18. Set Preliminary Value Proposition and Positioning: Inputs and Outputs

INPUTS	OUTPUTS
• Key solution benefits • Competitive analysis	• Preliminary value proposition • Preliminary positioning

Set Product and Marketing Objectives

The next step after the product management team crafts the product vision and the product strategy is to identify how progress will be measured. This exercise of setting specific objectives will help to identify one of three states after the product launches:

- Met or exceeded the initial plan. Time to set the next objectives.

- Have not yet met the objectives, but current indicators show positive progress. Maintain momentum.

- Have not met the objectives and current indicators show little or the wrong progress. Time for an adjustment.

Objectives are not the same as lofty goals that may be part of the vision, but rather are specific measures of success against a strategy step. For example, as part of the product vision, the company aspires to be the performance leader in its category. One of the strategy elements could be that it will invest in research and development activities for a specific core element of the solution with an emphasis on performance. An example objective would be to achieve a 20% improvement over the current performance within 12 months. This puts a stake in the ground for how the company knows it succeeded and when the measurement will occur. Objectives can also create a sense of urgency when dates are explicitly defined for when the measurement is due.

Objectives are also commonly called Key Performance Indicators (KPIs). A common framework for setting objectives is employing the acronym SMART, in which the letters stand for:

- **S**pecific – state exactly what is to be achieved and by whom

- **M**easurable — demonstrate whether (or how far) it has been achieved

- **A**chievable — be realistic given the circumstances in which it is set and the resources available to the business

- **R**elevant — be relevant to the people responsible for achieving them

- **T**ime-Bound — be set with a realistic time frame or deadline

At this point, the product team is looking for high-level drivers that will set the stage for quantifying early successes. They can set objectives for the product to achieve in two or three years, but they will also benefit by breaking their primary objective down into aligned sub-objectives that show results sooner, such as in the next six to twelve months. Example types of high-level objectives include:

- Product – specific capabilities that will be added, or levels of performance or cost that will be achieved

- Project – statement of milestones or deadlines, or budget and resource constraints

- Marketing or sales – response rates to marketing activities, qualified leads in a sales process, early customer pilots or trials, and initial unit or revenue targets

- Market – change in market share, change in penetration into a specific segment, or change in repurchases from existing customers

Setting objectives for the new product helps to clarify for the whole team what's important and where to focus. Coupled with the higher level product vision and product strategy, it will also align all of the stakeholders around what the team is trying to achieve.

Table 10-19. Set Product and Marketing Objectives: Inputs and Outputs

INPUTS	OUTPUTS
• Product vision and strategy	• Product and marketing objectives

Create Preliminary Launch Strategy

In addition to figuring out the product that needs to be built, an initial view of how the product will reach the market is needed. The purpose in this phase is to identify the high-level marketing and sales activities appropriate for the expected release of the product. The key questions to answer are:

- What is the specific market segment, or sub-segment of the larger market, that is being targeted for the initial launch?

- What general configurations of the product and pricing are being considered?

- What distribution channels are to be used, with what assumed discounts and commissions?

- What is the initial forecast for units and revenue?

- What are the key messages to communicate the value proposition and positioning of the product (often called the Unique Selling Proposition)?

- What are the primary messaging channels to be used, including advertising, press, analysts, social media, trade shows, and partners?

- What are the initial thoughts on sales, channel, and partner training and materials that will be required, including demos and tools?

- What is the initial estimate of launch budget required for resources and expenses?

10

The format of this information does not have to be a detailed document at this point if the product is leveraging current company assets for sales and marketing, though it is preferable. It may suffice that it is a list of assumptions and rationale in another document, such as the business case. However, if there is a significant mismatch between the go-to-market needs for this product versus the current capabilities of the company, then an investment in more detail and documentation is probably warranted to better develop the strategy. In either case, this is just an initial view of the plan, and it will get significant attention and refinement in subsequent phases beyond Conceive.

Table 10-20. Create Preliminary Launch Strategy: Inputs and Outputs

INPUTS	OUTPUTS
• Market requirements • Product requirements • Product vision and strategy • Value proposition • Positioning statement • Product and marketing objectives	• Preliminary launch strategy

Identify Product and Market Risks

The last component of the overall product and marketing strategy should identify the major risks the product faces. All products face some amount of risk. It is simply a part of doing business. Other risks are much more consequential and need to be identified, prioritized, and if possible mitigated. Some high-level questions to ask are:

- What are the risks in creating and delivering the product? Are there major concerns in technical feasibility, available resources, timeline or cost estimates, manufacturing or operational challenges, supplier or partner weaknesses, or legal or intellectual property issues?

- What market risks does the product face? Are there major concerns with market timing, barriers in distribution, macro-economic conditions, competitive moves, sales forecasts, or product acceptance?

- What is the likelihood of the risk occurring? Is it a lesser possibility or a high probability of occurring?

- What is the impact if it does occur? Is it a small "speed bump" that may cause some minor disruptions or is it a major brick wall hazard that will stop the team in its tracks?

- What is the mitigation for high-probability, high-impact risks? Is there a Plan B? Are there steps the team can take now to lessen the probability or impact of the risk? Is there a subset of the project, such as continued feasibility or market studies, that could be undertaken to reduce the risk before proceeding?

The need to resolve all of the major risks before exiting the Conceive phase is not a requirement, as they can be further investigated and plans put in place as part of the next phase: Plan. However, it's always better to identify them *upfront*, so that the appropriate resources and activities can be assigned to lessen the risks or plan alternative courses of action.

Table 10-21. Identify Product and Market Risks: Inputs and Outputs

INPUTS	OUTPUTS
• Product vision and strategy • Product and market objectives • Feasibility studies • Go-to-market plan	• Product and market risks • Mitigation plans

The product and marketing strategies are the core elements to come out of the Conceive phase to guide the product through the next phases in the product management lifecycle and on toward market success.

Table 10-22. Create Product and Marketing Strategies: Inputs and Outputs

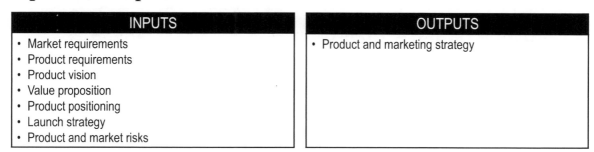

INPUTS	OUTPUTS
• Market requirements • Product requirements • Product vision • Value proposition • Product positioning • Launch strategy • Product and market risks	• Product and marketing strategy

10.3.6 Create Overall Project Charter

The project charter begins to lay out the overall plan for the solution delivery. It can be a separate deliverable or included in the preliminary business case. The information is a roll-up of specific project information that will be used going forward. The major questions to address are:

- What are the primary objectives of the project?

- Who are the project stakeholders?

- Who is on the core team? What supporting teams are needed?

- What are the high-level deliverables or activities? What is out-of-scope for the project?

- What are the major milestones planned and when do they occur?

- What are the major constraints on the project? What are the deadlines and resource or budget constraints?

- What is the risk management plan?

- What is the project communication plan? How will stakeholders and team members communicate?

The project charter will evolve into a full project plan as part of the activities in the Plan phase. The charter created in the Conceive phase will help jumpstart the team required for that activity.

Table 10-23. Create Project Charter: Inputs and Outputs

INPUTS	OUTPUTS
• Product and marketing strategy • Product requirements • Solution investigation • Operational assessments • Risk assessment • Resource plan • Budget	• Project charter

10.3.7 Create Preliminary Business Case

The *business case* provides the overall justification for the product, illustrating an internal cost-benefit analysis. It can range from a simple spreadsheet that shows the financial assessment of the project to a formal document set that weighs the trade-offs of entering into an entirely new line of business.

The business case can roll up much of the information that has already been discussed here, specifically the product and marketing strategy components. The financial analysis also rolls up the estimated revenues and costs that have been accumulating through each of the other activities, and the outcome of the operational assessment. Of course, at this point, the estimates for a new product are very high-level and can have significant error, but the overall goal is to get a quick assessment if this product has potential. Even if the numbers don't yet create a compelling financial picture, the product team might still decide to proceed based on other strategic factors or find a way to improve the financials. This is why a business case composed of just a financial analysis may be too restrictive.

The questions to be addressed by the business case include:

- What is the situation being addressed? What are the summary market needs being addressed and the supporting background information?

- What is the overall opportunity? How does the company benefit?

- What is the envisioned solution? How did the team arrive at this solution? How does it address the need? Why is it better than alternatives?

- What are the overall objectives being pursued? What business assumptions are being made?

- What are total costs of pursuing this opportunity? What resources are required?

- What is the strategic alignment of the product? Does it leverage the company's strengths? How does it align with the company's stated objectives or goals?

- What is the overall timing of the project? Does the timing satisfy the market need? Is now the right time to invest?

- What is the overall cost-benefit outcome? Does it make financial sense? Does it make strategic sense? What happens if the company does not proceed?

- What are the major risks the product and organization face? What are the contingencies?

- What investment is needed? What is the estimated overall investment required in delivering the product to the market? How much investment is required for the next immediate step?

Spending the time to perform high-level due diligence upfront can save significant time, effort, and cost down the road. The effort, however, should be balanced against the scope of the overall project and the downstream processes in place for further analysis, if required. The decision point the product management team is trying to reach now is whether they invest more resources into further definition of a high-potential prospect.

Table 10-24. Create Preliminary Business Case: Inputs and Outputs

INPUTS	OUTPUTS
• Market requirements • Product requirements • Product and marketing strategy • Solution investigation • Operational assessment • Project charter	• Preliminary business case

10.4 Exiting the Conceive Phase

In order to exit the Conceive phase, an approving sponsor or committee typically requires approval of the business case and overall strategy. During this major decision point, the concept can pass through the gate, be killed, be put on hold while other higher level projects are in progress, or recycled for more information or study. If there are lots of ideas in the company, then the approval meeting can be a routine event.

Every concept has its supporters and detractors. To rise above the opinions and politics the best approach for the product manager is to come into this meeting highly prepared and armed with objective data.

It also helps to have had a conversation with all of the approving stakeholders and their advisors, in advance. These conversations provide the opportunity to educate them on what the product team is trying to achieve, and receive input on their concerns and issues. If done well, there will be no surprises in the meeting and an open discussion and decision can occur.

Chapter 11

The Plan Phase

The Conceive phase initiates thoughtful activity for a new product or major enhancement. If the product concept is found to be worth pursuing, the Plan phase dives into further detail about the product, how it will be delivered, the marketing strategy, and the business case to support it. For many organizations, this culminates in the decision to invest a great deal of money and resources to produce the product in the next phase: Develop.

Due to the amount of time and money involved, the Plan phase can be quite rigorous and involve a large number of resources and time to execute. This can be especially true for hardware products, services, and systems comprised of multiple hardware, software, and service components. Even smaller projects requiring capital equipment or engineering expenditures can be a major decision for a company.

The contrary is also possible, especially for smaller companies in fast-moving industries. In this case, the Plan phase can be smaller in scope, as the risk and cost of changing direction is often low. This is particularly true for smaller product or service updates, or add-ons to an existing product. The amount of rigor required is typically much less significant due to the incremental nature of the development or operational activities required to support an established product. Due to this continuum of needs, this chapter will discuss the types of activities that are most often associated with the Plan phase, while leaving it to the practitioners to adapt planning activities and their depth to the needs of the organization.

11.1 Plan Phase Activity Groups

There are four major groups of activities that can occur in the Plan phase: Product Definition, Project Plan, Marketing Strategy, and Business Case. All of these activity groups evolve in parallel and leverage the outputs of the Conceive phase as their starting point.

Product Definition activities are focused on defining the product well enough to enable the product to be developed by the development organization. These activities should be driven by a deep understanding of customer needs and often supplemented in close partnership with user experience professionals with a focus on the end-to-end user experience and detailed user interface design. The activities can include refinement of the target market, a more focused description of all types of end users, and more detail about how they'll use the product. It can also include additional market testing and validation to ensure that the concept and requirements meet the targeted needs and deliver the intended value.

Project Plan activities are focused on the execution activities required to deliver the product to the organization. This plan outlines the boundaries of the project designed to create or enhance the product, including estimates of required resources, delivery milestones, and the anticipated cost of delivery. The plan should also include specific functional plans that provide for other schedule, resource, and cost estimates to deliver or support the product once it moves into the Launch phase and beyond.

For some products, the impact to existing systems and departments is minimal and thus the amount of project planning required is small and primarily focused on marketing activities. In other situations, the impact can be significant, such as requiring new manufacturing, test processes, equipment, supply chain partners, support of a new distribution channel, or changes in the business model or workflow for purchasing, delivering, and supporting the product. In this case, the project planning needs to be detailed.

Marketing Plan activities are focused on updating and expanding the initial market strategy and go-to-market plan with greater detail. This includes the target market and competitive information as well as further refinement and validation of the value proposition and positioning. It also includes updates to the distribution channels, anticipated pricing, and forecasts. Marketing Plan activities also include the initial iteration of the launch plan as the product manager begins to think through the details of how the product will be introduced into the marketplace, including sales channel rollout, public relations, advertising, and the estimated launch costs.

Business Case activities provide a roll-up of all of the cross-functional plans and costs into an overall justification for funding the product and/or project. It always involves a financial analysis that provides a full view of forecasted revenue, the estimated costs, the expected return on investment for the product, and a risk assessment. As with product and project definitions, the scope and depth of the business case can vary dramatically for different organizations or different product efforts, from very elaborate to a simple analysis.

The concept of a full *Product Plan* also exists for some organizations. The product plan is typically an integrated document suite that includes all four of the deliverables listed above in one central location. As part of this discussion, the product plan will be referenced as a potential output of the full Plan phase.

The subsequent sections will cover the four activity groups in more detail.

11.2 Product Definition Activities

The Product Definition activities consist of the product requirements and supporting processes, including user experience definition and requirements validation. For many products, the definition also includes a future-looking product roadmap.

11.2.1 Product Requirements

Product requirements are the primary driver of the technical development activities. In the Conceive phase, a high-level product solution is defined in a preliminary draft of the product requirements. The focus of the Conceive phase requirements were on identification of a preliminary solution defined at a high level.

The focus of the Plan phase is to create detailed functional and system level requirements with the goal of defining the product in enough detail to deliver it using the chosen development methodology. This detail will come from diving into deeper levels of capabilities beyond the high level captured during Conceive, including:

- More specificity on specific user actions and system responses
- More depth in non-functional requirements
- Potentially the full definition of the user interface design
- Completion of the whole product definition

Deeper definition of the solution also assists in the creation of a strong project plan and is necessary to flesh out the cost model required for the business case.

The focus of the product requirements document (PRD) is on the functionality provided by the product and other system-level qualities (often called the non-functional requirements). For software products, the major emphasis will be on the functionality to be provided, with the non-functional requirements defining the qualities and constraints for the system as a whole. For hardware products (including their embedded software systems), much of the emphasis will be on defining the physical attributes and the operating constraints. For services, the emphasis is on procedural or workflow changes along with any necessary changes to environmental, architectural, or material changes like interaction with new technology.

> **A Note on Agile Software Development**
>
> The substitute for the PRD is a product backlog comprised of prioritized user stories. A user story has the form "As a <persona>, I want <to accomplish something> so that <a benefit is realized>." As a user story is readied for the development team, more detail is added by the product owner in the form of acceptance criteria that defines testable success criteria for the user story. Other forms of documentation, including use cases and graphical documentation, can also accompany a user story to help define complex operations.

Prioritization is also a key part of the requirements process. Individual requirements, or groups of requirements, can be prioritized to indicate their relative importance and delivery sequence. Common methods include "High, Medium, and Low" or "Must Have, Important, and Optional" designators.

Alternatively, organizations can develop more sophisticated decision matrixes that weight various desired criteria in a fashion that ranks individual requirements in a manner that is meaningful to the organization. This helps the development team focus on those items with the highest priorities while providing for some flexibility in the capabilities to achieve cost or schedule objectives. In Agile software development, the requirements are stack-ranked in a linear priority backlog, with the opportunity to change priorities between iterations and releases.

The overall process of developing a PRD can be time-consuming, and is generally iterative with multiple reviews among various stakeholders. The PRD is also a fundamental driver of the project delivery plan, as development estimates are derived from the individual requirements given architecture and design assumptions.

It is not uncommon for requirements and requirement priorities to change in response to efforts to reduce project scope or risk as the plan is built. In some templates, the development project implementation details, such as resources, milestones, and costs, are included in the PRD. For this discussion, those items are deferred to the project plan section for simplicity.

The results of the planning process and development of the detailed PRD can also affect the original product concept. As the product is further defined and validated and as the project is scoped for cost and delivery estimates, the original product concept may be altered.

This can also affect the overall value proposition, competitive positioning, pricing, and other assumptions made in the Conceive phase as part of the product and marketing strategy that will need to be reconciled. The market requirements document (MRD) may also be updated or superseded by the PRD and marketing strategy documents.

Table 11-1. Product Requirements: Inputs and Outputs

INPUTS	OUTPUTS

• Experience design research
• Usability evaluation
	• Product requirements doc (detailed)
	  » User personas
	  » Functionality definition
	  » System qualities and constraints
	  » Prioritization
	• Agile user stories, acceptance criteria, and product backlog (alternate)
	• User interface definition (optional)
	• Mockups or prototypes (optional)
	• Market requirements doc (updated)

User Experience and User Interface

A key part of developing effective requirements is getting the user experience (UX) right for the targeted end user(s). The UX of a product contains not only the user interface (UI), but also the end-to-end experience in its acquisition, payment, installation, use, and support. For many products, especially web-based software, these activities are often intertwined with the product itself.

Methods for modeling and testing the UX/UI revolve around the creation of mockups and range from simple paper-based drawings used to illustrate product functionality or flow to elaborate high-fidelity prototypes that look just like the real product. These can be both software-based and physical mockups that simulate the look and feel of the product. Mockups are commonly used in discussions or demonstrations with focus groups or with individuals to ensure that the use goal is obtained. The mockups can also become part of the formal set of deliverables for the product requirements.

As part of the experience design process, user experience professionals conduct qualitative research that includes reviewing the target market segmentations' demographic and psychographic data necessary to establish the design direction. Designers also interview stakeholders, buyers, and the people who interact with the product and service, in order to gain insight into needs and goals. This information feeds directly into the types and characteristics of the personas that drive the design.

Usability Evaluation

Usability can be defined as the ease of understanding and learnability inherent to an experience. Usability studies enhance the elegance and clarity with which the interaction with an experience is designed. The primary objective of usability studies is to ensure that the user's experience of the product is:

- Learnable: How easy is it for users to accomplish basic tasks the first time they encounter the design?

- Efficient: Once users have learned the design, how quickly can they perform tasks?

- Memorable: When users return to the design after a period of not using it, how easily can they re-establish proficiency?

- Free of Errors: How many errors do users make, how severe are these errors, and how easily can they recover from the errors?

- Delightful: How pleasant is it to use the design?

The key principle for maximizing usability is to employ an iterative design approach, which progressively refines the design over time. Evaluation steps enable the designers and developers to incorporate client feedback until the product reaches an acceptable level of usability.

The preferred method for ensuring usability is to test actual customers on a working product and procedures. The most basic and useful process is evaluation, which has three components:

- Work with actual customers that meet the target persona.

- Ask them to perform representative tasks with the design.

- Observe what they do, where they succeed, and where they have difficulties with the interactions.

It is important to evaluate participants individually and let them solve any problems *on their own*. Any help or directing their attention to any particular part of the solution will bias the evaluation. Rather than running a big, expensive study, it's better to run many small evaluations and revise the design between each one so usability flaws can be fixed as they are identified. Iterative design is the best way to increase the quality of experience: the more versions and interactions that are evaluated with participants, the better.

Conduct usability evaluation early and often—usability plays a role in each stage of the design process. Don't defer evaluation until there is a fully implemented design because it's difficult to fix problems that may require "re-architecting" the product. Early designs should be fast, cheap, and easy to change. The best way to create a high-quality experience design is to start evaluation early in the design process and to keep doing evaluations every step of the way.

Before starting the new experience design, evaluate the old design to identify salvageable parts that should be kept or emphasized, and poorly performing elements that give customers trouble. Also evaluate competitors' experience to get data on the range of alternative designs. It can be helpful to conduct field studies to see how customers behave in their own typical setting instead of in a lab.

Consider making prototypes of one or more new design ideas and evaluate them—but the less time invested in these design ideas the better, because they'll need to change based on the evaluation results. Refine the design ideas that resonate with customers through multiple iterations, gradually moving from low-fidelity prototyping to high-fidelity representations. Inspect the design relative to established usability guidelines, whether from earlier studies or published research. Once the product management team decides on and implements the final design, it should be evaluated again. Subtle usability problems frequently creep in during implementation.

Evaluate early designs with a small representative sample of the target audience. As the product progresses along the continuum with higher fidelity prototypes and increased validation, sample size should be increased.

11.2.2 Product Roadmap

A product roadmap is common for products that can be delivered incrementally or in an evolutionary fashion, and high-level requirements are their building blocks. Product roadmaps act as the bridge between the product vision and strategy and the actual tactical product development projects that are undertaken in pursuit of attaining the product goals.

While the product vision and strategy from the Conceive phase outlines a desired future state, there can be multiple product development projects over a defined time frame that visually illustrate specific steps to take to achieve the vision. As business conditions and priorities change, so should the product roadmap—think of it as a "living document."

The roadmap can be visualized in two distinct time frames. In the short term, it's a record of planned releases and may extend two to four release cycles into the future. These activities are often represented by calendar year or on a rolling 12-month basis. See Figure 11-1 for an example of a product roadmap.

Figure 11-1. Product Roadmap Example

PRODUCT	Q2 YEAR	Q4 YEAR
Product Name	10.2 • Feature 1 • Feature 2	10.3 • Feature 1 • Feature 2
Product Name	12.1 • Feature 1 • Feature 2	12.2 • Feature 1 • Feature 2
Product Name	5.0 • Feature 1 • Feature 2	6.0 • Feature 1 • Feature 2

Some projects on the product roadmap may be already in active development, or some amount of planning has already occurred, and there is a high degree of confidence that most of the specified deliverables will happen.

The longer-term portion of the roadmap outlines product capabilities that reside outside the organization's current planning activities and are effectively queued while the current priorities are being developed. This section provides a *directional* view of where the product might head given current business conditions in the next 12 months or longer, depending on the industry. Any major changes in the current projects, the external marketplace, or internally in the business can change these envisioned future releases.

For products or platforms with relatively long lives or industries that are relatively slow-moving, the long-term view can project out multiple years or span a pre-determined lifecycle. For faster moving industries, such as software or consumer electronics, a multi-year look into the future may be much more difficult to assess with any degree of certainty, given the native rates of change, but it should remain directionally correct.

The primary internal objective of product roadmap activities is to gain organizational alignment so that resource and budget allocations can be planned in advance to enable effective execution. The main components of the product roadmap consist of 1) a defined time frame, 2) a solid understanding of market events or deadlines that will drive deliverables, such as the underlying sales cycle or product seasonality, 3) specific products, product capabilities, or themes phased over a period of time, and 4) associated development activities or resources impacted or required.

The internal product roadmap may also be the result of, or heavily influenced by, the product definition and project plan activities for the current release. Very often, the desired scope of envisioned capabilities to be delivered, in the current targeted time frame, far exceeds the team's human resources or budget, and so a prioritization exercise will be needed for what is delivered now—versus what can be deferred. Requirements prioritization may go so far as to further define a set of phases for future work, which becomes additional short-term and possibly longer-term aspects of the roadmap.

For some industries or products, especially those sold business-to-business, an external version of the roadmap may be required for customers. This is often the case where the product impacts a major operational or strategic capability of the purchasing company, or is deployed on a large scale across the organization. As the buyers are making long-term and/or major decisions for the company, they expect to see long-term product plans from the suppliers. Customers typically want to be sure that the organization will continue to invest in the products, and product roadmaps are often used as a means to measure the pace of investment.

External versions typically contain much less detail than the internal roadmap and can also be much less committal on specific dates. The most common representation depicts a high-level set of planned release milestones, in presentation slide format, and is often used to support internal or external communication—generally face-to-face.

An alternative is a *statement of direction* document that contains a high-level narrative discussion. It is rare that physical copies of these documents are ever provided to anyone outside the core product team, and if they are, it's typically done under a non-disclosure agreement.

The external roadmap can serve several purposes. One is to demonstrate thought leadership and open up discussions about future possibilities with customers and partners in order to collect feedback. Another is as a planning tool for the customer's budgeting and operational processes so that major expenditures can be planned for in the future. The external roadmap can also be used in high-impact competitive sales situations where it becomes one of several decision factors to help seal a deal.

Product managers need to exercise caution when it comes to developing, executing, and communicating aspects of a product's external roadmap. It is wise to embed a disclaimer that the information represented is the best view of the product's direction given current information and that it's subject to change without notice. Many customers perceive the roadmap as a *commitment* and if the direction changes, it can cause some difficult situations to ensue.

The second caution is that roadmap information is *confidential* and not to be disclosed. Even when roadmaps are clearly labeled confidential, expect that elements of the information will "somehow" end up in the hands of competitors.

The last caution relates to distribution across the sales channel. The external document should not be freely disbursed, but tightly controlled by the product management organization. It is not uncommon for the sales channel to latch onto "selling" future capabilities instead of the current product, and the roadmap becomes the reason to initiate a new conversation with a customer.

Table 11-2. Product Roadmap: Inputs and Outputs

INPUTS	OUTPUTS
• Product vision/strategy • Product requirements or product backlog (alternate Agile approach) • Development plan	• Internal product roadmap • External product roadmap (optional)

11.3 Project Plan Activities

The Project Plan activities primarily include the development plan for the product, but can also include several other functional plans, depending on the scope and organizational needs.

11.3.1 Development Plan

In the Conceive phase, an initial preliminary development plan may have been created in order to get rough estimates of potential development costs and timeline. Since the product definition at that point is very high-level, only a rough estimate of what is being built can be obtained. A major deliverable in this Plan phase is a more detailed definition of the product through the product requirements. These requirements, in conjunction with a more thorough project planning process, enable a more detailed pass at the development plan. The overall goal of the development plan is to identify how the product (including version or phase) defined in the requirements will be delivered via the project.

It is not the intent of this section to detail how a project will be defined and run, as this is outside the scope of this Body of Knowledge and ideally handled by project or program managers. Instead the focus of this section will be on the major project needs that are typically the output of development planning.

Once the product requirements are complete, or in parallel with their creation, the development team can begin assessment of what it will take to deliver the product. This may be fairly straightforward if the envisioned solution is similar to the capabilities or platforms that already exist, or it may require the invention of significant new capabilities for the organization. Therefore, the scope of any development activity can vary widely from previous initiatives.

The development plan is usually orchestrated by a project manager, but may also be led by a program manager or a functional manager/lead. Based on the product requirements, development estimates of effort or time are created to begin understanding the resource and budget needs for the project. Depending on the organization, these estimates can vary from very high-level to very detailed and low-level. The estimates themselves may come from the project lead directly or they may come from various individuals in the organization responsible for their delivery.

Once the estimates are obtained, a project schedule can be developed assuming specific resource assignments, availability, and loading. The schedule itself can become a formal part of the development plan, or high-level milestones derived from the schedule can be what are represented in the plan. In addition to the development activities, the plan should also account for any resources required to set up and manage the development environments, any testing and validation resources, any design or research resources, and product or technical documentation resources.

Typical resources included in a full development plan can include engineers/developers, project/program managers, architects, testers, experience designers, technical writers, business analysts, requirements specialists, product managers, product owners, Scrum Masters, quality assurance, and database analysts.

In order to support the business case and any budgeting activities required, costs are often derived from the overall estimates and schedules, plus additional costs for equipment, outside services, production tooling, prototypes, development tools, and any other costs required for the Develop phase.

A summary list of the common components of a development plan include:

- A list of resources or skill sets required for the project

- Estimates of overall time and costs required for all resources

- Cost of Goods Sold (COGS) estimates for manufactured or sourced products

- High-level list of project milestones and a detailed schedule

- Testing and product validation strategy, including alpha and beta testing

- Additional project costs outside of the direct resource costs

A final part of the development plan must also be risk assessment and mitigation. Identification of the key potential technical, schedule, and resource risks can be identified, with early warning indicators and risk mitigation plans determined in advance to help reduce fire drills down the road.

Table 11-3. Development Plan: Inputs and Outputs

INPUTS	OUTPUTS

• Project charter
• Product requirements
	• Development plan
	  » Resources required
	  » Schedule and cost estimates
	  » Delivery milestones
	  » Test strategy
	  » Development risk assessment

11.3.2 Other Supporting Functional Plans (Preliminary)

In addition to the development plan, other major functions within the organization may need to weigh in with their own high-level plans and costs. This may be a routine requirement of the development process, or it may be required for specific projects requiring activities or expenses outside the norm.

The following is a potential list of department plans that may be required for a specific product development project:

- Manufacturing Plan – Identifies the changes required to manufacture and test the product.

- Information Technology (IT) Operations Plan – Identifies changes in how a product or embedded software component is hosted or operated.

- Ordering or Billing Plan – Identifies changes in the business systems or processes.

- Support Plan – Identifies changes in needs for customer or technical support.

- Distribution/Logistics Plan – Identifies changes in how the product is fulfilled and delivered.

- Partner Plan – Identifies changes in external partner communities, such as service providers, Independent Software Vendors, or Developers.

Note that a specific marketing plan is broken out separately as it's nearly always a component required for new product activities. It also covers any changes required to sales channels, which may drive some of the requirements to the other department plans above.

In most cases, these functional plans will be preliminary and additional detailed work will be conducted in subsequent phases while the product is being developed. Some of these plans may also spawn additional projects for the organization. This is particularly the case for a new manufactured product that requires major changes in processes or required equipment. It can also be the case if there are major changes required in the IT systems that support a new product for operations, ordering, billing, or customer support.

11

The components of the plans are analogous to the development plan, with the intent of identifying the resources, schedules, and costs required to support the initial and ongoing delivery of the product once it is released from Development. This can also include supporting the product in the Qualify phase prior to launch.

A summary list of the common components of a cross-functional plan includes:

- A list of resources/skill sets required for the project

- Estimates of overall time and costs required for all resources

- High-level list of project milestones

- Additional project costs outside of the direct resource costs

- Risk assessment and mitigation plan

Table 11-4. Preliminary Functional Plans: Inputs and Outputs

INPUTS	OUTPUTS
• Market requirements • Product requirements • Marketing strategy • Development plan	• Department project plans (preliminary) » Resources required » Schedule and cost estimates » Delivery milestones » Project risk assessment

Cross-Functional Coordination

In a structured environment with a formal cross-functional project manager or program manager role, the managers are likely tasked with organizing all of the project planning activities across the organization and orchestrating the roll-up of department plans. In this scenario, the product manager may be a subject-matter expert to other organizations while the formal project/program manager drives aspects of the tactical planning process in collaboration with the product manager across the organization.

In less structured environments, the product manager may be the cross-functional lead to roll up the planning activities and results. It is also not entirely uncommon for product and program management roles to report to a single department that is looking across the product and delivery projects cross-functionally.

Given the potential number of deliverables and resources required for the activities in the Plan phase, it often needs its own project plan and project manager. As indicated earlier, the amount of analysis and resource requirements can be significant for the phase, especially across multiple functions.

It is recommended that the Plan phase have its own project charter defined with all key stakeholders identified and resources assigned. The risk of not treating the phase formally can be the loss of key information that may have material impact on the cost or schedule of the project. Additionally, the formal involvement of key stakeholders, early in the planning, will facilitate alignment and meeting objectives later in the delivery of the product to the marketplace.

11.4 Marketing Plan Activities

The Marketing Plan activities are focused on updating the marketing strategy based on parallel activities in this phase, and adding more detail to an evolving launch strategy to support overall planning and the business case.

11.4.1 Product and Marketing Strategy (Updated)

The product and marketing strategy that originated in the Conceive phase was the first attempt at defining how the product meets the needs of the target market, and the initial thoughts on how it'll be taken to market. These strategies helped to drive the product concept and initial business case estimates.

As the product requirements and development plan evolve throughout the Plan phase, there can be a significant change in the overall marketing strategy that results.

This can occur for several reasons. One is that more work has been done, resulting in increasingly detailed market segmentation, user research, competitive analysis, or requirements validation. The additional work may reveal that the initial need requires further refinement. Or the conceptual solution was inadequate to solve the market need or compete effectively in the market. Thus the product evolved differently than originally envisioned and directly impacts multiple aspects of the strategy.

Another common scenario is the trade-off of product capabilities versus development time or cost considerations. These trade-offs can reduce the value of the overall product, slip the original schedule plan, or defer major functionality into the future on a product roadmap. This can also have an impact on the product strategy. Regardless of the reason, the initial product and market strategy typically needs to be updated to adjust to new information uncovered during the Plan phase.

Typical updates include:

- Segmentation and initial target segment

- Value proposition and positioning

- Pricing and forecasts

Table 11-5. Updated Product and Marketing Strategy: Inputs and Outputs

INPUTS	OUTPUTS
• Product and marketing strategy (preliminary) • Competitive analysis (product features) • Product requirements • Development plan	• Product and marketing strategy (updated)

11.4.2 Launch Strategy (Updated)

The initial view of the launch strategy in Conceive now needs to be updated with more detail and changes.

This version of the launch strategy also expands information on pre-launch activities that may be relevant to the overall plan, including beta and pilot tests in the Qualify phase that could provide case studies and referrals for launch. A validation strategy can be defined that outlines the goals of market validation, from a marketing perspective, and any costs associated with the testing beyond those identified in the development plan.

The launch strategy components typically include thoughts on:

- Marketing collateral needs

- Sales tools and demos

- Social media and web marketing

- Advertising and demand generation

- Sales promotions

- Public relations (PR) initiatives and analyst reviews

- Tradeshows and digital events, industry conferences, sponsorships, and media partnerships

- Beta and pilot test strategy

- High-level launch timeline, milestones, and overall budget

Table 11-6. Updated Launch Strategy: Inputs and Outputs

INPUTS	OUTPUTS
• Marketing strategy (updated) • Launch strategy (preliminary) • Development plan • Department plans (preliminary)	• Launch strategy (updated)

11.5 Business Case Activities

The business case activities are focused on a detailed version of the financial analysis and an updated roll-up/summary of the overall business case.

11.5.1 Financial Analysis (Detailed)

The business case coming from the Conceive phase was an initial projection of the potential revenue and costs given some very high-level assumptions. The intent of the Plan phase is to evolve this projection significantly by understanding more fully the target market, need, and solution to be provided. More specifically, what product capabilities, in what time frame, and what it'll take to get there.

The typical update to the business case financials will include the following information and result in updated confidence factors:

- Updated target market sizing and growth parameters

- Supportable assumptions on target adoption and growth

- Pricing assumptions and revenue forecast

- Cost of sales/COGS estimates

- Development and Marketing launch cost estimates

- Manufacturing, Operational, and Support cost estimates to launch

- Ongoing Development, Marketing, and Operational costs

- Profit & Loss, Breakeven, Net Present Value, or some other Return on Investment calculations

The complexity and depth of the business case financials will vary significantly from company to company and project to project. In some organizations, the financial analysis is managed by a financial analyst with help from the product manager; in most it's completely managed by the product manager; and in others it's more of a conversation than a deliverable.

The output of the financial analysis is a major decision driver in many organizations. For relatively stable markets where historical market performance is available, they can also be fairly accurate if specific product assumptions are met. For nascent markets or those that are relatively small and growing, the ability to forecast adoption and revenue numbers is likely much more of a guess than science. In this case, the financial analysis results should be considered with caution and with less emphasis relative to other strategic factors in the overall business case.

Table 11-7. Detailed Financial Analysis: Inputs and Outputs

INPUTS	OUTPUTS
• Business case (preliminary) • Marketing strategy (updated) • Development plan • Department plans (preliminary) • Launch strategy (preliminary)	• Financial analysis (detailed)

11.5.2 Business Case (Updated)

The business case is the summarized roll-up of all the updated planning activities that have occurred, and rationalizes them relative to strategic drivers. In the Conceive phase, a preliminary version was developed and the goal in the Plan phase is to provide the justification for the overall product to move forward.

At the highest level, the business case should address the consideration of the product in context with the entire company investment portfolio and answer:

- Why this opportunity and solution?

- Why will we win?

- Why now?

- With what risks?

Typical components of the business case include:

- Summary of the market need and opportunity (from marketing strategy)

- Summary of the market and competitive landscape (from marketing strategy)

- Product capabilities, product vision, product strategy, value proposition, and positioning (from product and marketing strategy)

- Strategic leverage and alignment to objectives

- Summary development and go-to-market plans (from department plans)

- Summary financial analysis

- Summary risk assessment (from department plans and overall assessment)

- Open issues, conclusions, funding recommendations

Table 11-8. Updated Business Case: Inputs and Outputs

INPUTS	OUTPUTS
• Business case (preliminary) • Marketing strategy (updated) • Product requirements (detailed) • Development plan • Department plans (preliminary) • Launch strategy (preliminary updated) • Financial analysis (detailed)	• Business case (updated)

11.6 Create Preliminary Product Management Plan

The product management governing plan acts as the central repository for all of the materials that are created in support of the new product. The plan helps to ensure that the appropriate parties have access to the most up-to-date materials and can help in the transition process as new team members join or leave the team or organization.

Table 11-9. Preliminary Product Management Plan: Inputs and Outputs

INPUTS	OUTPUTS
• Product team charter • Business case	• Initial draft of the product management master plan

11.7 Exiting the Plan Phase

In order to exit the Plan phase all the deliverables defining the product and the plan to deliver it must be agreed upon. Funding and resources are then approved for the major Develop phase activities to begin. As indicated initially, the amount of information required to exit the Plan phase can vary significantly by product type, investment size, and organizational culture, but should be judged on the same set of objective criteria. Therefore, the process should be tuned to deliver "just enough information" to make the investment decision to proceed to the Develop phase or to decide not to pursue it.

11

Chapter 12

The Develop Phase

The Plan phase provided the groundwork for establishing the desired functionality of the product and overall business plan to create and launch it. The Develop phase begins a major investment cycle for the company with the assignment of product development resources to design, create, and test the product. The scope and duration of this phase can vary dramatically based on the type of product, ranging from a handful of development resources spanning a few calendar quarters to multiple dispersed teams spanning multiple years.

The product manager's involvement in this phase can also vary widely, depending upon how the various team members' roles are defined and the degree of specialization. It's not uncommon to encounter overlapping or poorly defined roles within the organization. Due to the variability in actual practice, this section will discuss the types of activities that are most often associated with the Develop phase, while leaving it to the practitioners to adapt these activities and their depth to suit the needs of the organization.

12.1 Develop Phase Activity Groups

There are four major groups of activities that can occur in the Develop phase, and this section will address each group separately. The activity groups are Product Development, Market Validation, Launch Planning, and Program Review.

Product Development activities are focused on monitoring and working with the Development organization as necessary to build, verify, and release the product while taking primary responsibility for product requirements refinement and prioritization.

Market Validation activities are focused on obtaining market feedback on the product's design and implementation, both during the Develop phase and in planning for the next phase: Qualify.

Launch Planning activities are focused on developing more detailed cross-functional plans to support the eventual launch of the product.

Program Review activities are focused on ensuring that the overall project plan is being executed based upon expectations.

The subsequent sections will cover the four activity groups in more detail.

12.2 Product Development Activities

Product Development activities encompass the overall implementation process in the Development organization, supporting product requirements refinement as required, product verification, and release and configuration management.

12.2.1 Product Implementation

For many organizations, there is a complete hand-off of the lead role between the Plan phase and Develop phase. During the Plan phase, the product management function takes the lead in defining the overall functionality and business rationale for the product, with the development function providing solution and implementation options and estimates of cost and time to support the business plan.

In the Develop phase, the Development function takes the lead role creating the actual product while the product management organization shifts its focus to the forward-looking phases of Qualify and Launch. Therefore, for product development activities, the product manager typically takes on more of a monitoring role and jumps in to resolve issues as they arise. However, alternatives exist when the product development team is executing on projects utilizing Agile product development methodologies. The implications of this variation will be discussed below, particularly as it relates to product requirements refinement.

The Development team dives into defining the details of the product and delivering the initial version, or working with vendors or partners to deliver portions or the entire product. As part of the overall process, the developers may create detailed design documents to share with others or to document the implementation. Overall documentation varies significantly by product type, industry, and the release process used by the organization.

Intermediate deliverables from the Development team include mockups and prototypes. Mockups are typically non-working models created early in the process to facilitate decision-making or to illustrate how the product may eventually look or function. For hardware or consumer products, it's common to mock up the overall packaging to capture the size, specific visual attributes, and look of the product. For software products, mockups illustrate portions of the user interface to capture the general functionality and/or look and feel. These mockups can range from a simple rough sketch to a fully simulated product. Regardless of the detail, the mockup can be used for early user testing.

Prototypes are typically early versions of the product that are put together to test the integration of multiple subcomponents or subsystems. They are often evolutionary versions toward a final product, have varying levels of the final capabilities, and can be of varying quality levels.

It is not uncommon to develop multiple versions of prototypes with increasing refinement, especially for hardware systems or manufactured products. These prototypes may also be used for Beta testing or other user-testing activities. For software, the product development team may start with low-fidelity paper prototypes and increase the fidelity of the prototype and sample size of the reviewers as they gain a better understanding of the design. The same is true for 3D models of spaces that may start with white foam-core models and increase the fidelity of the models by adding color, texture, and workable elements that demonstrate how people interact with the objects.

As the Development phase nears completion, the Development team works with Manufacturing or Operations to ensure a smooth hand-off of the released product and to signal readiness for these functions to begin ramping up their operational activities. Manufactured systems may have long lead items that need to be purchased, or capital equipment that needs to be designed and created, or procured, and installed to support building or testing the product.

In addition, the design of the physical packaging for retail and/or shipping will need to be created and sourced. Hosted software systems may require servers, software licenses, and hosting facilities that need to be acquired to support the product. Interior spaces may require interior designers, architects and engineers, and exterior spaces may require landscape designers—some may specialize with plants and others with lighting, hardscape, or other special skills.

Aside from the requirements refinement and verification testing, the product manager often has little day-to-day involvement in the details of the development

12

function activities, and the main source of status is through regular team meetings led by the project/program manager. The primary interest of the product manager is in ensuring that the product functionality is being delivered per the prioritized product requirements based upon actual market data and according to the project plan.

While there are some projects that move along without too many issues or roadblocks, it's not uncommon for major implementation or project issues to surface that impact the overall plan. These can be unanticipated design problems that force a change in the capabilities of the solution, a major underestimate of the schedule, or cost of an implementation, loss of key resources or partners, or the accumulation of many smaller issues that ultimately result in an overall product or project impact.

In this situation, the product manager needs to participate in the decision process to mitigate the issue. They may be requested to help generate alternative options that impact functionality, cost, or schedule (optimal outcome), or they may just be informed of the impact that was decided by the development function (least desirable outcome).

The ideal process includes the product manager leading the collaboration process with the developers to investigate all of the options and impacts, and to guide the team to the best outcomes considering the objectives established in the Business Case. Any major deviations to the plan or escalations that result from project issues will need to be addressed, usually through the program review process to be discussed later in this section.

Table 12-1. Product Implementation: Inputs and Outputs

INPUTS	OUTPUTS

• Product requirements
• Development plan
• Market requirements
• Product requirements (preliminary)
• Experience design research
• Usability evaluation
	• Project status
	• Mockups and prototypes
	• Potential project plan updates
	• Implemented product requirements doc (detailed)
	  » User personas
	  » Functionality definition
	  » System qualities and constraints
	  » Prioritization
	• Agile user stories, acceptance criteria, and product backlog (alternate)
	• User interface definition (optional)
	• Mockups or prototypes (optional)
	• Market requirements doc (updated)

12.2.2 Product Requirements Refinement

One of the major deliverables from the Plan phase is the product requirements document (PRD), and the breadth and depth of the deliverable can vary widely from project to project and company to company. During the Plan phase, some projects may completely define the product functionality in granular detail due to the nature of the industry or application, such as aeronautic or medical, while other projects may define them at a "good enough" level to create a conceptual solution with estimated costs and schedules.

In the detailed planning scenario, the requirements document from the Plan phase becomes the plan of record used to baseline revision control. Changing the requirements, in any way, is a formalized process, and is therefore highly resistant to change. In the "good enough" scenario, the requirements are intended to be evolutionary, with additional details defined as required in the Develop phase and through a much less rigorous change control process, if any. Due to this broad spectrum of possibilities for the requirements, the involvement of the product manager in ongoing requirements discussions can range from nil to active engagement.

Very often, the requirements are not changing in any significant way, but there are missing requirements or lack of enough detail for the developers to make an implementation decision when faced with a range of choices. The implementation choice may not directly affect the primary requirement, but could impact a non-functional requirement, such as performance or ease of use.

Another possibility is the requirement is vague, can be interpreted as having multiple meanings, or can have more than one technical solution. Additionally, there could be conflicting requirements and a priority needs be assigned between them or resolution of the conflict defined.

Finally, there may be a limitation in the implementation of the requirement and a change is requested by the developer. It will be the role of the product manager to deal with these requirements issues as they surface by whatever process has been established for the project.

Agile software methods are designed to handle evolutionary requirements. As part of the Agile process, requirements are detailed during the development process. The product manager can be in the role of product owner and thus is expected to be available on a continuous basis to the developers.

The product owner initially creates a set of prioritized user stories—one or more sentences in the everyday or business language of the end-user or user of a system that captures the goal or task they wish to accomplish—and testable acceptance criteria. These are compiled into a list known as the product backlog. As a developer begins to execute on each of the user stories, additional details are discussed and/or documented in near real-time with the product owner and built into the product within a sprint—a short iteration cycle of a few weeks. The product owner is on-demand for all of the developers with user stories or acceptance criteria under development during the iteration development cycle.

To offset this high demand on the product manager, organizations often split the product manager and product owner roles into more specialized functions. One way to compensate for this split is to add a business analyst as the product owner reporting to the product manager. The product manager provides the large user stories, referred to as epics, and features, for the release while the product owner breaks down the epics and features into smaller user stories for the sprint backlog.

The business analyst or product owner then works on a continual basis with the development team while the product manager oversees the work. This allows the product manager the necessary bandwidth to provide the additional planning and coordination required for the Qualify and Launch phases while continually monitoring market dynamics.

Another commonly used approach is to have the lead product manager oversee a less senior or more technical product manager as the product owner. Yet another possibility is the product manager is the product owner and begins to work more closely with a product marketing manager or program manager for the Qualify and Launch planning activities.

The situation does arise that requirements *change* during the Develop phase, as new or expanded requirements threaten to increase the original product scope that was approved during the Plan phase, also called "feature creep." These could arise in the form of new customer requests or in response to a new competitive offering or as determined during user testing.

In some cases, the development team may agree to take on the additional scope if it has minimal impact to their schedule. In many cases, however, the project impact may be too great and the responsibility will rest with the product manager to identify the preferred resolution. This resolution can include reprioritizing other capabilities to make room for the new functionality, deferring the feature to the future, or expanding the project scope and schedule through the formal program review process.

Table 12-2. Product Requirements Refinement: Inputs and Outputs

INPUTS	OUTPUTS
• Product requirements	• Updated requirements, as necessary

12.2.3 Product Verification Activities

To verify that product requirements are being delivered as agreed, the implementations are also usually tested by a separate Test and/or Quality Assurance team. The test strategy provided in the Plan phase is expanded in the Develop phase to a test plan that includes the details of how the product will be verified. It may also include the test cases used to verify the product. The test plan should provide specific reference back to the product requirements for traceability.

In order for the product to be released from the Development team, the product needs to pass a minimum verification level with acceptable results. These can include individual module testing of subcomponents or subsystems and full system testing of the integrated product. For complex systems, testing of the integrated product can involve a significant amount of effort and time.

For manufactured products, part of the verification process can involve a manufacturing test build that runs a limited number of units through a full manufacturing and quality control cycle. This is to ensure the product documentation is complete, the product can be manufactured and tested per the plans, and any process or product issues are identified before a major manufacturing cycle and investment is initiated.

A similar activity can be conducted for hosted software products, where the hosting operations group is responsible for verifying the system can be built and deployed in a staging environment. This is especially critical to ensure that an existing system can be upgraded and operational within a limited duration maintenance window to minimize system downtime. There may also be the need to test a major migration of user accounts or data between a legacy system and a new or upgraded system.

The product may also have to go through separate certification testing for compliance to standards, such as for safety, emissions, security, and specific industry requirements or government compliance.

In some scenarios, especially for contracted software products or more customized solutions for end customers, there is a formal user acceptance testing (UAT) or similar type of acceptance by customers. This testing usually involves a set of high

-level functionality and failure tests performed by the end customer to ensure the specification and contract obligations have been fulfilled.

The product manager is often heavily involved in product verification testing as a proxy user to ensure the overall functionality and experience is as envisioned. Many product managers are also involved in reviewing and prioritizing quality issues to determine which issues must be corrected prior to launch. They may also be responsible for a formal acceptance approval along with the test team. The product manager may also be directly involved with the customer in planning and creating the UAT.

Once all verification and compliance testing has been passed, the product is officially released to the supporting operational function.

Table 12-3. Product Verification: Inputs and Outputs

INPUTS	OUTPUTS
• Product requirements • Test strategy	• Test plan • Product verification passed

12.2.4 Release and Configuration Management

As indicated in the previous discussions, varying amounts of formality and control of the overall development process and documentation is required for different products. This process involves managing the lifecycle of requirements from initial approval to product release, ensuring compliance to requirements and required processes, transitioning the product from Development to Manufacturing or Operations, and capturing issues and resolutions beyond the development activities.

For software products, this process is often coordinated through Release Management. These activities can be centralized within an organization or partitioned across different functions or individuals for different aspects of the process. It is common to have a Release Manager role within the Development team. The major activities can include:

- Version control and change management of the product requirements and software components

- Maintaining development and testing configurations and environments

- Managing the software "build" process for ongoing development and testing activities

- Packaging and validating the finalized components for distribution or Operations

- Ensuring all required process steps for release have been completed, including security audits, operational tests, and documentation

- Defect tracking, triage, and issue tracking process and systems

For manufactured and complex system products, the process is often coordinated through Configuration Management. It typically is managed through a dedicated group as part of the overall QA activities. The major activities can include:

- Version control and change management of the product requirements and system components

- Bill of materials and Stock Keeping Unit assignments and management

- Management of product build and use documentation

- Ensuring all required process steps for product release have been completed, including testing and issue resolution

The direct involvement of the product manager in these overall activities is usually minimal, though they are likely involved at a deeper level on individual activities.

Table 12-4. Release and Configuration Management: Inputs and Outputs

INPUTS	OUTPUTS
• Product requirements • Development plan • Test strategy	• Completion of product release checklist • Released product

12.3 Market Validation Activities

The Market Validation activities relate to obtaining market feedback and include the development of a Beta Plan or Market Plan to be executed during the Qualify phase and usability testing performed during development.

12.3.1 Beta Plan/Market Plan

Prior to doing a full product launch, it's common to first do some form of product validation in the market to verify the product is ready. This is often called a Beta test or Pilot and is performed as part of the next phase: Qualify. The Develop phase is a good time to create a Beta Plan to get alignment in the organization about the goals of the testing to be performed and the logistics of how it will be conducted once the product is ready for release.

Some internet companies choose to publically launch their initial version of the product and call it a Beta release in order to set market expectations on the feature or quality level. For this discussion, a Beta test is a limited test run before formally releasing the product or service to the full market.

Depending on the goals and scale of the planned test, the effort and resources required could be significant and would need to be incorporated into the Launch schedule. Collaboration with a project or program manager for these planning and scheduling activities can help ensure success. Beta tests can range from a handful of users to thousands, and it's not uncommon that dedicated resources need to be assigned for larger tests.

Sometimes there is a dedicated leader for this effort—a Release Manager—or it may fall onto the product marketing manager's list of responsibilities. It is also important to find testers who are motivated to test the product. The testers should match the product personas—be part of the target market user group and are often early adopters or some of the leading edge customers.

There are multiple reasons or goals for performing a Beta test prior to launch. The Beta can also have multiple phases that each address different goals. Some of the results that can be obtained from a Beta include:

- Product functionality verification – Ensures that the product performs as expected across different users and environments to gain broader verification test coverage before launching.

- Marketing validation – Provides feedback on various aspects of the product messaging, positioning, value proposition, and pricing, and provides early customer testimonials to use at launch.

- Supporting system readiness – Allows end-to-end testing of the full customer experience, including purchase, delivery, use, and customer support.

- Usability validation – The product is effective (key tasks are completable), efficient (key tasks can be completed in a timely manner), quickly learnable, and delightful (positive emotional associations).

- Sales support – Pre-launch demonstrations or prospect trials to accelerate purchases.

Of course, the single primary reason to go through the effort of a Beta test is to provide data to make an important decision, which is to launch the product or not. Therefore, the Beta test can be one of the major drivers in choosing one of three options for the readiness of the product:

1. The product is ready to launch and the Launch phase begins.

2. The product is not ready and additional work is needed before a launch is approved.

3. The product does not or cannot meet market or business needs and the launch is cancelled.

The Beta Plan created in this Develop phase typically includes answers to the following questions:

- Why are we doing this test? What results are we trying to achieve?

- Who are we targeting for the test? How many testers are we seeking?

- How will we find and recruit testers? How will we incent them?

- What will we be providing to the testers? Do we plan on getting the product back and how?

- What do we want them to test (general operation, specific functions or environments)?

- Who will be managing the test, including setting up the testers and supporting them?

- How will we communicate with them and how often? How will they provide feedback?

- What are the activities, schedule, logistics, resources, and costs of the test? Who pays for it?

- What legal documentation do we require, including confidentiality or licensing agreements?

- How do we plan on incorporating the results of the feedback prior to launching the product?

- What are the measurable success criteria for the test?

To help flesh out the product functionality prior to doing a Beta test, an Alpha test is often also performed. An Alpha test is usually an in-house-only validation of the product using internal staff outside of the development function. It can also include "friendly" external testers, such as partners or leading edge customers who will be very tolerant of the state of the product. If an Alpha test is also planned to be performed, the logistics should be included in the Beta Plan.

12

The Beta Plan can be implemented as a stand-alone document or can roll up as a section in the launch plan discussed later in this section. Be sure to account for any incremental costs that have been identified in the updated business plan and project budgets.

Table 12-5. Beta Plan: Inputs and Outputs

INPUTS	OUTPUTS
• Launch strategy • Test strategy • Development plan	• Beta plan or launch plan • Business plan (updated)

12.3.2 Usability Testing

As discussed in the Plan phase section, usability evaluation should be occurring throughout all phases of the product development cycle. In the earlier phases, low-fidelity rapid prototyping or mockups helped vet assumptions and validate design direction. As the team gets closer to the end of the Develop phase, the fidelity of the prototypes increase, as do the sample size and exactness of the personas matching the target customer. The focus of the usability moves from overall workflow to more exact tasks and interactions.

During the Develop phase, the product is being actively created and is still at a point where changes can be made to the product design fairly easily. The further the product moves down the development path, the more difficult and costly it'll be to make changes. Therefore, it's advised to test early and test often as pieces of functionality are implemented. The opportunities will vary widely based on the product or service, such as hardware or software, or interior or exterior space.

The preferred method for ensuring usability is to test actual customers on a working system or place and procedures. It's important to evaluate participants individually and let them solve any problems on their own. Any help, or directing their attention to any particular part of the solution, will bias the evaluation. Rather than running one big study, it's better to run many small evaluations and revise the design between each one to fix more usability flaws. Additionally, it's better to conduct three iterative studies with five participants than one with fifteen.[51]

Table 12-6. Usability Testing: Inputs and Outputs

INPUTS	OUTPUTS
• Product requirements • Test strategy • Mockups and prototypes	• Usability test results • Updated product requirements or designs

---

[51] Nielsen, J., & Landauer, T. (2000). Why you only need to test with 5 users. *Jakob Nielsen's Alertbox*. Retrieved from http://www.useit.com/alertbox/20000319.html.

12.4 Launch Planning Activities

Launch Planning activities include expansion of the preliminary launch and supporting functional plans developed in the Plan phase, plus beginning the work on product documentation and marketing/sales materials required for launch.

12.4.1 Launch Plan (Detailed)

The launch strategy provided in the Plan phase provides the basis for the detailed Launch Plan in the Develop phase. In the launch strategy, the intent was to identify a general launch philosophy and a high-level set of tasks and costs to support the business plan.

The Launch Plan moves to a more tactical view that begins to nail down the specific messaging and positioning of the product, with the necessary projects to support a launch from a marketing perspective. Most of these projects will occur in the Qualify phase leading up the actual launch of the product.

The Launch Plan components typically include detailed information on:

- Overall launch strategy and objectives (including forecasts)
- Planned messaging and positioning of the product
- Pricing and discounting policies
- Sales promotion plans
- Marketing collateral requirements
- Sales tools and demo requirements
- Advertising and demand generation activities (including social media, search engine optimization, and web marketing)
- Public relations (PR) activities
- Industry analyst rollout and reviews
- Tradeshows, industry conferences, and digital events
- Beta Plan (or as a stand-alone plan)
- Detailed project milestones and overall cost update

The authorship and contributions to the Launch Plan can be accomplished in many ways. The product manager can be the primary driver and owner or he/she can work with a product marketing manager as the beginning of a hand-off

12

for go-to-market activities. Other marketing specialists can also be contributors to the plan, or can take a lead role with product expertise support provided by the product manager. Ultimately, having a single individual responsible for the launch increases the odds of success and enables more effective measurement of the results.

Table 12-7. Detailed Launch Plan: Inputs and Outputs

INPUTS	OUTPUTS
• Launch strategy • Marketing strategy	• Launch plan (detailed) • Business plan (updated)

12.4.2 Other Supporting Functional Plans (Detailed)

The preliminary functional plans provided in the Plan phase provide the basis for the detailed functional plans in the Develop phase. Similar to the Launch Plan, the preliminary plans from affected organizations were developed to support the initial business plan. Now the plans need to be updated for specific project activities that need to occur to support the product launch and beyond. These all include milestones, resource assignments, and costs.

The following is a potential list of functional plans that may need to be evolved with more detail:

- Manufacturing Plan – Identifies the changes required to manufacture and test the product.

- Information Technology (IT) Operations Plan – Identifies changes in how the product is hosted or operated.

- Ordering or Billing Plan – Identifies changes in the business systems or processes.

- Support Plan – Identifies changes in needs for customer service or technical support. It also identifies the product training plan for the support staff.

- Distribution/Logistics Plan – Identifies changes in how the product is fulfilled and delivered.

- Partner Plan – Identifies changes in external partner communities, such as Independent Software Vendors (ISVs) or Developers.

Table 12-8. Detailed Functional Plans: Inputs and Outputs

INPUTS	OUTPUTS
• Supporting functional plans (preliminary)	• Supporting functional plans (detailed) • Business plan (updated)

12.4.3 Documentation and Materials

In addition to the Launch Plan delivered above, work can also begin on some of the deliverables defined in the plan. As with the overall plan itself, these deliverables can be provided by the product manager, product marketing manager, or other marketing specialists.

Product documentation is often required to support the installation, setup, use, and support of the product. This documentation can take many forms and have different user audiences, and therefore can have multiple delivery paths, including from the Development team or product management function. Very often, a dedicated documentation or writing group is involved under the direction of one of these groups. The product documentation is also often required for any Beta testing that will occur, and is typically in draft form to allow for changes.

Marketing collateral is another major deliverable that can be started during the Develop phase. A marketing function typically organizes the overall design process and delivery, but the product manager likely plays a key role in providing the content and reviews collateral to ensure accuracy.

A number of sales materials may be required for a product, particularly to support a direct sales force. These can include sales presentations, competitive assessments, product whitepapers, demos, and cost-of-ownership/ROI calculators for more complex solutions. These may all be driven by the product manager or with support from product marketing or a sales operations team. A major culmination of the development of all of these materials is sales training conducted just prior to launch.

Support materials and training may be required for all staff required to provide direct customer support. The product manager typically works with support training leads to identify what material is needed. The actual training material creation and delivery is usually conducted by the support staff.

The involvement of the product manager in pricing activities can vary widely across organizations. In some, pricing is controlled by other groups, including finance or executive committees. In most organizations, the product manager is directly responsible for pricing, including analysis, the supporting business case, and publishing the price list. While the pricing may not be finalized until just before launch, the discussions and analysis likely start in the Conceive phase.

Finally, the product manager may be involved in several different discussions with the legal staff about product terms and conditions, end user licensing agreements, service level agreements, and actual sales contracts terms and conditions.

12

Table 12-9. Documentation: Inputs and Outputs

INPUTS	OUTPUTS
• Product requirements • Launch plan	• Product documentation • Marketing collateral • Sales and support materials • Pricing • Contracts and legal documents

12.5 Program Review Activities

The Program Review activities include ongoing review checkpoints and potential updates to the Development, Other Functional Plans, or Business Case.

12.5.1 Review Checkpoints

The Develop phase is often one of the longest phases and has the highest opportunity for issues that need to be addressed. For this reason, a periodic program review is highly warranted. The intent of the review is to get indicators that the project milestones and business plans are both on track and within acceptable deviations. If deviations are beyond acceptable limits, the reviews provide an opportunity to make corrections and adjustments in time *before* product launch. In addition, these reviews can provide stakeholders and senior management the ability to course correct or remove roadblocks that are outside the authority of the project team.

As discussed in the Product Implementation section above, a number of issues could arise that affect the schedule for the effort, the scope of the functionality, or the cost and business case as originally estimated. Finding out at the end of the Develop phase that major changes have occurred is usually a costly and an unpleasant surprise.

Outside of the Development team, other issues can also arise related to any of the supporting function's plans relative to the initial preliminary versions from the Plan phase. Manufacturing or Operations may need more time or have higher costs than anticipated. Other business systems to support ordering or fulfillment may have issues. Support may need different processes than planned. All of these can have a major impact on the overall project plan and business case for the product.

The project/program manager should be responsible for coordinating these reviews with the appropriate stakeholders and rolling up the overall status. In addition, the program manager is responsible for risk management and issue resolution with support from the various teams and subject matter experts.

Table 12-10. Review Checkpoints: Inputs and Outputs

INPUTS	OUTPUTS
• Other functional plans (detailed) • Development plan • Business plan	• Periodic reviews and issues addressed • Updates to individual plans

12.5.2 Business Plan Update

The business plan provided in the Plan phase provided the overall justification for the approval of the project to proceed to the Develop phase. As the project progresses with more detailed product designs and detailed cross-functional plans, there may be major changes to the business plan that need updating and potential review. There may also be changes in the external market regarding the competitive situation or macro-environment that need to be documented.

Potential areas of change for the business plan include:

- Marketing strategy
- Development plan
- Other functional plans
- Launch plan
- Financial business case
- Risk assessment

Table 12-11. Updated Business Plan: Inputs and Outputs

INPUTS	OUTPUTS
• Business plan • Updates to specific functional plans • Updates to external environment situation	• Business plan (updated)

12.6 Exiting the Develop Phase

In order to exit the Develop phase, the product must be created, tested, and released per the specific processes required by the individual company. It is highly recommended that market validation activities are undertaken during the Develop phase to ensure the product is meeting marketing needs during a time when adjustments in requirements and implementation can be made more easily.

Chapter 13

The Qualify Phase

The Qualify phase can be defined as the transition from the development of the product to the market launch. This phase *should* be a formal period within an organization's approval process. Alternatively, it can be a set of activities tacked onto the back of the preceding Develop phase or onto the front-end of the subsequent Launch phase. The important point is that validation occurs—ensuring the product delivers the intended value—*before* a full-scale launch.

There are three major groups of activities that occur during the Qualify phase. The first is Market Validation, in which the product is externally tested, in a controlled fashion, to ensure it meets the market needs. The second is Launch Preparation to ramp up all internal processes and systems, and to prepare the sales and marketing channels to engage. The third is the Launch Readiness Assessment, which evaluates if the product and company overall are ready for launch.

As with previous phases, the product manager's involvement in this phase can vary widely. The level of engagement often depends upon how the various team members' roles are defined and the degree of specialization. Due to the variability in actual practice, this section will discuss the types of activities that are most commonly associated with the Qualify phase, while allowing practitioners to adapt these activities and their depth to suit the needs of the organization.

13.1 Market Validation Activities

Market Validation activities are centered on obtaining market feedback and include the execution of a Beta test or other market testing planned during the Develop phase.

13.1.1 Beta or Market Test

The Beta Plan created in the Develop phase provides the basis for obtaining market validation through a formal Beta test. As discussed in the Beta Plan section of the Develop phase, the scale of the Beta test can range from a handful of participants over a few weeks to hundreds over a period of months. The goals for the test can also vary between verifying the product functionality and its usability to identifying the most attractive marketing messages and product price points. It can also test that internal systems are ready for launch.

The Beta test can also be implemented as a pilot or similar concept. A pilot is a full end-to-end test of the system within a limited environment. One example is within a handful of early customers who implement the product for their use and provide feedback on the results. This is a fairly common practice for information technology products for internal business systems or processes. The pilot can be useful for obtaining market validation of your solution, a set of references for future sales opportunities, and even a set of case studies as part of the sales materials.

Another pilot example would be to perform market testing in a limited geographic area, such as a specific city or region. This allows the set of product and support systems to be tested on a smaller scale, with lower risk exposure than a full product launch. Pilots of this nature can be valuable for verifying that the product works as expected, the required infrastructure for sales and support are available, and the product messaging and pricing are sufficiently fine-tuned.

Another form of pilot testing is a *soft* launch. This type of launch is similar to either of the pilot examples above, and includes the caveat that limited or no marketing is done to create demand. It is purposely low-key to assess the product, its performance, and some adoption and conversion factors *before* moving to the more formal hard launch.

The product manager is often highly engaged in market testing. The primary role of the product manager will be the overall definition and guidance of the market testing and assessment of the results. While it's recommended that a dedicated project manager handle the day-to-day testing logistics, the product manager will have significant involvement in supporting the issues and questions that arise. It is also not unusual that Development and/or a dedicated test team are also on standby to support the testing. The product manager will be the person to roll up the final results and recommendations from the test.

As discussed in Beta Plan development, the primary reason to go through the effort of a Beta or Market test is to answer the question of whether the product should launch or not. Issues that can be found during testing include:

- Portions of the product functionality or usability do not meet requirements and additional development work is needed before launching. This can recycle the activities back to the Develop phase, as either a planned event or as an extension to the project schedule. An alternative is to document the deficiencies of the initial release to customers and continue the launch, while planning to correct the deficiencies in the next release. This is fairly common in software products due to their flexibility in incrementally adapting the functionality.

- The supporting infrastructure for the product is not ready. This can include the sales channel is not able to sell, order, or process payments for the product, the manufacturing or operational systems are not able to fully deliver the product, or the support systems are not able to adequately provide customer support. The origin of these issues may be missing requirements that were not identified during the Plan phase.

- The success metrics defined for the test are not achieved. The defined metrics for the test can vary widely, but a few higher level indicators can be used to determine the overall likely success of the product after launch. One measure is customer satisfaction with the product. Does it provide a solution that meets the customer needs and in a way that's satisfactory for the users? Would they recommend it to others? If not, where does it have gaps in functionality or benefit? A second measure can be the value of the product—its level of benefits versus the cost. Would customers be willing to purchase the product themselves and, if so, at what price? If not, why not? A third measure could be for those tests aimed at the product messaging. Are the response and conversion rates for purchase or use meeting the goals?

The results of the Beta test are rolled up as one factor to consider in the overall decision to proceed to the Launch phase.

Table 13-1. Beta Test: Inputs and Outputs

INPUTS	OUTPUTS
• Beta plan	• Beta test results

13.2 Launch Preparation

The Launch Preparation activities include specific activities occurring in Marketing, Manufacturing/Operation, Sales, and Support to prepare for launch in addition to completing the required product documentation.

13.2.1 Marketing Launch Preparation

The detailed Launch Plan completed during the Develop phase becomes the basis for marketing activities in the Qualify phase. A new product launch, or a major update to a product, typically requires several marketing activities happening in parallel to be able to align them to a specific launch date. This requires cross-functional coordination and a dedicated resource that provides singular focus to these activities.

This may be someone in a product marketing role or a project/program manager. Some organizations have a similar role filled by a Marketing Operations team whose main focus is to coordinate these activities. It is also not uncommon for the marketing team to work with outside agencies for support of specific deliverables when the company may not have in-house expertise or available resources.

The product manager will work with the identified resources to help the product successfully maneuver through the process. The product manager may also be directly providing some of the key deliverables, such as the content for marketing collateral and needed sales materials. A product marketing manager can also be the primary point person for coordinating all of the product-related information and materials to the marketing or marketing communications team.

To close out the Qualify phase, the Launch Plan may need to be updated to reflect changes in launch activities and expenses and rolled up to the final business plan. An update to the launch metrics that will be tracked post-launch may also need revising based on the results of the market testing or limitations of system readiness identified by the other functions.

At the conclusion of the Qualify phase, all of the marketing deliverables and the marketing channel should be fully prepared for the launch.

Table 13-2. Marketing Launch Preparation: Inputs and Outputs

INPUTS	OUTPUTS
• Launch plan	• Marketing readiness assessment • Launch plan (updated)

13.2.2 Manufacturing and Operations Launch Preparation

For tangible products, the units need to be built, tested, and shipped. Product packaging and logistics also need to be designed, developed, and available. For web-based software services, they need to be hosted on servers and general administration provided. For other types of services, a combination of equipment, personnel, and processes may need to be provided to ensure smooth operation. All of these capabilities require planning and implementation time prior to being available for a commercial offering. Manufacturing, in particular, may require a long lead time for availability of raw materials, parts and equipment, and to make needed changes in the manufacturing flow.

In addition, there are supporting processes and systems in parallel that need to handle specific customer touch points, including ordering, inventory management, and fulfillment, payments and support. These also need to be primed and ready to go prior to the formal launch.

The product manager generally serves as a subject matter expert to the functions that will be delivering these capabilities, rather than providing any hands-on activities directly. A common area for the product manager to be involved is ordering part number(s), configuring definitions, pricing, and getting the elements into the required systems.

Occasionally, the product requires changes to the way a company traditionally implements its other products, and the involvement of the product manager may then need to be higher. There may be issues that develop and work-arounds to the original plans that need to be implemented with the help of the product manager. There may even be some impact to the product itself that needs to be addressed or resolved. The further the product strays from the established capabilities of the delivery organizations, the more likely the product manager will need to stay close to the teams to facilitate the transition.

Functional plans should be updated to reflect any changes in the deliverables, timing, or costs originally envisioned and rolled up into the final business case.

At the conclusion of the Qualify phase, all of the delivery systems should be *fully* prepared for the launch.

Table 13-3. Manufacturing and Operations Launch Preparation: Inputs and Outputs

INPUTS	OUTPUTS
• Manufacturing plan • Operations plan • Ordering and payment plan • Distribution and logistics plan	• Delivery system readiness assessment • Functional plans (updated)

13.2.3 Sales and Channel Launch Preparation

The product manager's initial thoughts on supporting sales activities are typically captured in the initial launch strategy and subsequent launch plan in the previous phases, with the focus being on what's needed from the product and marketing teams to support the sales efforts. During the Qualify phase, there is often active participation from the Sales organization to facilitate the rollout.

The type of sales channel activities required for the product will heavily dictate how the product manager engages during the Qualify phase. If there is a direct sales force and/or third party solution partners, the product manager or product marketing manager may be directly engaged with the sales team in order to provide tools and training. If the product is sold online or through indirect retail channels, then the product manager may have far less involvement and support the sales through the marketing channels team.

In a similar manner as the marketing activities, in some companies a Sales Operations team may exist to work with the product manager in developing the appropriate content. Content can include:

- Sales presentations, competitive assessments, and product whitepapers
- Price lists and sales contracts
- Product demos
- Cost-of-ownership/ROI calculators and other sales tools

These may all be driven by the product manager or with support from product marketing or the sales operations team. A major culmination of the development of all of these materials is often sales training conducted just prior to launch.

During the Qualify phase, or perhaps even prior to it, a sales plan may be generated by the Sales organization that goes into more detail as to how the product will be rolled out. This plan may cover items such as individual quotas, geographic or regional phasing of the rollout, how the sales force is to be supported, and specific compensation and sales promotion plans to promote the new product.

There may also be additional sales channel partners that need some or all of the materials presented to the internal sales force. These would typically be retailers, wholesalers, and manufacturer's representatives, also finished-goods manufacturers, system integrators, or value-added resellers or independent software vendors who bundle the product into other products or provide associated products and services into a more comprehensive package.

Another related partner channel is a software developer program where documentation on ways to write software applications for the product is required. The applications may also require a certification process and even a dedicated sales implementation to facilitate distribution, as is now common for mobile content and devices. These efforts can be so large that they require dedicated product management resources and are effectively a supporting product to the main product being delivered.

Any changes to the Launch Plan that have been impacted by revised forecasts or costs should be captured to roll up to the final business plan.

By the end of the Qualify phase, the sales channels should be fully prepped for the product launch.

Table 13-4. Sales and Channel Launch Preparation: Inputs and Outputs

INPUTS	OUTPUTS
• Launch plan	• Sales channel readiness assessment • Launch plan (updated)

13

13.2.4 Customer Support Launch Preparation

The Support organization for some companies requires major pre-launch activities as there is significant end-customer contact involved. This can be the case for many consumer-related products and services. Even when the support required is not at a high-volume level, but required at a technical level, a significant amount of product training may be required.

Support materials and training may be required for all customer-facing staff. The product manager typically works with support training leads to identify what material is needed and a "train-the-trainer" approach is taken to facilitate knowledge transfer. The actual training material creation and delivery is usually conducted by the support staff to the rest of the support organization.

There may also be a need to update or enable the information technology systems used by the support staff to effectively support the product. At a minimum, the ability to record issues associated to the product and report on them is generally targeted. There may also be online knowledge bases to facilitate finding the appropriate answer to common questions. Finally, support personnel may need direct access into specific administrative functions of the product, such as for online software products, to be able to modify or adjust operational issues for the customer.

The support plan should be updated to reflect any changes in the deliverables, timing, or costs originally envisioned and rolled up into the final business case.

By the end of the Qualify phase, the support organization should be fully prepared for the product launch.

Table 13-5. Customer Support Launch Preparation: Inputs and Outputs

INPUTS	OUTPUTS
• Support plan	• Customer support readiness assessment • Support plan (updated)

13.2.5 Product Documentation Delivery

The Development organization typically handles all of the required documentation to build and deliver the product from manufacturing and/or the operations functions. User documentation may also be a deliverable from the development team, or it can be provided by marketing.

Typical documentation includes user guides, user manuals, warranties, license agreements, installation and configuration manuals, and other technical documents. There may be several different user groups for different sets of documentation, including end users, administrators, resellers, service and maintenance personnel, and third-party software developers. The scope of the documentation can also vary dramatically, depending on the complexity of the product and the channels that it needs to go through.

There may also be a large effort in language localization required on the documentation, in addition to the user interfaces on some products, to support an internationally distributed product. If the documentation is included with a physical product, then it must also be printed and available on the bill-of-materials for the product, so printing and manufacturing lead time must be taken into account.

Any changes to the launch plan that have been impacted by revised forecasts or costs should be captured to roll up to the final business plan.

By the end of the Qualify phase, the required product documentation should be available for the product launch.

Table 13-6. Product Documentation Delivery: Inputs and Outputs

INPUTS	OUTPUTS
• Product requirements • Launch plan	• Product documentation available • Launch plan (updated)

13.3 Launch Readiness Assessment

The Launch Readiness Assessment activities include an update for a final version of the business plan and a formal launch decision process.

13.3.1 Business Plan Update (Final)

It's been a journey, likely with several twists and turns along the way. During the Qualify phase, more changes to the original thinking likely have occurred. Market validation activities may have turned up issues with the product or customer acceptance that could affect early adoption forecasts. Or perhaps the value proposition has to be tuned or even repositioned to a slightly different initial target market. Or pricing could change, which would impact the financial analysis. Or any number of other project issues could have occurred in the preparation activities for manufacturing, operations, marketing, sales, or support. Or there may be changes in the external market that need to be taken into account, such as competition or macro-environmental factors. Or maybe your overall sales forecast is being raised due to great results, and you need to account for being able to scale faster than planned.

Whatever the situation, this is the time to update the business plan and any financial analysis accompanying it to validate the product is still within the intended results. It is also wise to do a final risk assessment.

Table 13-7. Final Business Plan: Inputs and Outputs

INPUTS	OUTPUTS
• Business plan • Launch plan (updated) • Updates to specific functional plans • Updates to external environment situation	• Business plan (final)

13.3.2 Launch Decision

The decision to launch is the culmination of all the activities from the Qualify phase, including the results from the Beta test and the functional readiness assessments.

The outcome of market testing is one of the major measures of the product's readiness to go to market. If the product does not meet the success criteria defined for testing, then a major decision has to be made regarding the fate of the product launch.

The product can still be launched, with the risk of wasting precious launch resources, budgets, and potentially company reputation. The product can be recycled back to the Develop phase for further development or modifications and the launch deferred. Or the product launch can be cancelled and the project terminated. The latter decision, while painful, may sometimes be in the best interest of the company if the road ahead looks too risky. The resources and attention may best be utilized on another project, despite sunk costs.

The readiness assessments from each of the functional areas also indicate whether the launch should begin. These assessments typically do not weigh toward outright cancelling of the launch, but rather delay or reduce its scale until the required readiness is achieved. It is not unusual for one or more functions to have some limitations in supporting the launch, and so a risk mitigation plan may be created by the project manager to guard against certain envisioned scenarios.

The final business case should identify the major changes to plan that have occurred and should set expectations on what is expected to be achieved. As with the market testing, if the results are significantly below what had been envisioned, it may be better to direct the company resources toward better opportunities. Otherwise, it's full steam ahead.

The decision to move to the Launch phase is similar in magnitude to the decision to move to the Develop phase in terms of importance. The costs for the launch are often significant, as is the impact on company reputation. This decision should not be taken lightly and should have the expressed consent of all affected functions.

Table 13-8. Launch Decision: Inputs and Outputs

INPUTS	OUTPUTS
• Beta test results • Business plan (final) • Functional launch readiness assessments	• Launch decision

13.4 Exiting the Qualify Phase

In order to exit the Qualify phase, the product should meet the market validation criteria established, meet the acceptable level of business viability established in the final business plan, and achieve launch readiness from all of the affected supported functions.

Chapter 14

The Launch Phase

Now that a product has been developed to meet market and customer requirements, it's time to take it to market. The Launch phase is one of the most critical phases of the product management lifecycle process. It is the point where the product management lifecycle phase of Launch aligns with the product lifecycle stage of Introduction.

A product launch can fail due to many reasons, such as overconfident estimates, recent competitive activity, under-allocated resources, and market shifts. Launching a product is more than following a standard checklist. It requires a carefully crafted strategic and tactical foundation in the preceding phases, particularly Conceive. A successful product launch is still not guaranteed even though all the preceding phases may have been executed according to plan and care taken to ensure the product meets market and customer requirements. A successful product launch is the result of *many* carefully planned steps by a focused, coordinated team. These teams can be further supported by product planning tools that enable cross-functional collaboration ensuring product management, marketing, sales, and other customer-facing teams are on the same page throughout the product launch process.

14.1 The Importance of Market Type in Setting Launch Strategy

The finalized launch plan requires much forethought. One of the key areas to consider is market type. Is this an existing market or a new market? Or is it a market that has been re-segmented to capitalize on the company's unique capabilities? The type of market will determine the launch strategy, budget, and resources required.

For example, if it's an existing market, the launch team may want to consider a full frontal assault using every available demand generation vehicle. This type of launch requires a sizeable budget upfront for ads, public relations, tradeshows, direct mail, etc., in addition to a high level of commitment from the entire company characterized by maximum exposure at a single point in time. Such an aggressive launch is required in an existing market where the cost of entry is high. The launch team must dedicate and focus all the marketing and sales resources available to grab a share of the marketplace.

In the case of a new market, a targeted low-cost approach may make the most sense. Online marketing and social media are the most popular approaches today for a new market given the cost versus reach considerations. The company needs to continually educate the market on how they can solve an existing, unsolved problem with the new product through long-term thought leadership and awareness programs, while investing in tactical demand generation programs and campaigns to gain sales momentum. Either way, the final goal is to create a tipping point in customer demand.

In the case of re-segmenting the market to create a niche for the product or service, the launch strategy will depend on various factors. For example, are there customers ready to buy in the new segment? Does the market clearly see the difference in this product or service versus existing offerings? If the new market is immature, treat it like a new market launch. If the market segment is more mature and ready to buy, then consider a full frontal assault. For a niche launch, invest all marketing dollars in acquiring a single, identifiable market segment and customer.

Bottom line, invest time in studying the market type upfront and tailor the launch objectives and plan accordingly. This is the single most important consideration that can determine the success or failure of the product or service in the market.

14.2 Product Launch Activity Groups

With less than 50% of product launches successful, the risk of product failure is high. Mitigating and managing execution risk is critical for a successful product launch. Specific risk areas that companies need to consider when planning a product launch include: selecting the right launch strategy, allocating resources appropriately to match timing and constraints, managing execution dependencies across multiple teams and regions, and ensuring product and marketing teams are well coordinated across all stages of the launch.

The two activity groups of the product Launch phase can be categorized as follows:

Launch activities begin with the product and marketing teams collaborating on the product narrative and finalizing the key positioning messages for the launch. This includes working cross-functionally to prepare for market readiness, including the development of customer and market-facing collateral, website messaging, select analyst and customer briefings, press relations readiness, product demonstration tools, and SEO. As these are being done, it's also critical that sales and channel partners are trained and enabled to appropriately position and sell the product with the required sales tools and access to final marketing collateral.

All customer-facing teams, including operations and customer support, are provided with the necessary documentation and product details to enable them to effectively deliver and support the product. Finally, any manufacturing-related readiness factors are considered to ensure a timely delivery and distribution of the product. Once complete, the product is officially launched in the market with clearly defined selling, delivery, and support processes.

Post-Launch activities occur once the product has been officially launched. It is time to promote the new offering to gain maximum attention and interest, and ultimately to create a desire to buy. The product is now showcased in relevant industry events, tradeshows, and advertising efforts conducted per the launch plan. It is now time to execute and fine-tune demand generation strategies to gain the prospective customer's attention and interest, and convert this interest into sales and market share — the goal of the Launch phase.

Upon the successful execution of these activities and before the transition to the Deliver phase, it's also important to monitor, evaluate, and refine the launch activities to ensure any corrective measures are taken to finalize and tighten for a successful launch. This includes measuring product launch progress with indicators that can identify unforeseen launch issues and respond before they become big problems.

14.2.1 Launch

Behind every successful launch is invariably the support of key executives from all the represented functions as well as a dedicated budget to support launch activities. Gaining access to needed resources is a critical step that needs to be completed *before* proceeding with the launch.

With executive support and financial resources secured, representatives from each of the functions are identified and a core team is formed. The functions that need to be actively involved in the launch process include product management, product marketing, operations, manufacturing, customer service, and sales. The team members need to be briefed on the level of commitment required until the completion of the launch. Ideally, product marketing leads the launch and coordinates the key activities with the rest of the team. The high level of activity to be coordinated across a large number of cross-functional groups may indicate the need for a project manager to assist the team.

Once these activities have been completed the emphasis shifts to positioning. Product positioning defines the space in the market that the company wants to own in the future. Very closely associated with positioning are the value proposition and the key messages that amplify the value proposition. The value proposition is a one- to three-sentence summary of the compelling reasons why the customer should buy the product or service solution as opposed to someone else's. The key messages, ideally limited to three, amplify and provide more detail in support of the value proposition.

These messages should be backed up with facts and figures that prove the point. The brand positioning statement, value proposition, and key messages need to fit on one page. This document becomes a one-page product story that is articulated in every communication with the target audience (e.g., websites, advertisements, direct mail, sales presentations, collateral, and other communication vehicles).

It is important to establish the exact value proposition the company wants to convey to the market. The value proposition and key messages are central to the success of the new product. Invest in the right advertising, collateral materials, and sales tools. Precisely articulating the product's value proposition, key messages, and substantive facts supported by the right collateral and sales tools provides the best chance to achieve the marketing objectives.

The launch team should make a list of all the key influencers, leading analysts, and thought leaders in the space who can act as product champions. They should develop a briefing deck that communicates the value proposition and clearly explains why the product is different from the competition.

> **The Importance of Marketing Materials**
>
> Sales people depend on professional marketing materials to drive business. How much effort and planning has gone into ensuring that the key product messages translate right through the documentation chain from engineering specification to user documentation, product brochures, and white papers?
>
> In order to avoid sales and marketing efforts separating themselves from the engineering and documentation sections, the launch team has to implement a system that facilitates information flow through the business. Good marketing materials will enforce the key product features and messages that are found in engineering, support, and user documentation, and contribute to market readiness.

Collateral is developed to support the sale of the product and influence the customers' opinion of the company or product. Product collateral typically includes:

- Product brochure or sell sheets – Created to highlight the unique aspects of the product and provide customers a reason to purchase this product over the competition.

- Product fact sheet – Developed to present compelling facts about the product, often at a more detailed level than a brochure or sell sheet. The product fact sheet typically highlights favorable characteristics of the product down to the actual features and functions.

- Press release – An announcement of major news events related to the product, such as a new release, new version, product line extensions, partnerships, high-profile customer acquisitions, or other relevant news.

- Return on Investment Calculator – A tool created to demonstrate how quickly the product will provide a return on the customer dollars invested. This tool is most appropriate for B2B and more expensive consumer purchases.

- White papers – Educational or research-orientated documents that are used to support the product's value proposition by highlighting key aspects of the product or countering a competitor's advantage.

- Websites – An effective channel for communicating the information listed above.

14

- Product demo or video

- Competitive product comparison

It is important to enable sales and channel readiness by equipping the sales and channel teams with needed training and tools to successfully sell the product. Product marketing should lead these cross-functional efforts, coordinating closely with product management and key internal stakeholders.

Operational and support readiness ensures that the operations and support teams are ready to deliver and maintain the product post-sale. Typical steps to consider ensuring operational and support readiness include:

- Integrating procedures for operations, quality, logistics, and production functions

- Developing procedures that improve the availability of any system, database, and tool

- Implementing all operations programs and procedures

- Ensuring the system integrity of the applications, that the applications are tuned for best performance, and that the daily services are working as expected

- Helping the business to find better ways of working and exploiting or improving the application

Product support readiness includes:

- Establishing the product support functions:

  o Level one help desk – assist users of products with basic questions

  o Level two and three – assist users of products with advanced technical issues

- Enabling users to utilize the product effectively by providing process and applications training

- Preparing policies, procedures, databases, and support systems needed for vertical launch and operating success

- Creating online support vehicles

- Preparing automated email and telephone response systems

Manufacturing readiness applies to many types of products and is the ability to achieve an operational capability that satisfies company objectives in the quantity, cost, and quality needed for a successful product. The process technologies, facilities, workforce, tooling, and supplier base must be ready for effective transition from development to production.

Successful product design follows a proven process that complies with the applicable regulatory standards, depending on the product and industry. Certain industry regulations require that a comprehensive management system be established and maintained to monitor and mitigate risks from product inception through design transfer and into production. For instance, pharmaceutical products require significant legal and regulatory procedures to ensure compliance.

At the point of design transfer to a manufacturing environment, most of the identified risks will have been eliminated or mitigated usually by the design, process control, and labeling stages. The design history file is complete with supportive verification testing data, and the documentation to procure, fabricate, tool, build, and test has been released in support of a production lot build.

A manufacturing readiness review is a key tool that determines whether the output of the design process, along with the manufacturing, supply chain, and quality team preparedness, meet all the requirements to move to a production environment.

Moving through this phase without completing all the elements could result in costly engineering changes, rework, and product recalls in the future. Moving too slowly through this phase could cause product launch delays and potential erosion of market share. This is why a well-planned and executed product development process with meaningful product decision points that culminate in a manufacturing readiness review leads to a smooth design transfer to production.

14

Table 14-1. Launch Activities: Inputs and Outputs

INPUTS	OUTPUTS
• Messaging and positioning inputs • Preliminary analyst briefings • Sales inputs on training, marketing campaigns	• Market positioning document • Marketing collateral • Sales tools • Analyst/PR briefing document • Demand generation plan • Tradeshows and events plan

14.2.2 Post-Launch

Now is the time to line up and conduct press interviews. The goal of this step is to make sure all key analysts, industry influencers, relevant media publications, and online resources, such as influential bloggers, are aware of the product launch and serve as a platform for promotion.

The launch team identifies all the tradeshows, conferences, and digital events that are relevant to the industry to showcase the product and include in the plan, and budget as appropriate. They speak at events and have staff on-hand to demonstrate and evangelize product capabilities and benefits. They undertake a road show, if budget permits, showcasing some early customer victories. The team uses social media and digital event opportunities to extend their reach.

The launch team prepares a demand generation plan to reach out to the target audience by region. They develop an integrated demand generation plan with key messages by role and segment at every stage of the campaign. Deciding on the right sequence and promotion mix is very important. For example, the launch team may start by sending out an email message inviting prospects to a webinar announcing the launch followed by a reminder as the date draws closer. At the end of the webinar, there may be a call to action followed by an offer or online promotion and next steps. The purpose of these demand generation campaigns is to capture the prospect's attention and interest, and then convert interest into desire and action, leading to a sale.

Table 14-2. Post-Launch Activities: Inputs and Outputs

INPUTS	OUTPUTS
• Analyst inquiries to clarify positioning, competitive landscape • Tradeshows, events • Demand generation ideas—sales, marketing discussions	• Analyst briefings/PR plan • Tradeshows/events plan • Demand generation plan

14.3 Exiting the Launch Phase

In order to exit the Launch phase, all the deliverables defined in the two activity groups must be agreed upon. As each of these stages is reviewed, launch activities are evaluated and refined. The team's project manager reviews the deliverables for each of the above stages, ensures completion, and conducts an exit review. The team obtains executive sign-off before moving into the Deliver phase.

Chapter 15

The Deliver Phase

The Deliver phase is the point where the product management lifecycle intersects the "product lifecycle" stages of Growth, Maturity, and Decline. While represented as a serial or linear phase in the product management lifecycle— as each successful product must pass this phase and continue on ultimately to the Retire phase—it can also be thought of as a circle or spiral because the product is adapted throughout its lifetime to meet the changing customer, organizational, and market needs.

The exact length of this phase and the number of iterations undertaken is highly dependent upon the product's market. Durable products can last for decades whereas technology products can last a few months as new technologies rapidly replace existing ones. The challenge for product management professionals is to understand the underlying market dynamics and optimize the company's product investments to increase the value of the product during the Growth stage and then regulate investment in the Maturity stage while realizing that minimal or no investment may be warranted in the Decline stage. Product managers continuously balance investment and return throughout the Deliver phase.

Once a product has been successfully launched, it will then progress through the rest of its lifecycle similar to how we as human beings go through infancy, childhood, adulthood, and old age. This sequence of progressive stages from a product's launch to growth, maturity, and decline is associated with changing market conditions and evolving customer requirements that impact a product's marketing strategy and mix. These factors continually shift depending on where the product is in its lifecycle. For example, consumers are regularly bombarded by

15

advertisements announcing exciting new features of existing products, such as a car with standard satellite radio or a cereal that now comes in additional flavors. Yet, there are thousands of products in stores that are not advertised at all.

Some established products are regularly given makeovers and generous marketing budgets, while others are left to sell themselves because product managers and product marketers are acting according to where the product is in its lifecycle.

For example, during the earlier parts of the product lifecycle, the cost of promoting the product may be greater than the revenue it creates. However, if that investment results in a product that meets its objectives for market share, unit sales, and cost targets, the product will likely become increasingly profitable during the Growth and Maturity stages. And as the product enters the Decline stage, marketing investment tapers off or is diverted to different versions of the product depending on its end-of-life plan and exit strategy.

This section provides insights into these types of questions and can help you make the right product, feature, and marketing decisions and ensure that the product maximizes its profitability across the entire lifecycle.

15.1 Product Deliver Stages

As discussed previously, products go through the three stages of Growth, Maturity, and Decline after they are launched. Each stage requires a different mix of marketing activities to maximize the lifetime profitability of the product.

Growth – During the course of its launch, a product spends a considerable amount of time in market where customers and potential consumers get familiar with its capabilities and start buying the product or consuming it. As demand for the product increases the product enters the Growth phase and product marketing activities focus on expanding the market for the product into new segments, usually either geographic or demographic. These new segments frequently result in enhanced product features or introduction of newer versions, such as new variations, sizes, or software releases.

As a successful product steadily grows in the market, it gains strength and faces increasing levels of competition. The competition now offers a greater range of choices to the customer in the form of different product types, packaging, and prices. This competitive situation offers an opportunity for new products to differentiate themselves. The market base expands as more customers buy the product. Now is also the time to enter new regions and target new industries, depending on product-market fit. More channel partners are willing to sell the product and one generally observes a softening of prices towards the latter stages of the Growth phase.

At this time, the company increases operations and manufacturing in order to scale. There are fewer product bottlenecks, hence cost is lowered. To remain competitive over a period of time, the firm initiates product improvements or modifications to suit new target markets or segments, but profits taper off at the end of this phase.

Maturity – Upon the completion of the Growth phase, the product now enters its Maturity stage. By the time a product reaches maturity, overall market growth is flat and the company typically seeks to increase profits by reducing costs while investing enough to maintain customer loyalty in order to entice customers to the next generation product. The Maturity stage *is the most important phase of Deliver* from a financial point of view because this is the period when the product is most profitable.

There are a number of reasons for a product entering the Maturity stage. For example, entry of a disruptive new product that may be offering better quality at a cheaper price and has induced a consumer shift may cause a product to enter its Maturity stage. This calls for some effective product and marketing strategies to revitalize the product so that it stays alive in the market.

During the Maturity stage, strategy shifts again to focus on reinforcing the current market position, revitalizing the brand, and increasing sales. Product marketers try to come up with ways to defend their market positions against possible in-roads by competitors.

In addition, the product's features may continue to be augmented, and there will still be some promotional activity to differentiate the product from the competition and increase market share. However, marketing activity and expenditure levels may be much lower than in the Growth stage.

At this point of the Maturity stage, it is important to recognize that it's difficult to survive, as there are new entrants that are now offering better quality, more features, and lower priced products. Product maturity often leads to the decline of the product, and this is the time when the company starts incurring losses on its production. A clear indicator is dwindling profits, signaling decline.

Remember, while a product is contributing to the growth of the company, it will continue to be produced. But when the carrying and marketing costs are higher than the return from the product, production needs to stop and the product is often discontinued.

15

Decline – Dwindling sales and profits bring the product to the Decline stage when sales slow down dramatically and profits fall off. The product may be dropped to make way for new products and the cycle recommences. Finally, once the product begins to decline, marketing support may be withdrawn completely, and sales will entirely be the result of the product's residual reputation amongst a shrinking market sector. Staunch brand loyalists, for example, may continue to buy the product despite zero marketing or advertising.

By this stage, the most important decision that needs to be made is when to take the product off the market completely. It can be tempting to leave a declining product on the market—especially if it served the company well in its time and there's often a certain sentimental attachment to it. However, it is essential that the product is not allowed to start costing more than it takes to produce and market. This can easily happen if production and marketing costs increase as volumes drop.

More importantly, the old product's very existence can absorb the entire product team's time, energy, and valuable resources and can discourage or delay the development of a new, potentially more profitable replacement product. This is in addition to other customer-facing teams required to keep the product in the market, including customer support, customer relationship management, and sales renewals.

The following sections outline the steps within each product lifecycle stage in more detail.

15.1.1 Growth

Now that the product has been successfully launched, it's time to stress differentiation to solidify the product's position and gain market share. This stage is characterized by growing market acceptance and increasing profits. Marketing objectives and strategies change rapidly during the growth phase as competitors begin to enter the market and sales begin to increase.

Companies concentrate on optimizing product availability and making it easy to reach the customers. The primary objective at this stage is to stimulate "selective demand." This is an attempt to stimulate demand for a specific product instead of the entire product line or category. The focus is on obtaining additional market share by swaying significant numbers of the mass market (early and late majority) to the new product.

Here are some key considerations to ensure the product stands out during the Growth stage and solidifies its market position:

- Modify and enhance the product as required to exceed market and customer expectations. Correct weak or omitted attributes in the product and build capabilities that will ensure competitive differentiation and help gain traction.

- Adopt a pricing strategy that will ensure parity with competition, especially if a price-skimming strategy has been adopted previously. Set premium pricing only if the differentiation is very clear to the customer, or you will run the risk of being perceived as an expensive provider missing out on an opportunity for rapid customer acquisition.

- Build loyalty for the product. Ensure marketing communications stress the competitive differentiators of the product. Since consumers are more aware of the product's benefits and there is more competition, it's imperative to clearly and consistently differentiate the product from the competition.

- Move toward intensive distribution. Expand the channel partner network as the product category is more familiar and the product is now more accepted. Intermediaries are therefore more inclined to accept the risk associated with the product and will be willing to invest in its growth.

Product managers and product marketers ensure that the sales organization has the appropriate amount of product information and the necessary tools to enable a quickening rate of revenue capture. Product managers may also lend support to the sales organization by assisting in the sales process with key clients in order to close deals that contribute significantly to the organization's revenue stream.

Profits begin to flatten out late in the growth stage. Product marketers and managers will need to pursue further segmentation in order to continue growing, albeit at a slower rate, before the product enters its Maturity stage.

15.1.2 Maturity

The rate of sales growth slows down during the Maturity stage as the product has already been widely distributed and has hit peak sales during the Growth stage. The company now focuses on creating product line extensions and promotion offers to boost sales. New product research is critical to ensure future sales as product managers uncover new market needs and specific capabilities to meet them. During the Maturity stage, the sales curve peaks, severe competition ensues, and consumers are now experienced users of the product.

Several marketing strategies can be adopted to ensure that the product still continues to be profitable as it progresses during the Maturity stage. An additional strategy for extending growth and maturity is to expand and add new products within the same product line. These new products can carry the same product line or brand name as their parent products, or can be given different names.

Price cutting or promotional discounts may be called for as competitive pressure intensifies. Defending market share and profitability becomes the main focus and purpose of the product marketing team.

When products reach maturity they are well known. However, as competing products enter the market, mature products can begin to look old and tired. Action must then be taken to refresh the product's image. For example, a product may be rejuvenated through a change in packaging, introducing new models or versions, or making aesthetic changes. Repositioning can create new appeal for existing customers or attract new customers.

Repositioning strategies are used to respond to changes in customer needs or market conditions, or a change in competitor strategy. The extent of the repositioning will depend on the level of change in customer requirements, needs and supporting technologies, and on how well competitors are doing.

Firms also can modify the augmented product to extend growth and maturity. Services can be added where none existed before—adding free set-up and delivery are good examples.

15.1.3 Decline

After the Maturity stage the product now enters the Decline stage where sales fall off rapidly. This can be caused by new technology or a market trend. Product managers and marketers can justify supporting the product as long as it contributes to profits or enhances the effectiveness of the product mix.

Sooner or later, however, companies need to decide whether to eliminate or reposition to extend the product's life. This is the stage when some of the competition drops out.

Decline poses serious challenges to all competitors still remaining in the market. The major strategy employed during decline is *harvesting*. Expenses are reduced as much as possible to squeeze out all remaining profits from the brand. Costs are cut back in all areas of the marketing program, including advertising, sales promotion, personal selling, and channel support.

One of the major causes of product decline is the advent of a new technology. New technologies have led to a long list of products that are no longer relevant, for example the impact touch-tone phones had on the rotary dial, or what laptop computers did to the sales of word processors. The rotary dial phone and word processor entered their decline stages and faded into history.

Once a product enters the Decline stage, the company must consider its potential deletion from its product mix and start thinking about the end-of-life plan. There are multiple deletion strategies companies can employ when anticipating a product's removal from the market, such as the following:

- Harvest the Product — Harvesting usually signals the company's future intention to drop the product. Harvesting entails finding ways to cut production and marketing costs to a bare minimum. The product is eliminated from unprofitable distribution channels and market segments. All forms of marketing promotions and activities are cut back. Most sales promotion is eliminated and advertising is refocused to serve only as a reminder to the customer that the product is still available. The company knows that harvesting will effectively hasten the decline of the product, but any remaining sales will be more profitable.

- Discontinue the Product — A company can simply discontinue the product, just as Apple does with unprofitable laptop models.

- Sell the Product — The product can be sold to other companies to augment or complement *their* existing product line. For example, GE sold its small appliance line to Black and Decker.

Here are some key considerations when a product enters the Decline stage and becomes a candidate for deletion:

- The potential impact of the product's withdrawal on the sales of other products in the company's mix must be examined. Most companies sell entire lines of products, not single products. Generally, these products complement one another. If so, yanking one from the market potentially can hurt the sales of the other items.

- Sometimes it's better to keep the declining product on the market because it leads to higher levels of sales of other products in the company's mix.

- Honoring warranties and service contracts, as well as providing replacement parts for existing product owners, is a must when products are deleted. The company may choose to provide parts and essential services itself, or may contract these out to other companies.

15

15.2 Controlling the Length of Product Lifecycle Stages

The duration of each stage of the lifecycle can be influenced or controlled to a certain extent. This is particularly true of the Maturity stage as this is the most important one to extend from a financial point of view because this is the period when the product is most profitable.

In addition to the marketing strategies discussed in the section earlier, typical tactics designed to extend the Maturity stage include:

- Increasing the amount of the product used by existing customers or expanding its user base to other divisions within an enterprise

- Adding or updating new product features and functionality

- Price promotions to attract customers who use a rival product

- Advertising to encourage trial of the product targeted at people who don't use this category of product at all, for example web-based trials

- Acquiring competitors—Oracle and Seibel, for example

If the product management team understands how to manage the product lifecycle for individual products, then they are in a better position to manage the company's entire product portfolio to ensure that the overall mix of products generates the highest possible returns for the firm.

Products entering decline must be balanced with products that are in their growth and maturity phases. This is the only way the companies can maintain stable levels of overall sales and profits. Individual product lifecycles must complement one another and the result is a strategic product mix that will ensure the company or product line's market dominance.

15.3 Exiting the Deliver Phase

In order to exit the Deliver phase, all the key indicators must be defined and agreed upon. Key indicators can include any of the following:

- Low product demand – Due to lack of demand or a significant drop in demand, the product is no longer profitable.

- Consumption decline – Long-term consumption for the product type is expected to significantly decline due to a change in customer behavior. This market trend impacts all direct competitors that do not have a substitute product.

- Market uncertainty – Due to market uncertainty, significant consolidation occurs with direct and indirect competitors through mergers and acquisitions.

- Business strategy change – Due to changes in the business strategy, the product strategy no longer aligns. This may happen when a company is in survival mode and the product is not a significant revenue stream.

If the product manager reviews the status data and concludes that demand for the product has begun to decline due to an irreversible shift in market forces, an exit review will be conducted to confirm that all the indicators have been examined before moving into the Retire phase.

15

Chapter 16

The Retire Phase

Retiring a product is a difficult and complex task. Product managers have spent the majority of their professional careers focused on driving growth and creating and maintaining value throughout all the previous phases of the product management lifecycle. So market withdrawal is often difficult personally and professionally.

In fact, many organizations underestimate the complexity of the task, including the amount of time and resources required. Retiring a product successfully, with a minimum of customer disruption, can be one of the most difficult aspects of a product manager's job.

Market decline occurs when there is an absolute reduction in unit sales over a sustained period of time. An absolute decline means that it impacts all direct competitors or rivals in the same industry. Revenues drop to the point where it's no longer economically feasible to continue developing the product.

Market decline is not the only factor influencing the decision to retire a product. Other reasons can include strategic business considerations, regulatory changes, fine-tuning the company's product portfolio mix, mergers and acquisitions, or simply determining that the product is no longer central to the organization's business model. Regardless of the reason, any of these factors can lead to a product's retirement.

Once product retirement is agreed to by the key stakeholders, the product manager must now decide when and how to gracefully withdraw the product from the market and ideally migrate existing customers to an alternative product. The product will formally reach its end-of-life when the parent organization is no longer marketing, selling, or sustaining it, and may also be limiting or ending its support.

16

The duration of a product's lifetime depends on the product and on the customer's perception of how long a product should last. Different products have different expected lifetimes. For example, on average, toys from fast food chains may last a few weeks, cars may last ten years, and mobile phones may last up to three years.

In some cases, the life expectancy of a product is considered at its inception so that all the stakeholders within an organization understand when to begin planning for its market withdrawal. This is referred to as *planned obsolescence*. For example, Intel introduces a new microprocessor every 18 months as they announce the end-of-life for previous versions.

While planned obsolescence is an established part of the overall product lifecycle management process for many organizations, each product entering its end-of-life prompts a company to review key indicators that signal the need for withdrawal. Companies frequently rely on portfolio analysis tools to monitor and visualize these indicators.

16.1 End-of-Life Plan

Once a determination to withdraw the product from the market has been made, the company organizes activities into a structured End-of-Life (EOL) plan. This EOL plan is the reverse of a Launch plan. It outlines the company's plan for gracefully withdrawing a product from the market while minimizing the impact to existing customers who may utilize more than one of the company's products.

The actual components of the EOL plan will vary based upon industry, but there are several key areas of consideration that must be taken into account. The first is that ending the life of a product requires effective communication to all impacted internal stakeholders, as well as externally to the market. Customers and business partners will need to understand the schedule for full market withdrawal in order to find alternatives or prepare accordingly.

Legal considerations and contract terms also can play a big role in dictating the appropriate approach and timing of the product's retirement. This is particularly true in business-to-business environments. Organizations that manage this process well often develop a targeted project plan to help manage the components of market withdrawal to ensure that the goal is attained and that all the associated complexities are fully planned out and effectively executed.

Another factor to take into consideration is product support. While a company may choose to withdraw a product from the market, it is not uncommon for organizations to maintain some level of product support past the point of the product's actual retirement.

For example, hardware may have an expected lifetime of ten years after production ends, and the company may choose to maintain product support by making spare parts, technical support, and service available. This approach is often profitable for the organization, although the cost of parts production is likely to increase as manufacturing volume drops.

A well-thought-out EOL plan helps customers plan and manage their transition to alternative products. It also communicates the role that the company can play in helping them migrate to a replacement product or solution. It clearly identifies external impacts on the customers/users, distribution channels, key partners, and suppliers. It also identifies factors internal to the company, such as cost analysis and impact on customer support, operations, or manufacturing functions.

16.1.1 External Areas of Impact to Consider in End-of-Life Plan

External areas of impact are identified by looking at the company value chain (Table 16-1). This chain includes companies on the supply side of the value chain, such as key partners and suppliers that the organization relies on to reduce time to market or manufacturing and operations costs. This also includes companies on the demand-side of the value chain, such as distribution channels, which the company relies on to deliver products to customers.

Table 16-1. External Areas of Consideration for an EOL Plan

Customers	Distribution	Partners/Suppliers
• Contracts • Upgrade offers • Upgrade logistics • Warranties • Training	• Contracts • Training • Promotions • Order systems	• Licensing agreements • Contracts • Acquisition plans

16.1.2 Internal Areas of Impact to Consider in End-of-Life Plan

Internal areas of impact include all departments and functions involved within an organization that support the product that is being retired (Table 16-2). This includes, but is not limited to, development, quality assurance/control, customer service, manufacturing, operations, marketing, and sales. This may also include deployment teams, supply chain management, and distribution channel management.

16

Table 16-2. Internal Areas of Consideration for an EOL Plan

Marketing/Sales	Customer Service	Manufacturing/Operations

• Competitive positioning
• Pricing strategies
• Communication plan
  » Termination, migration, or upgrade strategy
  » Promotion plan (if appropriate)
• Marketing and Sales materials
• Order systems
	• Customer service procedures
	• Training
	• Spare parts and service
	• Maintenance documentation
	• Troubleshooting documentation
		• Procurement plans
		• Production plans
		• Inventory
		• Training
		• Documentation

EOL plans are an essential tool for ensuring that all parties are aware and appropriately engaged in the often difficult transition to retirement. Product portfolio analysis tools coupled with competitive analysis and relevant financial data can point to the need to retire a product that is winding down its market relevance. The resulting EOL plan provides the necessary structured framework to ensure that the product is terminated efficiently and with a minimum of market and customer disruption.

If a replacement product is offered, a migration plan will be needed to communicate to internal and external stakeholders how customers can migrate from the terminated product to the replacement product.

Table 16-3. End-of-Life Plan: Inputs and Outputs

INPUTS	OUTPUTS
• Product portfolio management analysis • Profit and loss (P&L) or financial reporting • Competitive analysis • Market trends • Customer satisfaction survey data	• End-of-Life Plan • Product termination

16.2 Phase Review

The Retire phase is successfully exited when the good or service is withdrawn from the market in accordance with the end-of-life plan.

SECTION 3:
Key Product Management Tools by Product Lifecycle Phase

Section three provides an overview of some of the key tools used by product managers throughout the product management lifecycle. The intent of the section is not to provide every conceivable tool or to explain each tool in minute detail, but rather to describe the general nature of the tool, the underlying components, and the characteristics that distinguish a strong tool from a less robust version.

Chapter 17   Product Management Tools

Chapter 17

Product Management Tools

17.1 The Conceive Phase Tools

There are a number of tools product managers are expected to know, particularly in the conceptualization phase. These tools often provide product managers with a more strategic view and reveal insights beyond the boundaries of individual products and their features.

17.1.1 Product Portfolio Management

The product portfolio connects the overall corporate strategy to a specific product strategy. The product portfolio contains the overall suite of products, both existing and planned. The active management of planned and existing products helps to ensure that the company achieves its stated goals and objectives.

The portfolio management process provides the linkage from high-level corporate resource/budget allocation down to the strategy initiatives encapsulated in one or more product roadmaps. The overall portfolio management process is also coupled to a more tactical project portfolio management discipline that approves and tracks *specific projects* supporting the product portfolio initiatives.

The portfolio management processes and activities involve the analysis of the suite of products in the portfolio relative to strategic corporate goals. The methods used to analyze the product suite and the measures used to evaluate success can vary significantly among companies.

Knowing where to invest (and not to invest) is perhaps the most important contribution made by product leaders. In fact, Steve Jobs once famously said "Deciding what not to do is as important as deciding what to do. That's true for companies, and it's true for products."[52]

[52] Isaacson, W. (2011). *Steve Jobs*. New York, NY: Simon & Schuster.

For example, one common and easily understood method used to communicate the analysis visually is illustrated by the Boston Consulting Group (BCG) Growth-Share Matrix, as shown in Figure 17-1.

Figure 17-1. BCG Growth-Share Matrix

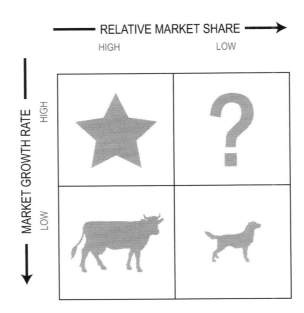

The matrix has Market Growth Rate on the vertical axis and Relative Market Share on the horizontal axis with respect to the market (segment) leader. Products in the lower right quadrant (those in low growth markets and with low market share) are referred to as *dogs*. These "dog" products are ripe for disinvestment or divestiture and can free up resources and management attention for more attractive options.

In the upper right quadrant are products in a growth market but with relatively low market share, referred to as *question marks*. Question marks typically require an investment of some sort to improve their market position with no guarantee of success.

Products in the upper left quadrant have high growth markets and strong market share and are referred to as *stars*. Stars also require investment to capitalize on any market opportunity and to maintain or grow share.

In the lower left quadrant of the matrix are products in lower growth markets with relatively high market share, referred to as *cash cows*. Cash cows are typically successful mature products with limited additional potential, requiring a minimal amount of investment to maintain market position or maximize profitability. Profits and resources from cash cows are often used to fund investments into stars and question marks, as shown in Figure 17-2.

Figure 17-2. Profits from Cash Cows Fund Investments in Question Marks and Stars

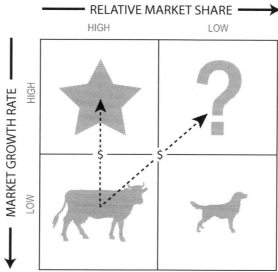

Over time, stars become cash cows as market growth begins to slow, and cash cows become dogs as newer and better solutions gain relatively higher market share, as shown in Figure 17-3. Thus, the portfolio must have investments and products in the question mark stage with the potential to replace fading stars. A major problem in many maturing companies is the lack of a pipeline of new products positioned in new growth markets to offset or replace products in the maturity or decline stages.

Figure 17-3. Progression from Star to Dog over Time

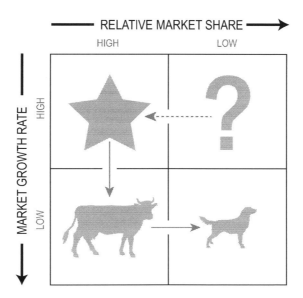

Another similar tool is the GE-McKinsey Matrix, which extends the BCG approach by expanding the definitions of the labels on each axis. Replacing Market Growth Rate on the vertical axis with Industry Attractiveness creates the opportunity to define elements that are more company-focused, including size of the market or competitive intensity in addition to market growth. The approach also allows weighted combinations. On the horizontal axis, Market Share is replaced with Competitive Position. The definitions can expand market share to include other corporate strengths, including brand equity, core competencies, and distribution strength. The GE-McKinsey Matrix expands the grid to a 3 by 3, giving nine possible options. These alternatives range from a clear investment opportunity to exiting a product, as shown below in Figure 17-4.

Figure 17-4. GE-McKinsey Matrix

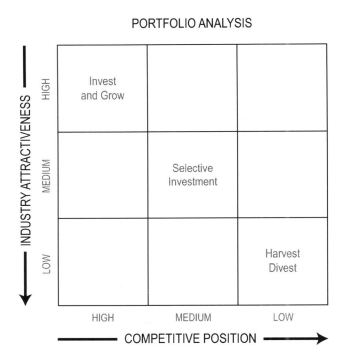

Regardless of the analysis method chosen, elements of a good Product Portfolio Management process include:

- Allocation of resources aligned to strategic corporate objectives across the various product activities.

- A balance of product activities that diversify across current and future products, current and future markets, and short-term versus long-term revenue.

17.1.2 Product Concept Identification

SWOT Analysis

A great tool for understanding the product's current and potential standing in the competitive market place is the SWOT analysis. The acronym stands for **S**trengths, **W**eaknesses, **O**pportunities, and **T**hreats. A SWOT analysis is the process of assessing the current situation for a company, a product, or a competitor, and is used to help formulate strategy. At a high level, the analysis involves the assessment of various components of the external and internal environments, and looks at them from both positive and negative perspectives.

The results of the analysis can be rolled up into a 4-by-4 matrix shown in Figure 17-5.

Figure 17-5. SWOT Matrix Example

	+	-
Internal Origin, Now	**Strengths** • Product capabilities • Company competencies • Market position • Key resources • Strong processes/quality • Key partnerships	**Weaknesses** • Product capability gaps • Missing competencies • Lack of market position • Missing resources • Ineffective processes • Ineffective partnerships
External Origin, Future	**Opportunities** • Market expansion • Competitor weaknesses • New technology • New resources/partners • Environmental changes	**Threats** • Weakening markets • Competitive incursions • Replacement technology • Lost resources/partners • Environmental changes

The matrix lists Strengths and Weaknesses in the upper row. The strengths and weaknesses are internal to the company or product under analysis and are focused on the current view. *Strengths* are considered positive attributes for the company, while *weaknesses* are considered negative. The matrix in Figure 17-5 lists common categories for assessing the internal view, including product capabilities, company competencies, market position, key resources, strong processes or quality, and key partnerships.

Opportunities and Threats are listed on the bottom row. The opportunities and threats are external to the company or product, and are trends or events that may impact the company at some future point in time. *Opportunities* are those

17

factors providing a potential positive impact, while threats are factors providing a potentially negative impact. This analysis focuses on changes occurring in the market, competition, technology, processes, resources, and partners.

It is important to remember that strengths and weaknesses are about the product and company in the competitive landscape, whereas opportunities and threats are related to trends and situations in the markets the company serves. For example, "we might not deliver on time" is a weakness, not a threat; "technical literacy is expanding in our markets" is an opportunity.

The information provided by the SWOT matrix by itself does not tell the product team what to *do*. The next step in the process is to assess the options from a strategic perspective to address the opportunities and threats being faced, while being mindful of the specific strengths and weaknesses present in the organization.

An extension to the SWOT analysis is the TOWS matrix (TOWS is SWOT spelled backwards). The reverse order is intended to illustrate that the assessment of the external environment (Threats and Opportunities) is the primary focus and should be done first, followed by the assessment of *relevant* internal capabilities (Weaknesses and Strengths). This approach helps to remove or mitigate the risk of focusing on internal elements that may not have any impact on the potential opportunities or threats. For the actual TOWS analysis, the focus becomes what strategy options best leverage the strengths while minimizing or overcoming the weaknesses. The strategy options can be developed as shown in the TOWS matrix in Figure 17-6.

Figure 17-6. TOWS Matrix with Strategy Options

	STRENGTHS Good Now [Maintain, build, leverage]	WEAKNESSES Bad Now [Remedy, stop]
OPPORTUNITIES Good Future [Prioritize, optimize]	**S-O Options** [Future Growth] How do I leverage my Strengths to take advantage of the Opportunities?	**W-O Options** [Internal Fixes] How do I overcome Weaknesses that prevent or diminish the pursuit of the Opportunities?
THREATS Bad Future [Counter, minimize]	**S-T Options** [External Fixes] How do I use my Strengths to reduce the likelihood and impact of the Threats?	**W-T Options** [Survival] How do I address Weaknesses that increase the likelihood and impact of the Threats?

Each of the TOWS quadrants assist in the development of options from a strategic perspective that matches with outputs from the SWOT analysis. The left column shows potential strategies that can leverage strengths to take advantage of identified opportunities and/or threats.

For example, one strength element could be a strong technology development capability with expertise in a specific area. The product team might be able to leverage technology development capabilities by expanding the product line into an adjacent growth segment. Or identified strengths might be able to be utilized to counter an emergent competitive threat.

The right column shows strategic options the product team could pursue that address the opportunities and threats and that minimize or overcome weaknesses. For example, addressing an attractive growth market with a new product line could offset an identified weakness of the maturing or declining current market. Addressing the competitive threat of a new low-cost competitor could lead to the creation of a low-cost or simplified version of the existing product, which could offset cost and pricing pressures on the core product or product line.

Once the product team has a full set of options, they can be prioritized by rolling up options that leverage the most strengths and diminish the most weaknesses in addressing the opportunities and threats. The top options can then inform the strategy initiatives to support the overall product strategy going forward.

A good SWOT analysis includes:

- A comprehensive view of the external environment along with major factors that impact the business, and the opportunities and threats projected.

- An honest assessment of internal strengths and weaknesses relative to the future opportunities and threats identified.

- A set of strategy options generated by leveraging strengths and diminishing weaknesses for each of the opportunities and threats.

- A prioritized roll-up of the strategy options into initiatives that will drive the specific project selection going forward.

The product team should be prepared to defend assessments of weaknesses. This area may offend the people who are responsible for the items that the team has noted. In general, collecting relevant customer quotes and meaningful data can help ensure that the right decision is made.

17

The Product Concept

The Product Concept is the first step toward connecting a high-level set of market needs to a specific conceptual solution that could be developed to satisfy the need. It proposes the potential market opportunity, the way in which the company might create and deliver the solution, and the value the solution delivers to the market.

The Product Concept statement is typically a lightweight, living document that answers the following questions:

- What market problem are we attempting to solve?

- How big is the opportunity if the problem is solved?

- Who specifically has the problem? Who are the buyers and users?

- What are the benefits for the customer? What are the benefits to the organization?

- What evidence have we collected that demonstrates that we correctly understand the problem and that prospects would really buy our solution?

- What is the market window for the opportunity?

- What is the competitive situation for the solution?

- What are the main features of the solution and key success factors?

- What are our key differentiators?

- How would we take the solution to market?

- What metrics should be utilized to determine product success?

The objective of the Product Concept is to provide enough information about how a company might approach a market need in order to justify continuing the investigation at a deeper level with additional resources. Therefore, a good Product Concept statement will:

- Contain enough research into the market segment to document the current situation and market needs.

- Provide an understanding of the competitive situation and an explanation as to why the market gap exists.

- Provide a conceptual solution that aligns with the company's capabilities and strategic objectives.

- Define how the solution will provide enhanced customer value beyond what existing competitors or products offer.

- Define the financial and long-term benefits that the company should expect.

A popular tool for a product concept document is the Business Model Canvas.[53] It is a visual chart with elements describing a firm's value proposition, infrastructure, customers, and finances. It assists firms in aligning their activities by illustrating potential trade-offs.

Idea or Feature Prioritization Matrix

Every product team, no matter the size, must learn to choose from a wide range of possible options. After all, organizations have limited resources. A Prioritization Matrix is a scoring mechanism that is used to assess alternative product concept ideas. When product ideas are developed and submitted for review, a systematic approach can be helpful in determining which ideas should move forward for further study. The same systematic process can be utilized to determine which proposed product features may or may not provide value.

The matrix can be developed using any criteria that makes sense for the specific goals and strategy of the organization. Here are some possible criteria:

- Market attractiveness

- Competitive attractiveness

- Timing for entering the market

- Market value

- Differentiation

- Projected return on investment over a defined period of time

- Strategic alignment with company goals and objectives

- Estimated cost of development relative to the size of the opportunity

17

[53] Osterwalder, A., & Pigneur, Y. (2010). *Business Model Generation: A Handbook for Visionaries, Game Changers, and Challengers*. Hoboken, NJ: John Wiley & Sons.

An example of a prioritization matrix is illustrated in Figure 17-7.

Figure 17-7. Example Idea Prioritization Matrix

CRITERIA	SCORING	IDEA ONE	IDEA TWO	IDEA THREE
Market attractiveness	3=High, 1=Low	2	1	3
Competitive attractiveness	3=High, 1=Low	2	1	3
Market timing	3=Good, 1=Bad	3	2	1
Solution value proposition	3=High, 1=Low	3	2	1
Solution differentiation	3=High, 1=Low	3	1	2
Potential company gain	3=High, 1=Low	1	1	2
Strategic alignment	3=High, 1=Low	2	3	1-Stop
Total score	Minimum 14 No Stops	16	11	13

Each of the selected criteria is scored using the illustrated measurement scale. It is best to specifically define each measure to eliminate individual subjectivity. For example, for market attractiveness, high = market growth > 5% + market size > 2M potential customers. Each idea is then scored on the available scale and totaled.

In most cases, the scoring will be somewhat subjective and that's okay. At this point, the product team is not building a financial forecast but looking for the best opportunities to explore further.

There can also be some automatic stops built into the evaluation process. An example of a hard stop might be if the proposed solution is not in line with company strategy, then the proposed solution would be dropped from consideration. Finally, there should be some minimum score criteria, so that projects that do not score a minimum of X are also dropped from further consideration. A systematic approach provides increased efficiency and a more effective use of resources. It is not unusual for a company to discard the majority of the ideas submitted for review.

17.1.3 Product Concept Investigation

Personas

Before the product team can build a product, they need to answer the question, "For whom?" *Personas* represent groups of customers that possess a set of characteristics. A persona is a way to bring an individual (or homogenous group) to life via an archetype or character. Personas provide a common frame of reference for team members on the project. The persona allows team members to understand for whom a product or service is being developed. The characteristics and behaviors of the persona helps team members make decisions during the planning and development of a product. Information to create the persona is obtained through primary research and Voice-of-the-Customer activities.

A persona can range from a very lightweight user profile, containing just enough information to gain a basic understanding of a homogeneous group of individuals, to a very elaborate description of behaviors and characteristics that attempts to capture activities and motivations for decision-making purposes. Information contained in personas can vary between business-to-consumer and business-to-business products and services. Common information found in a persona includes:

- A made-up descriptive name and optional photo or caricature

- Demographic information (gender, age, marital status, location)

- Education, work, income

- Lifestyle or work factors and goals

- Domain competence or experience in the product category

- A quote or slogan that captures personality or personal drivers

- Typical activities that may influence the product use, especially pain points

- Other related products or solutions currently used

- Values, attitudes, and motivators that influence the decision process

- Other collaborators related to reaching goals

- Frequency of activity toward goals

17

Buyer personas represent specific types of buyers that the sales channels are targeting. Examples include an end user, a department manager, and a purchasing manager for a business product. Personas drive the development of the important components, functionality, and benefits of the value proposition. Personas may also impact and influence the messaging and sales materials development.

User personas represent specific types of users who will use the product in different ways or have different expectations of it. An example is a group administrator who installs and sets up a software product for the end users, versus the end user who uses it for the job on a daily basis. These personas help drive decisions and prioritization for product capabilities and functionality, as well as specific design decisions impacting usability, look and feel, etc.

The overall goal of the persona is to provide a tool for understanding a typical customer for the product. Successful personas will have the following characteristics:

- Provides relevant information that gives insight into the customer's world, including the challenges and goals they are trying to achieve related to the product.

- Focuses on the primary buyers and users of the products, typically achieved with just a handful of personas.

- Driven from market research or Voice-of-the-Customer activities over a sufficient number of customers to realize trends or common tendencies.

The product team should be especially cautious of "creative writing." Many teams build elaborate personas based entirely on internal opinions and perhaps one or two customer interviews. Creative writing is not appropriate for business documents.

Problem Scenarios

Personas have problems that the product is intended to solve. *Problem scenarios* represent one method for describing the market problem. They are an easy way to describe, at a high level, a typical situation that a typical customer encounters and the challenge the customer faces in achieving a goal. For example, a customer may need to provide a quick, healthy, and tasty meal for the family before running off to gymnastics practice and a baseball game. The need is for a quick meal. The challenge is to provide a healthy and tasty meal within time constraints.

Scenarios can take several forms, depending on the type of product being developed and the level of detail needed to capture the information. One common format is a simple story consisting of a few paragraphs or bulleted steps in a sequence.

In this story, some key elements should be identified as follows:

- Primary persona for the scenario. There is typically only one, but occasionally multiple personas can be involved if they are interacting with each other and have different perspectives on the problem. An example would be an online doctor/patient interaction where both have specific sets of information to share in order to assess symptoms and make a diagnosis without an office visit.

- Setting for the scenario. The location and time frame of the scenario, such as in an office during a normal workday.

- Goal of the persona. The high-level objective that the persona is trying to achieve in this situation, such as "easily listen to music while jogging" or "quickly get some cash at a convenient location." This goal sets the high-level context that helps the product team focus on the problem and potentially generate entirely new solution options.

- Most common steps to achieve the goal. These are high-level activities the persona would do to achieve the goal, with focus on the most common flow that illustrates challenge or frustration. These steps describe what the persona currently does using existing solutions or competitive offerings. The steps should illustrate a full end-to-end set of activities providing a comprehensive view of the situation and an overall context for developing a solution.

- Major decisions the persona needs to make in the workflow. For more complex or interactive products, such as software or services, there may be multiple paths that can be taken depending on choices the persona needs to make. For example, if the product team was attempting to create an ATM for obtaining cash, some common decisions a persona would need to make are from which account to withdraw, the amount of the withdrawal, and whether he or she would like to know the resulting account balance.

Another method for illustrating the problem is through a storyboard that combines graphical illustrations with individual steps, much like an illustrated story or cartoon. Storyboards help to capture information and context much more rapidly than reading a story, though attention should be paid to the potential loss of detail that might be conveyed more completely through text.

Alternatively, for process-oriented solutions, a *flow diagram* may be useful for capturing the series of steps and decisions required to achieve a goal. Flow diagrams are especially useful if there is collaboration required between individuals or departments within an organization, where flow diagrams can graphically depict steps and hand-off points.

The purpose of the problem scenario is to illustrate the challenge a user has in achieving the goal, including the limitations of existing solutions. A successful scenario ensures:

- Understanding of the context in which the user is attempting to achieve a goal, and a definition of the goal itself.

- Understanding of how the customer pursues the goal today, and the frustration and/or latent needs associated with current solutions.

- Opportunity to stimulate ideas for solving the frustration or need, including the potential for a radical or breakthrough idea that could significantly improve the customer experience.

Competitive Analysis Matrix

In SWOT analysis, the product team examines the offering at the product level. A competitive analysis matrix drills down further to the feature level. A competitive analysis matrix is a comparison of features across a set of competitive solutions in the target market. The competitors are usually other companies offering comparable solutions, but could also be existing alternative ways users achieve their goal through entirely different means.

The matrix is usually in a tabular format (in a spreadsheet or document) that has a list of features on one axis and a set of competitors on another. A rating is provided for each feature and against each competitor for the level of support. Figure 17-8 illustrates a high-level competitive analysis matrix:

Figure 17-8. Example Competitive Analysis Matrix

PRODUCT FEATURE	MARKET IMPORTANCE	YOUR SOLUTION	COMPETITOR 1	COMPETITOR 2	COMPETITOR 3
Feature 1	High	√√√	√√√	√√	√√
Feature 2	High	√√√	√√	√√√	√
Feature 3	Medium	√	✗	√√	✗
Feature 4	Low	✗	√	✗	✗
Platforms	Medium	√√	√√√	√√	√
Support	High	1 year free	1 year free	1 year $$	1 year $
Price	3=Hi, 1=Lo	$$	$$$	$$	$

In the example, there is a column corresponding to the importance of each feature to the target market. Not all features have the same level of importance. Some are capabilities required to provide the fundamental value proposition. Others have varying levels from "somewhat important" to "not important at all." Competitors may have included features to appease an important customer or simply because other competitors included these capabilities. Features add costs. Unused or low-value features should be eliminated. It is essential that every capability or function earn its way onto the features list. Market importance can also drive prioritization across the features. If the product team finds itself short on resources or time to complete all of the desired features, then the first ones to be removed would be those features that are of less importance and value to the customer.

The ratings in figure 17-8 are not simply a "yes" or "no" that a feature exists. Just because a feature is included doesn't mean it is implemented well by a competitor. The product team should attempt to attain more granular information for identifying how its competitors execute on each capability. Levels of criteria should be created that describe a well-executed feature versus a mediocre or poor feature. Ratings represent performance, completeness, quality, etc. The product team may find opportunities to surpass other solutions for those features marked as important to the customer. The product team may also consider including features at a reduced performance level that may be less important to customers. Feature inclusion options enable the product team to fine tune allocation of resources to the capabilities providing the biggest impact in terms of assisting customers in achieving their goals.

The purpose of the matrix is to help identify gaps in competitive offerings relative to specific features that are important to the customer. The matrix therefore helps in positioning and prioritizing the feature set. A useful matrix will include:

- High-level feature sets, spanning a dozen or so for a simple product, and potentially dozens for a complex product. It is often useful to group related features that support a high-level value being offered. While it may be tempting to capture a comprehensive, detailed view, the team may get bogged down by the detail and lose sight of the major value the product is offering.

- End-to-end customer view. The matrix should include attributes beyond characteristics of the physical product or capabilities for an interactive product, and include attributes that affect the entire user experience. This can include how the product is purchased, delivered, installed, maintained, supported, and disposed. This can open the door for differentiation beyond the delivered product to those that satisfy the expected whole product.

- Measure of "how well" features perform. A "yes/no" rating does not provide insight into whether the feature implementation is complete or useful.

17

- Measure of the market importance. It is very likely the competition has features that are not of high value to most customers. If the product team can identify them, they can deprioritize these to maximize the focus of limited resources on those features that are highly valued in the market and less than completely addressed by the competition. The assumption that the company needs to match competition on all features is the easy, but often unnecessary and wasteful, approach to developing a truly valuable product offering.

The product team should focus their efforts on those items that are valued the most by customers, regardless of what the industry expects or the competitors offer.

The Market Requirements Document

The Market Requirements Document (MRD) is probably the most important deliverable from product management in the creation of a new product or major extension to a product. The MRD identifies the overall target market and need or gap that exists. The MRD also goes beyond illustrating just the specific set of problems by attempting to capture the market expectations across a number of product attributes that would be necessary for a successful solution.

The actual implementation of the MRD can be in many forms, including a document, a spreadsheet, a wiki, a specialized software tool, and possibly others. The size and scope of the opportunity and individual company processes and capabilities will dictate the actual contents required. The core of the MRD typically contains the following information:

- Definition of the target market, specifically the buyer and user profiles or personas.

- Problem scenarios highlighting the major issues or gaps that exist for the personas. Note that the buyer and user may have different motivations and different needs, so they likely will need different problem scenarios documented to illustrate the gaps in achieving their goals.

In general, requirements fall into two major types:

- *Functional* requirements are used for capabilities that have interactivity with the user and describe the specific high-level functions the user can perform.

- *Non-functional* requirements describe performance factors and design constraints placed on a product. Performance requirements specify "how well" a product needs to perform for specific measurements. Constraint requirements include "how much" a product needs to support.

Many categories of non-functional requirements exist and are industry-specific. The list below includes some common categories:

- Physical requirements are typically for manufactured products and include maximum or minimum dimensions and weight, portability or mobility needs, ruggedness, and packaging.

- Environmental requirements are typically for manufactured products and include the operating or storage environment, such as temperature ranges and humidity, exposure to water, tolerance to chemicals or gases, exposure to or omitting noise, etc. Power needs could also fall into this category, such as the typical voltage and current limits and stability and noise limitations. For system-based products, this category can identify the operating environment, such as a lab or data center.

- Performance requirements can address a number of different types of parameters, including how fast specific operations need to be, how many over a period of time, lifetime expectations for usage, scalability for how large the system needs to be able to grow, etc.

- International requirements describe where the product will be sold and used, including requirements for language, currency, power supply, and any special localization needs.

- Compatibility requirements describe how the product needs to work with other products or systems, including any standard or non-standard interfaces that need to be provided.

- Documentation requirements describe the type, formats, and delivery methods for product documentation.

- Support requirements describe how customers will obtain help in installation, operation, repair, payments, maintenance, and disposal of the product.

- Legal, regulatory, and compliance requirements describe any special laws, standards, rules, certifications, or other government- or agency-imposed requirements.

- Distribution and packaging describe how the system will be distributed and any requirements for how the product needs to be packaged for different channels.

A successful MRD should convey the market gap that exists and also a broad assessment of the market expectations for a potential solution. Specifically, the

MRD should:

- Capture a definition of the target market, specifically the buyers and users, their goals, and the market gap that exists.

- Provide a comprehensive list of market requirements that would be expected from the solution.

- Suggest objective measures of success for each of the requirements, preferably in quantitative forms.

- Prioritize requirements from the market's point of view. Not all requirements are of equal or high importance. There is always a hierarchy of importance from "must have" to "optional." Attempt to prioritize major feature groups first, and then sub-prioritize within each group.

- Focus on the market problem, not an envisioned solution. It is easy to confuse the two. The solution is discussed in the Product Requirements Document (PRD).

- Target a time frame for introduction and communicate a supporting rationale.

Product Vision and Strategy

The Product Vision is a high-level definition of what the product will aspire to be beyond where it is today. It sets a target for the ultimate value the product will deliver to the market.

The Product Strategy defines the high-level actions or activities needed to achieve the product vision. It helps the organization understand the fundamental path it will take toward the product vision, and provides boundaries that define what will not be undertaken.

A Product Vision and Strategy can be delivered as individual documents, and incorporated into other documents, including the Marketing Requirements Document and Product Requirements Document.

The product vision and strategy should provide:

- A future, ideal statement of what the product will be or will deliver to the market.

- A set of high-level actions or initiatives that will be undertaken towards realizing the future state.

- A set of measurable objectives that define both short- and long-term goals.

The characteristics of a good product vision include:

- A picture of the future, at least a year and possibly many years depending on the product lifecycle, which can endure for the entire product's life.

- A definition of the target customer and the ultimate problem(s) the product solves or the value derived from the product.

- A high bar that pushes the need for innovation from the product team. Reaching the bar might even appear impossible given current solutions or capabilities.

- A sufficiently high level that doesn't change every time a market dynamic shifts.

The characteristics of a good product strategy include:

- Clearly defined phases that are stepping stones toward realizing the vision. This is quite common and helps to set up the product roadmap. The product strategy will further detail key activities or major programs the product team will undertake toward realizing their aspirational product vision. The product strategy can change over time depending on current business and market conditions, while the overall product vision remains a constant.

- Measurable product objectives with time lines that are usually associated with business metrics around customers, the market, the competition, or financials.

- Measurable project objectives that typically define some shorter term milestones for specific deliverables and the next few steps in the journey.

17

Product Roadmap

The Product Roadmap is an envisioned set of phases or activities that illustrates the potential steps that will be taken in executing the current product strategy. The roadmap typically extends for multiple product development cycles into the future and defines high-level targeted deliverables or product objectives. The product roadmap can be communicated in many ways—a presentation, a spreadsheet, a document, etc. The primary purpose of the roadmap is to ensure internal alignment, performance measurement, and resource assignments. An external version of the roadmap may be prepared for partner, supplier, and customer use.

A typical Product Roadmap contains the following elements:

- A time line aligned to major development or business cycles, such as quarters or years, which extends into the future for multiple cycles.

- Market drivers are external events or milestones that may drive specific deliverables on the roadmap. For example, annual tradeshows for new product introductions, or seasonal periods of high sales like holidays or summer, or effective dates for new legislation or compliance rules.

- Business objectives or product themes that partition the larger time line into phases with specific alignment to the overall product strategy in realizing the longer-term product vision. Objectives help prioritize the major activities that will be the focus during specific time frames.

- High-level features within each of the phases identified that act as a high-level set of major product capabilities that are being targeted for delivery. The capabilities may be expressed as major market needs that will be addressed, as opposed to the specific solution that will be delivered. The roadmap projects into the future and suggests the likelihood that additional products and/or services will be developed to continue to address identified market needs.

- Technology roadmap (optional) that will indicate specific technology platforms that are impacted by each of the major phases and feature lists. The technology roadmap gives further visibility into major resource allocation requirements. This type of roadmap can be useful to align the product and technology groups in longer-term strategy development.

A good product roadmap includes the following:

- Serves as a guide for each of the planned phases and project prioritization.

- Aligns with and provides a plan for delivering the product vision and product strategy.

- Contains a plan and resource requirements that are explicitly supported by the executive team.

- Allows for updates on a regular basis as progress is made and changes occur in the product strategy.

The biggest issue relating to roadmaps is who they should be shared with. If a roadmap is provided to sales, they are likely to share it with customers. If a roadmap is left with customers, they could share it with competitors. The best practice for roadmap distribution is to have two roadmaps: one for internal use with more detail and one for external use with much less detail. In general, don't put anything on the external roadmap that is likely to change or be unachievable. The external roadmap is perceived by all to represent committed projects. Never share an internal roadmap with customers or externally facing employees.

Positioning Statement

A positioning statement unites the overall value proposition and positioning of the product into a high-level set of statements that summarizes the overall solution. The positioning statement is sometimes called an *elevator pitch*, to imply it needs to be a quick but comprehensive statement of the product's intrinsic value. A useful framework for product positioning comes from Geoffrey Moore in his book *Crossing the Chasm*.[54] Table 17-1 conveys Moore's framework.

Table 17-1. Positioning Statement Framework

STATEMENT	DESCRIPTION
FOR <target market>	A concise definition of the market segment
WHO HAVE <this problem>	The problem statement indicating the underserved need or market gap
OUR PRODUCT IS <solution category>	A generic name to help categorize the solution to the market
THAT PROVIDES <key benefits>	Key benefit(s) and the value provided
UNLIKE <reference competition>	Defines the primary alternative market solution(s)
OUR SOLUTION <key advantages>	Identifies how this product differentiates from the competition in a way that creates customer value

A successful positioning statement has the following elements:

- Identifies the overall purpose of the product and added value the product delivers to fill a market gap, and the ways in which it's better than the current alternatives.

- Provides enough information for someone who is unfamiliar with the product to gain a good understanding in just a few minutes.

- Contains analogies to other existing solutions to help create an image and understanding of the solution.

- Focuses on benefits and value provided, not features or specific implementation methods.

17

[54] Moore, G. (2002). *Crossing the Chasm*. New York, NY: HarperCollins

There are other formats for positioning, including the simile and the user-story format. The "simile" approach is perhaps the quickest way to convey a message. This approach explains the product by utilizing a familiar context: *It's like* [reference product in another category] but for [new application]. An example is the Amazon Kindle Paperwhite: *It's like* an iPod *but for* books.[55] Agile teams are very comfortable with the user-story format, so they can write positioning like any other user story, but at a product level: As a [persona] I want to [solve a problem] So that [professional benefit statement] Plus [personal benefit statement]. Regardless of the format chosen, create a positioning statement that resonates with customers and helps focus the development and marketing of the product.

Launch Strategy

The Launch Strategy document encapsulates the approach to taking the product to market. Launch strategy can originate in the Conceive phase and evolve towards a detailed launch plan developed in later phases. The intent of this effort is to document all marketing and sales assumptions for launching the product so that an estimate of scope, resources required, and budget needs can be developed for updating the business case. For a new product, the cost of the launch can sometimes be larger than the product development effort.

The focus of the launch strategy is on the breadth of coverage across all of the envisioned activities so that overall costs and initial timeline can be developed. The plan must address four key points:

- Who will you reach (top priority audiences)?
- How will you reach them (top priority outreach activities)?
- What will you say (messaging)?
- To produce what result (objectives)?

Typical components of the launch strategy include:

- Targeted sales channels
- Marketing collateral needs
- Sales tools, demos, and training requirements
- Advertising and demand generation activities
- Sales promotions
- Public relations, industry, and social media initiatives

---

[55] Amazon, Kindle, Kindle Fire, the Amazon Kindle logo, and the Kindle Fire logo are trademarks of Amazon.com, Inc. or its affiliates.

- Tradeshows and event needs

- Social media and community activities

- Field testing strategy

- Sales forecast by channel

- Measurable launch objectives

- High-level launch timeline, milestones, and overall budget

Subsequent revisions to the launch strategy will update assumptions while adding depth and details from a tactical perspective.

A successful launch strategy will have the following characteristics:

- Confirms audience and competitive targets

- Confirms messaging

- Aligns launch plans to the overall product strategy and development plan

- Prioritizes the go-to-market activities to gain focus on those that are most impactful

- Provides measurable short- and long-term criteria to assess the success of the launch

- Aligns to the marketing and distribution strengths of the organization

- Identifies any new activities or capabilities that need to be sourced or developed

- Provides inputs and support from targeted channels

Project Charter

The project charter identifies, at a high level, the scope, objectives, deliverables, schedule, required resources, communication plan, risk management, and project management monitoring and controlling procedures for the project.

The project charter establishes the authority of the project manager, especially in a matrix environment. A good charter should be clear and concise. The charter should contain information about the purpose of the project, the benefits and objectives, a measurable set of success criteria, the name of the project sponsor, the list of stakeholders, budget, and the product description and deliverables.

17

The project charter typically includes the following:

- Reasons for undertaking the project

- Objectives and constraints of the project

- Identities of the main stakeholders

- In-scope and out-of-scope items

- High-level risk management plan

- High-level communication plan

- Target project benefits

- High-level budget and spending authority

The product team knows it has a good project charter when:

- The project stakeholders approve the charter and assign the necessary resources to begin.

- Any new executive can reference and evaluate the charter.

- There are clear decisions on who owns the budget and who is managing the budget.

- There are measurable and achievable objectives that the execution team agrees to be accountable for.

17.2 The Plan Phase Tools

17.2.1 Product Requirements Document (PRD)

The Product Requirements Document (PRD) provides the level of detail needed by the development team to understand the features, functionality, and capabilities required. The level of detail varies significantly, depending on whether development is focused on a new product or enhancements to an existing product.

The general questions the PRD should answer are:

- *Who are the users of the product targeted for this release?* What market need or gap is the product addressing? What are the characteristics of end users that this product targets and how will end users utilize the product? End users are often portrayed via the use of personas.

- *What actions will the users take with the product?* The actions are often called the functional requirements and are specific activities the users perform through interactions with the product. Functional requirements may be as simple as buttons and indicators or it may be a computer display. For other products, specifically services, interactions can be defined using a process flow of various activities that different end users perform. Requirements are often captured in a hierarchical set of use cases or user stories in Agile methodologies. Other forms of documentation that illustrate the flow of events or information, such as flow diagrams, data diagrams, context, and entity relationship diagrams, are also often included within the functional requirements document.

- *What are the performance requirements and design constraints of the product?* These are often called the non-functional requirements. Performance requirements define how well or how much the product needs to perform along some measureable criteria. These can include performance, capacity, scalability, and so on. Constraints define boundaries within which the product must be developed and/or function. Constraints can be physical, environmental, other platforms the product supports or interfaces with, specific geographies, legal or compliance needs, etc. The list of non-functional requirements for any product is typically industry-specific and can be extensive for large systems or complex products.

- *What accompanies or supports the product?* Support items can be any additional items that are not directly related to the specific operation of the product, but are necessary to support a full end-to-end user experience. While often captured in the non-functional requirements section, this provides a check that everything has been accounted for. Support can include documentation, accessories, shipping or packaging needs, installation or maintenance tools, and replacement parts. Additionally, support can define how the product will be maintained in terms of customer service issues, including troubleshooting, maintenance, and repair.

A good PRD defines both the breadth and depth of the product capabilities in enough detail such that:

- The development team sufficiently understands what should be designed and built. An indicator for this is when questions about "what to build" shift to "how to build."

- Given the definition of what the actual product will be, the supporting organizations understand what they need to deliver with the product.

- A complete end-to-end customer experience is defined for the new capabilities.

- The requirements are aligned to the business objectives set for the product release.

Additionally, good product requirements should be:

- *Verifiable* — the requirements can be verified or tested. This means that requirements can be validated and that they perform as intended. This also means that requirements are measurable rather than subjective.

- *Clear and Concise* — understandable for all team members. The document is easy to understand and does not have multiple possible interpretations.

- *Complete* — contains all of the necessary information. The document communicates the entire scope of the needed product or enhancement. In addition to scope the details for individual requirements, such as units of measure, are effectively conveyed. The document does not require making assumptions to fill in missing gaps. The definition of completeness will vary based upon the method chosen to create the product.

- *Consistent* — there are no conflicts between requirements. Terminology is defined and used consistently and there are no duplicate requirements that might confuse the reader.

- *Traceable* — all requirements can be traced back to a source of the market need. The document includes discrete numbering or annotation of individual requirements and hierarchical structure that allows breaking requirements into smaller units while maintaining ability to associate with higher level requirements. The document also includes version control to trace changes in requirements.

- *Viable* — the requirements can be met and are feasible. The product can be delivered with existing technology, skills, capabilities of the organization, and within schedule and budget. This may be a negotiated or iterated agreement based on further analysis.

- *Necessary* — requirements must be present for the system to achieve its purpose. Removing the requirements would create a deficiency in the system. This often leads to prioritization discussions with explicit and transparent criteria.

- *Free of Implementation* — defines *what*, not *how*. Does not decide how a requirement is implemented. Leaves the choice to the designers except where the market demands that the product meet certain standards.

17.2.2 Project Planning

Formal planning has a positive influence on innovation and product management activities. Two kinds of plans are critical to product development success: project plans organize the activities required to reach the defined near-term product objectives, and product management plans set out longer-term goals and define the cross-functional activities required to optimize the product and deliver business value.

Project Plan

At a high level, a project plan is the deliverable that explains *how* the product team is going to execute, manage, evaluate, and communicate change in the project. The project plan *organizes* the project work, reducing risk and increasing predictability.

The project plan for a new or expanded product is typically cross-functional to account for all of the interdependencies required to deliver the product. Sub-projects within the overall project plan can include:

- Development — identifies how the development team will create the product
- Manufacturing — identifies the changes required to manufacture and test the product
- Information Technology (IT) Operations — identifies changes in how the product is hosted or operated
- Ordering or Billing — identifies changes in the business systems or processes
- Support — identifies changes in needs for customer or technical support
- Distribution/Logistics — identifies changes in how the product is fulfilled and delivered
- Partner — identifies changes in external partner communities, such as Independent Software Vendors (ISVs) or Developers

The project plan is designed to remove ambiguity by clearly mapping out activities against expected outcomes relative to time. Identifying the interdependencies between deliverables and functional teams early in the process will better determine which teams should be more integrated and when, relative to the overall product development process.

17

This document is a high-level view of deliverables, resource assignments, estimates, and dependencies based on core team members and overall project success criteria. It is a plan in which all team-member deliverables are recognized and related back to the customer's needs and requirements. The plan is designed to ensure the project team understands the context behind the project.

The primary purpose of the project plan is to be the single authoritative source of information to ensure a shared understanding of all project parameters:

- Scope

- Timing

- Assumptions/Constraints

- Risks/Issues

- Resources

- Quality

- Special Considerations/Exceptions

- Development Methodology considerations

- Team Members and associated Roles and Responsibilities

- Policies and Procedures

Additionally, the project plan defines the technical and managerial processes to be utilized. It is a living document and will be revised as necessary during the course of the project.

In order to ensure all project components are addressed, a project plan, at a minimum, should include the following:

- Quantifiable success criteria for the project — Role clarity and shared objectives can be further translated, at the project level, into success criteria. Success criteria need to be understandable, measurable, and achievable by the project team and project stakeholders. Define *who* is going to benefit from *what,* and *how* they're going to measure it.

- Project trade-off matrix (scope versus schedule versus cost) — Documents the options available when critical trade-offs must be made among the scope, schedule, and resource/cost parameters. The matrix captures both stakeholder and product management guidance.

- Work Breakdown Structure (WBS) — The WBS breaks down activities and tasks into management work units. Each descending level of the WBS represents an increasingly detailed definition of the project work. It is a hierarchical decomposition of the project work into smaller and more manageable work units. At the lowest level of this breakdown are project *deliverables*.

- Roles and responsibilities broken down by deliverable – The RACI matrix is used to describe the roles and responsibilities of various teams or people involved in developing and delivering a product. The matrix should also include the stakeholders and any extended team member needed to deliver the project. The RACI matrix is to be used as a tool to help plan and break down the work even further, so that the right people are doing the right work at the right time. The RACI matrix splits tasks into four participatory responsibility types, which are then assigned to different roles in the project. These responsibility types make up the acronym RACI:

  o **Responsible** — The individuals who do work to achieve the task. There can be multiple resources responsible.

  o **Accountable** — The individual ultimately accountable for completing the task. There must be exactly one "**A**" specified for each task. The Accountable role is accountable for the creation of the deliverable and the communication associated with the deliverable. The person accountable may or may not also be responsible for the task, but typically it is a person in a functional or team leadership role.

  o **Consulted** — The individuals whose opinions and feedback are sought. The role is focused on two-way communication. These are often individuals who provide approval on a deliverable. Consulted parties sometimes turn into Accountable parties in the next stage of the project.

  o **Informed** — The individual(s) who are kept up-to-date on progress. The role typically involves one-way communication of information.

- Communication plan/stakeholder management plan — A quantitative and qualitative approach for communication to internal and external stakeholders during the course of the project.

- Risk management plan — Must include identification, prevention planning, contingency planning, and ongoing monitoring of risk. The goal of risk management is to head off problems before they become events changing the course of the project.

17

- Budget management plan — Designed to address both capital and operating costs relative to the project. The plan is typically broken into components for granular visibility and transparency of tracking cost. Typical components in a budget management plan are:

  o Estimates of overall time and costs required for all resources, such as internal labor (plan vs. actual) and external labor (plan vs. actual)

  o Hardware/Software

  o Procurement costs and any third-party development partners that may be used throughout the project

  o Cost of Goods Sold (COGS) estimates for manufactured or sourced products

- Change management plan — Project Change Management is a process for identifying, assessing, controlling, and documenting proposed changes to the project. A "project change" is any modification to the project that will potentially affect the project schedule, cost, resources, and/or risks.

The product team knows it has a good project plan when the entire core team understands the meaning of the word "done" as it relates to the tasks that make up the project schedule. All the ambiguity in roles and responsibilities has been removed and activities against expected outcomes, relative to time, have been clearly mapped out.

Product Management Plan

The product management plan acts as the central repository for all of the materials that are created in support of the new product. The plan helps to ensure that the appropriate parties have access to the most up-to-date materials and can help in the transition process as new team members join or leave the team or organization.

The plan includes:

- Product charter (goals, objectives, and organizational alignment)

- Product scope (market and product requirements)

- Product roadmap

- Strategy (Organization, Business, Customer, Product, Marketing/Launch)

- Preliminary phase review product schedule

- Cross-functional team requirements

- Cross-functional team staffing (core team members assigned)

- Product communication plan

- Product risks/contingencies

- Optional - Preliminary product procurement plan (purchase/acquire)

All members of the team and stakeholders have easy access to the key information and plans for the product and the project regardless of changes taking place on the team or within the organization.

17.3 The Develop Phase Tools

During the Develop phase, it's important to test the product on different audiences using a variety of validation methods that are ideally iterative in nature.

17.3.1 Usability Evaluation Methods

Usability evaluation assesses the degree to which the product, process, and/or system can be used by customers. The evaluation validates that the customer can easily complete the job or task required. Not only should the customer find that the product helps accomplish the job, but that using the product is easy and intuitive. If the product solution does not make the task easier, then the solution is most likely not ready for the marketplace.

Large companies in mature markets may have several usability labs and teams that are constantly testing solutions with customers. Smaller, more nimble companies may or may not have someone who is evaluating usability with the same rigor or formality as a larger, well-established company.

Usability testing is at the heart of ensuring that the company delivers a viable market solution capable of gaining and retaining market share. Retaining market share is also dependent on constantly evaluating and improving upon the original product. If the original company fails to improve on the product, a competitor will, and market share will be lost.

When conducting a usability evaluation, the product team should begin by identifying the target audience. The target audience consists of one or more user groups or personas. For example, a single website or application may have content for consumers and a separate log-in area for site administrators. It is likely that these two user groups perform different tasks as part of their normal activities. Each user group should be given tasks to perform during testing that reflect their different usage patterns.

17

Typically, participants will perform a set of tasks within a session or through the use of instrumented apps. Tasks should represent the most common user goals. Well-defined tasks include clear success criteria, where the participant should begin the task, and how task completion will be measured. Measurements include task completion, time on tasks, learnability, and satisfaction.

When conducting user evaluations, the usability engineer reads a participant one task at a time, such as, "Find out how to contact technical support," and allows the participant to attempt to complete the task without any guidance. To prevent bias, the same script is used with each participant.

Part of the testing may include asking the participant to "talk aloud" as he or she works on a task to better understand the participant's mental model—what they're thinking—while completing the task in real time. Several methods for conducting usability studies are described in the following sections.

Usability Lab

Some companies have a usability lab; others employ an outside lab to run their usability studies. The lab is usually designed to simulate the target user environment. For example, a living room to test a remote control, a retail counter to test a service, or an office to test a software experience.

A lab provides a controlled setting and more exact comparative analysis. However, since the lab is not the real setting, "in the field" factors like ambient lighting, sound, interruptions, and other conditions cannot be easily measured.

Onsite Usability

Conducting a usability study onsite allows the product team to observe the solution in the context of real-world interactions. They can observe how factors like ambient lighting, sound, hardware, and other conditions affect the user and the quality of the service or product in this environment. There is more of a challenge in conducting these studies because these various factors can interrupt the study and metrics. There are also costs associated with travel expenses, scheduling issues, and inconvenience for the customers when planning and executing onsite usability studies.

Remote Usability

Remote usability studies are more cost effective and easier to run than lab or onsite studies. The most common way to conduct a remote usability study is to host a web meeting, turn the controls over to the participant, introduce the tasks, and record the interactions. There are also online services that may be used. Participants are able to participate from the comfort of their home or office.

In the case of any of these methods, when all participants have completed the study, the usability engineer will compile the data to determine the severity of each usability issue that was encountered and provide prioritized recommendations for the development team to meet usability requirements. For example, a user experience engineer can identify the most frustrating parts of a software-related task and suggest ways to improve the interaction to better support the user by analyzing participants' facial expressions, the number of mouse clicks made, the users' verbal statements, and the navigation path used to complete a task. If the study was recorded, clips of the recording can be added to the study to illustrate the issues.

17.3.2 Alpha and Beta Plans

An Alpha test plan illustrates how the product will be tested internally, usually by quality assurance professionals with pre-selected customers and often in-house customers as well. When a release candidate is tested by internal personnel, this is known as an alpha test.

The Beta Plan describes how the product will be tested in the market by end users prior to possible commercial product launch. The goal is to ensure the product meets the needs of the customer as articulated in the market research, competitive analysis, and project charter. Beta testing includes executing the product functionality and assessing the overall completeness in terms of the product meeting intended goals. In addition, the level of product quality and usability is tested to ensure its readiness for commercial use.

Beta test execution during the Qualify phase can vary dramatically from a few weeks with a handful of users to several months with hundreds or thousands of users. The resources and level of project oversight and management required will be directly proportional to the defined scope.

The overall Beta Test Plan identifies the goals and objectives of the testing, all of the resources required to execute the test, and project-level detail for milestones and major activities.

The Beta Plan typically includes answers to the following questions:

- Why are we doing the test? What results are we trying to achieve?

- Who are we targeting for the test? How many testers are we seeking?

17

- How will we find, recruit, and compensate test participants?

- What will we provide test participants? Do we plan on retaining the product or giving it to test participants?

- What do we want participants to test (general operation, specific functions, or environments)?

- Who will be conducting and evaluating the test, including setting up the test participants and supporting them throughout the test?

- How will we communicate with test participants and how often? How will test participants provide feedback?

- What are the activities, schedules, logistics, resources, and costs of the test? What part of the organization is responsible for paying for the test?

- What legal documentation do we require, including confidentiality or licensing agreements?

- How do we plan on incorporating the results of the feedback prior to launching the product?

- What are the measurable success criteria for the test?

A good Beta Plan provides both the strategic reasons and objectives for conducting market testing and tactical planning. The Beta Plan provides a discussion and a plan for how the feedback will be used in the overall product readiness assessment. Unfortunately, some Beta tests are only a checklist item in a product development process with no plan for incorporating feedback into the launch readiness decision. A well-executed Beta test can provide real insight into the likely success of the product launch and beyond. Beta testing can provide early indication of achieving expected product results.

17.3.3 Launch Plan

The Launch Strategy provided in the Plan phase provides the basis for the detailed Launch Plan in the Develop phase. In the Launch Strategy, the intent is to identify a general launch philosophy and high-level set of tasks and costs to support the Business Plan. In the Launch Plan, the product team moves to a more tactical view that nails down the specific messaging and positioning of the product, with the necessary projects to support a launch from a Marketing perspective. Most of these activities will occur in the Qualify phase leading up to the actual launch of the product.

The primary goal is to define how to launch the product, including resources and subprojects required from a marketing perspective. The Launch Plan includes detailed information on:

- Overall launch strategy and objectives

- Planned messaging and positioning of the product

- Pricing and sales promotion plans

- Launch forecasts

- Marketing collateral requirements

    o Sales tools and demo requirements

    o Advertising and demand generation activities

    o Public relations activities

    o Tradeshows and event needs

- Social media

- Internal/channel sales training

- Detailed project milestones and overall cost update

A successful launch plan aligns all parties on how the product will be introduced to the market. The plan drives the budgeting, resource allocation, and milestones planned for the eventual launch.

17.4 The Qualify Phase Tools

17.4.1 Launch Readiness Checklist

Launch preparation activities include specific activities occurring in the areas of Marketing, Manufacturing/Operations, Sales, and Support. To facilitate the decision as to whether the product is ready to go to market, a high-level checklist is prepared to make the assessment across a broad set of criteria.

The checklist categories can vary by overall scope of a product and the needs of any specific organization or industry. Potential candidate categories and checklist items include:

- Product Readiness

    o All Development and Quality milestones have been achieved

o All compliance and certifications required are complete

o Market validation objectives have been successfully achieved

o All required documentation and associated deliverables are complete or scheduled

o A product roadmap is in place for Development to move to the next set of deliverables

- Marketing Readiness

o Clear messaging and positioning have been defined

o Product naming, including trademarks, are finalized

o Marketing collateral and website are complete and available

o Point-of-Sale materials are complete and available

o Advertising and demand generation activities are ready

o Press releases, media and public relations activities are ready

o Frequently asked questions and Q&A documents have been prepared to anticipate friendly and not-so-friendly questions

o Whitepapers and in-depth discussion/education materials are available

o Case studies and customer testimonials from early testing are available

o Tradeshows and event activities are planned and scheduled

o Social media objectives are defined and channels ready

o Launch objectives are defined and measurements in place to assess success

o Customer and channel feedback mechanisms are in place to collect input

- Sales and Channel Readiness

o Pricing, volume discounts, and promotions are formalized

o Sales compensation, channel discounts, and sales incentives are formalized

o Sales/Channel training has been completed

o Sales presentations, materials, pricing/return on investment tools, and demos are available

o Sales contracts and other legal documents are available

- Manufacturing/Operations/Legal Readiness

  o Inventory, manufacturing, testing, and packaging are ready for production units (physical products)

  o Operational systems to support hosting or operating the product are ready (service or hosted software products)

  o All legal contracts with suppliers and vendors are in place

- Support and Repair Readiness

  o Customer and Technical Support training are completed

  o Customer Support systems are ready

  o Product Repair personnel are trained and systems ready

- Orders and Payments Readiness

  o Product ordering systems with defined product configurations, pricing, and options are in place and functional

  o Payment systems for required payment options are ready

- Distribution and Logistics Readiness

  o Systems and vendors for product delivery and returns are ready

- Other Required Systems or Programs

  o Reporting systems in place to assess status and product results

  o Professional Services or outside partners used for installation or customization of the product are trained and ready

  o Other industry-specific supporting programs are ready, such as Developer Programs, Partner, or Trade Association Programs

- Final Business Plan Update

  o Planned sales and revenue forecasts and adjustments have been made and factored into all of the supporting functional area plans

  o Final costs have been captured and factored into the overall profitability model

  o Overall financial business case has been updated and meets business objectives

  o Major business risks have been updated and have mitigation plans going forward

17

The overall goal of the checklist is to ensure that the company is aligned around delivering a successful product to the marketplace. The measure of a successful launch is always after the fact. Successes and unpleasant surprises or outcomes should be recorded to inform the next product launch. A final meeting should be scheduled to review lessons learned and to update the process and the checklist.

17.5 The Launch Phase Tools

As discussed in Section 2, Launch is one of the most critical phases of the product lifecycle process. Hence it becomes absolutely critical for product teams to ensure the right tools and methodologies are in place to enable success.

In addition, product managers and product teams need to know when and where to apply tools and methodologies. A codified set of tools and methodologies can help the team move forward confidently and go to market successfully.

Within each deliverable listed in this section are specific descriptions that are vital for decision making at every stage of the launch process. For those individuals not familiar with the launch process, this section serves as a comprehensive guide to take the product team step by step towards a successful launch. For more experienced product managers or marketers, the launch strategy, plan, and checklist serve as a reference and guide to ensure that all critical product launch decisions, issues, or management questions are considered at every stage.

17.5.1 Product Launch Plan

The Product Launch Plan is a blueprint of *how* the product or service will be delivered to the marketplace. In addition, the product launch plan serves as a checklist to guide all product launch activities. The plan ensures that all activities are on track to support the launch. The plan is centered on product management and sales and marketing, and involves all critical functional areas, including Engineering, Manufacturing, Product Support, Operations, and Implementation. The launch plan establishes accountability with concrete actions and timelines that ensure alignment, consensus, and ultimate success. Typically, the Product Marketing function owns the product launch plan.

The primary questions a Product Launch Plan should answer, at minimum, are grouped into three main areas:

1. Strategy

   • What are the product launch objectives?

- What product launch strategy provides the best chance to meet the objectives?

- What are the main customer needs that will be met?

- What are the main product differentiators?

- What is the competitive landscape?

- What is the positioning and messaging strategy?

- What is the market awareness and promotion strategy?

2. Planning

   o Who should be involved in the product launch?

   o Who are the key stakeholders?

   o Whose approvals do we need?

   o Who are the assigned resources by functional areas? (These are often referred to as the core team members.)

   o What is the allocated and approved budget for the product launch?

   o What are the go-to-market activities in priority order?

3. Execution

   o What are the timelines and major milestones?

   o Who is responsible for monitoring, tracking, and reporting on execution?

   o How is launch effectiveness measured?

A great Product Launch Plan should:

- Define launch objectives clearly and in measurable terms

- Explain the launch strategy, action plan, budget, and timeline

- Help structure and organize resources for a well-executed and on-time launch

- Communicate market, customer, and competitive intelligence

- Position the product appropriately and differentiate effectively

- Ensure marketing, sales, and channel readiness

- Provide a mechanism to track, monitor, and report on execution

- Establish an ongoing process that measures performance and adjusts dynamically

17

17.5.2 Messaging and Positioning Platform

The messaging and positioning platform is the core communications document used for interfacing with industry media, creating web copy, improving search engine results, pitching investors, and developing marketing material.

Without a messaging and positioning platform, execution of marketing communications is random and leads to ineffective messaging. Worst of all, different mediums convey different messages about the product, which confuse customers, as well as the sales and support teams.

A messaging platform helps protect the product team from these problems. It will make the launch and ongoing marketing endeavors easier. It will also give the team more comprehensive and coherent messaging. Product Marketing usually owns the messaging platform efforts and documents.

The questions an effective Messaging and Positioning Platform should answer are as follows:

- What are the clearly defined objectives?
- How should the company best position the product?
- Who is the target audience?
- What is the category for the product in the marketplace?
- What are the main product differentiators?
- What is the strategic direction of the product?
- What is the company's brand promise and how does the product fulfill that promise?
- What are the key market drivers and challenges?
- What are the main product features and benefits?
- Who is responsible for execution and evaluation of messaging?

The product team can leverage earlier concept and planning phase work to create the Messaging and Positioning Platform by referencing the problem scenarios, personas, value proposition, and positioning statement.

An effective Messaging and Positioning Platform should:

- Provide a foundation for category, company, solutions, and product-level messaging and positioning

- Describe the problem to be solved

- Articulate the value proposition and product positioning

- Describe the market drivers, target audience, and their needs

- Describe the barriers to adoption and major objectives

- Define the category that the product or service fits best

- Differentiate the product or service effectively from the competition

- Reinforce how the product or service delivers on the brand promise

17.5.3 Sales and Channel Readiness Plan

The Sales and Channel Readiness Plan ensures that the sales and channel teams are ready, enabled, and equipped with the proper training and tools to successfully sell the product. Product marketing often leads this effort in coordination with product management and the marketing organization.

The questions an effective Sales and Channel Readiness Plan should answer are as follows:

- What objectives are we trying to achieve?

- What sales tools and collateral do we need to precisely articulate the product value proposition, positioning, features, and benefits?

- What are the training requirements for the sales and channel teams?

- How do we conduct the training most effectively?

- What is the training schedule and major milestones?

- Do we go to market with existing channels or do we need to recruit new channel partners?

- What is the sales cycle and what are the main objections at every step in the sales process?

A Sales and Channel Readiness Plan should:

- Provide a clear schedule and delivery mechanism to train the sales and channel teams

17

- Describe the sales tools and collateral to be developed by sales stage

- Outline the entire sales process and objections to be overcome at every stage

- Identify new channel partners and agreements to be put in place (if required)

- Reinforce pricing strategy, discount terms, contract negotiation process, and all the approvals required to complete a sale

17.5.4 Demand Generation Plan

The purpose of the Demand Generation Plan is to provide a blueprint or a set of campaigns that describes the trends, themes, targets, and tactics to be used to capture the customer's attention. The goal is to convert interest into desire and action, leading to a successful sale. The Demand Generation Plan covers target audiences by region with key messages by role and segment at every stage of the campaign. Deciding on the right sequence and promotion mix is important. For example, the product team may start by sending out an email message inviting prospects to a webinar announcing the launch, followed by a reminder as the date draws closer. At the end of the webinar, there may be a call to action followed by an offer and next steps.

The questions an effective Demand Generation Plan should answer are as follows:

- What are the objectives?

- What are the current market trends?

- What are the primary marketing and demand generation themes?

- Who is the target audience?

- What are the specific programs and tactics we will use to generate awareness and create desire?

- What are the objectives of each campaign or program?

- What industry associations and experts need to be engaged to create buzz?

- What are the key metrics that need to be tracked for lead conversion?

- Who is responsible for execution and monitoring of the plan?

An effective Demand Generation Plan should:

- Articulate the major demand generation themes for the campaigns to be developed based on market research and trends

- Outline the specific campaigns and programs on a timeline with key objectives and actions

- Show the entire demand generation program's calendar and schedule

- Provide a snap shot of campaigns and program's progress over a quarterly timeline

- Explain the budget and resources required for a successful program

- Combine all promotion vehicles—direct mail, email, webinars, social media, telesales—to arrive at the optimal marketing mix by campaign or program

17.5.5 Analyst Relations Plan

The purpose of the Analyst Relations Plan is to make sure all key analysts, industry influencers, and relevant media publications are aware of the product launch and can lend their support and influence.

The questions an effective Analyst Relations Plan should answer are as follows:

- What are the objectives of the plan?

- What industry influencers and analysts need to be made aware of the launch?

- What industry associations and experts need to be engaged to support messaging?

- Who are the major analysts covering the space?

- What are the major briefing themes?

- What is the analyst briefing plan and schedule?

- What are the key metrics that need to be tracked for analyst coverage?

A great Analyst Relations Plan should:

- Identify the key analysts and industry influencers that can serve as champions for the product

- Outline a specific briefing timeline with key objectives and messages

- Reinforce the major themes and the strategic direction of the product that need to be promoted as part of the analyst and industry influencer's briefings

17

17.5.6 Public Relations and Media Plan

The primary purpose of the Public Relations Plan is to serve as the basis for the public relations program. It can be either company-wide or may focus on a specific product line, product, or service. The plan needs to make sure all relevant media publications are aware of the product launch and can lend their support and influence.

The questions an effective Public Relations Plan should answer are as follows:

- How can we preserve or augment our corporate and brand identity?

- What is our media strategy?

- What should be the major briefing themes?

- What industry influencers and media publications need to be aware of the launch?

- Who are the key spokespeople in the company?

- What should be in the press kit?

- What are the key metrics that need to be tracked for public relations coverage?

- Who is responsible for plan execution, monitoring, and reporting of results?

A Public Relations Plan should:

- Identify the key media publications that are relevant and can promote the product

- Outline a specific media/roadshow schedule on a timeline with key objectives and messages

- Reinforce the major themes and the product's strategic direction that need to be promoted as part of the media briefings

17.6 The Deliver Phase Tools

The Deliver phase of the product management lifecycle is centered upon continuously optimizing a product or a group of product's market performance throughout the growth, maturity, and decline phases of the product lifecycle. This requires careful consideration and proactive management of the marketing mix and product investment.

The marketing plan needs to have the flexibility to adapt to changes in the business environment as the product advances through the growth, maturity, and decline phases. The competition may change, technology may rapidly advance, and products and services will likely require modification over time. The product team must think about contingency plans for ways to adjust the marketing strategy to changing conditions to ensure that the product has the adaptability for lasting success.

This section provides an overview of some of the key tools that are commonly utilized to make the right product, feature, and marketing decisions and ensure that the product maximizes its profitability across the growth, maturity, and decline phases.

17.6.1 Market Analysis Template

Total product sales, measured in volume or in value, are the most direct measure of the market's behavior and response. Product sales analysis by itself, however, can be misleading since it does not reveal how the product is doing relative to competition operating in the same market or region.

For example, an increase in sales may be due to a general improvement in market conditions and have nothing to do with the product's performance, or the increase may be hiding a decline in the product's position (e.g., if it has grown but at a lesser rate than competition). Thus, product sales analysis must be complemented by a market share analysis.

The reason for measuring market share is to eliminate the impact of any environmental factors and consumer behavioral patterns that exert the same influence on all competing products, thus allowing a proper comparison of the performance of each product.

Quality market analysis helps predict future performance. The critical question addressed is: What makes up our market share? Traditional market share measures in units or in value should be complemented by an analysis of the customer base. Market share is simply calculated as follows: A Product's Unit Sales divided by Total Market Unit Sales for all vendors. While the calculation is easy, finding the total unit sales for a market can be very difficult. The product team can often get this information from industry analysts.

A strong Market Analysis helps marketing, sales, and finance teams forecast the market share for a new product or service. A quality market analysis template can be used to forecast annual revenue and gross margin based on the market share forecast, and to generate charts that illustrate revenue and gross margin trends.

A great product market analysis should provide three- to five-year market share projections by competitors. It should also provide the number of active and converted customer projections for the same period. Product market analysis should also contain a financial projections section with direct and channel mix by percentage and revenue projections by direct sales teams and channel partners. The final part of the financial projections should provide a gross margin analysis by channel and direct sales.

The information will help the product team make the right market and channel decisions to maximize the product performance during the Deliver phase. It will help the team decide which product lines to retire, and when to retire them, so that they don't continue to manufacture, market, and support products that are under-performing and negatively impacting the company's profitability.

17.6.2 Channel Strategy and Plan

A channel plan is a document that can be used to consolidate the channel analysis and choose the optimal strategy and sales channel(s) to increase the product's reach. The plan will enable the product team to proactively manage the growth phase of the product and ensure that it is being distributed appropriately in targeted markets and geographical regions via preferred channel partners.

The channel plan should document the channel strategy and outline how to measure the results of the respective channels and evaluate each for effectiveness. The important elements that should be included in the Channel Strategy and Plan are:

- Clearly Support Corporate Goals – The channel plan and strategy should be clearly linked to the organization's corporate goals and objectives and communicate the rationale for the indirect channel(s) selected.

- Segment Target Markets – Determine the targeted markets and identify the size and priority of them.

- Channel Selection – Analyze channel profitability and capability to ensure that product objectives can be met.

- Partner Selection – Identify and qualify that the correct partners are selected with careful considered criteria and competency requirements, including how success is to be measured.

- Clearly Define Roles – Determine who is in charge of the channel and identify who is running the program.

- Create a Business Plan – Develop an annual operating plan to achieve targeted goals as defined in the success criteria.

- Define the Capabilities of a Partner – Include important factors that will enable the partner to work with the indirect sales channel team.

A Channel Strategy and Plan should provide a blueprint to:

- Penetrate new geographical territories

- Reach more customers at a lower cost point

- Penetrate specialized market segments that require particular skills or specialized knowledge

- Test new markets with reduced levels of risk

- Scale the sales operation very quickly in response to new or unexpected demand

A well-defined channel plan outlines all the various channels that encompass the partners or resellers with whom the company works to successfully extend sales coverage and reach.

17.6.3 Pricing Comparison Chart

A meaningful pricing comparison chart should contain pricing options available based on the usage of the product. For instance, a table showing the right options and features for small business or big business, or comparing the configurations for teachers against those for students.

If the product has multiple versions or bundles—Basic, Advanced, Deluxe—then the pricing comparison chart should also help compare those options side by side. TurboTax® is a great example of this type of comparison, making it very easy for customers to buy.[56] At the back of every TurboTax product is a listing of the options and features available—"Which TurboTax is right for you?"—helping customers make the right decision quickly. Three to five bundles is probably best; more than five is overwhelming.

17.6.4 Product Demos

The challenges most product and marketing teams face include letting potential customers experience the product without giving it away or explaining a complex

---

[56] TurboTax is a registered trademark of Intuit Inc., registered in the United States and other countries.

product in a simple yet effective manner. Alternatively, some organizations offer a variation on this theme by allowing users to access a downgraded version of the product as a demo/trial.

Product Demos are becoming an increasingly critical part of a company's marketing arsenal due in part to more savvy and well-educated buyers. Many companies spend time and money on website and marketing material explaining why their product is better than competitors.

But what if some buyers *only* want to see a demo, skipping all of the marketing speak and metaphors on the website? Expectations about what potential buyers can see and experience about the product is increasing daily. Many buyers want to learn about new products taking the "just show me" approach. Unfortunately, this is where a lot of companies fail in the online product experience.

What does an effective product demo do? It provides an introduction, presents a challenge, offers a solution, walks the buyer through the resolution process, and summarizes the benefits. A demo should:

- Last no more than five minutes. Cut out all unnecessary content. Answer the buyer or user's most critical questions and demonstrate results in the shortest time possible.

- Tell a story. Don't just click and navigate to hit every feature. Make it as real as possible with use case scenarios. What was their problem? How did they use the product to solve it?

- Make the product exciting. Show people using the product. Try to show how using the product resulted in a happier customer. People like to see real results even in a virtual world.

- Show live people in a demo. Showing individuals talking about a product and/or using a product in the demo strongly engages users and strengthens the connection with the people on screen. People are less likely to click away from an on-screen personality looking them in the eye, compared to viewing text or narration.

17.6.5 Analyst Strategy and Briefings Plan

Before the product has launched and is gaining traction in the marketplace, the product team should develop an analyst strategy that will continue to promote and support the product momentum. An analyst briefing is an opportunity for product vendors to present their products, services, and business strategies with analysts that cover either the vendor specifically or a related technology or market. During an analyst briefing, the flow of information predominates from vendor to analysts and is not particularly interactive. Analysts may ask questions of clarification during a briefing session; however, analyst feedback is not the goal of this meeting.

Analyst firms like Gartner and Forrester schedule briefings based on an interest in the company, technologies, and marketplace, not because of any fee or contractual relationship, which gives them credibility as an impartial third party. The product team can make the most use of this forum by highlighting the problems the product solves and how it makes the customers' lives easier.

The product team should make a list of all the key influencers and leading analysts in the space who can act as product champions. They should develop a briefing deck that addresses the value proposition and clearly explains why the product is different from the competition.

So what does a typical analyst briefing entail? The list below includes some of the topics that may be covered in these briefings:

- Company Overview — brief history, financial performance, operating principles, organizational structure, value proposition, vision statement

- Market Positioning — assessment of market drivers or business issues, category description (software integration, consultant, data-mining solution provider, etc.), competitive position, description of target markets, go-to-market strategy (direct, indirect sales model), partner strategy, points of differentiation

- Capabilities — customer benefits, delivery model, methodologies, portfolio review, success stories, tools

- Strategic Intent —growth plan (organic, partners, acquisitions), investment strategy, vision for future directions

Some other best practices for effective analyst briefings are as follows:

- Supporting Materials — E-mail the presentation materials to the analysts attending the briefing at least three days in advance of the scheduled briefing. If certain information is confidential or embargoed, that should be noted on the document and cover letter.

- Web Demos — What kind of demo is most appropriate for the audience and can be delivered reliably? Web demos should be used to demonstrate software, databases, and tools only. Electronic slide presentations should

17

still be e-mailed to the vendor briefings specialist and the attending analysts in case analysts are unable to access the web demo due to technical difficulties or travel. Analysts prefer the electronic presentation as they can write comments while the briefing is taking place and presentations are posted to their archival database.

17.6.6 Public Relations and Media Plan

As the product is gaining traction in the marketplace, a well-planned public relations campaign is critical to sustain the momentum and growth.

The product team should consider the following steps when planning and developing an effective public relations (PR) and media campaign:

- *Step 1: Define and write down the objectives for the publicity or media plan.* In order for the PR and media plan to be successful it is very important to first determine and define the objective. With a clear objective in mind, the product team lays the ground work for an effective PR and Media plan. Consider the following question: Why is the product team designing the plan? Is the primary objective to:

  o Establish expertise/thought leadership among peers, the press, or potential clients or customers?

  o Build goodwill among customers, suppliers, or the community?

  o Create and reinforce the brand and professional corporate image?

  o Inform and create good perceptions regarding the company and services?

  o Assist the company in introducing a new service or product to the market?

  o Generate sales or leads?

  o Mitigate the impact of negative publicity and/or corporate crisis?

- *Step 2: Define the goals to achieve the above objective.* It is important that the goals be specific, measurable, results-oriented, and time-bound. These goals must be in line with the overall business, marketing, and sales objectives.

- *Step 3: Determine the target audience.* Who does the product team want to reach with the PR campaign? What are the key messages?

- *Step 4: Develop a schedule for the public relation campaigns.* Create synergy by coordinating the public relations plan with other marketing and sales efforts.

- *Step 5: Develop the plan of attack.* What communication vehicles will be used to get the message to the public? Select from the following list and begin researching and developing the approach:

  o Press Releases

  o Bylines and Articles

  o Customer Success Stories

  o Blogs

  o Press Conferences, Interviews, or Media Tours

  o Radio, Television, or Press Interviews

  o Seminars or Speaking Engagements

  o Event Sponsorships

- *Step 6: Build a media area on the web site.* Assuming the press and analysts will write about the product, the best screen shots, official icons, and promotional product art need to be available. A media area doesn't have to be only for the press and analysts. Assume social media followers, bloggers, and customers will go there too.

- *Step 7: Put measures in place to track the results of the PR Campaign.* Review the results after each campaign. Were the defined objectives and goals of this campaign achieved? Should the product team consider modifying the PR plan?

17.7 The Retire Phase

Most of product management is focused on planning and delivering products, but the importance of a plan for retiring products is often underappreciated. When the financials no longer make sense, it's time to retire (or "sunset") the product.

17.7.1 End-of-Life Plan

The End-of-Life Plan (EOL) outlines the plan for gracefully withdrawing a product from the market. It is, in its most basic form, the reverse of a Launch Plan. The plan describes the sequence of events that need to be executed by the product manager with the support of cross-functional teams to withdraw a product from the market while minimizing the impact to the organization, customers, suppliers, and distribution channels.

17

The EOL describes internal impacts to the company, including impact on revenue, manufacturing, operations, customer support functions, and external impacts, such as minimizing excess inventory for suppliers and distribution channels. It also can describe the level of support required to migrate customers to a replacement product. It identifies internal communication and key activities needed to avoid serious economic impact to the organization.

The general questions the EOL Plan should answer are:

- Which product or product line will be withdrawn from the market?

- Why is it being withdrawn from the market?

- What is the impact to the company's product portfolio?

- What is the preferred strategy for this product: divest, spin off, harvest, or retire?

- What are the legal implications?

- What are the key risks to the plan and how will the risks be mitigated?

- How will the revenue stream impact be offset?

- Who are the impacted customers and end users?

- Which internal functions are impacted by this action?

- What key resources need to be redeployed or repurposed?

- Which partners, suppliers, and distribution channels need to be informed?

- Will there be a replacement product? If yes, include a brief description. What level of support will be provided to help customers migrate to the replacement product or solution?

- What are the key milestones and critical dates? Who owns these activities?

- What are the critical success factors?

An effective EOL Plan includes all of the following:

- Product or product line name — list of SKUs or product IDs

- Reasons for withdrawing from the market

- Description of selected strategy — divest, spin off, harvest, or retire

- Brief description of any replacement product or solution – proposed migration plan

- Internal communications plan — planned end-of-manufacturing date, planned end-of-sales date, planned end-of-support date, planned date for discontinuing renewal of contracts, planned discontinuance date

- External communications plan — what will customers and channel partners be told, and when?

- Description of external impact — customers and users, distribution channels, key partners and suppliers

- Description of internal impact — revenue, excess inventory, marketing and sales, customer and technical support, development, manufacturing, operations

- Cost analysis — inventory write-off, support costs, maintenance costs

- Risk analysis — risk factors and impact

A strong EOL Plan has a number of finite characteristics. The plan must be:

- Clear and concise — Everyone on the team ranging from senior executives to those supporting the product's market withdrawal must be able to understand the plan and get behind it. This includes clearly spelling out key milestones, owners, and critical dates.

- Complete — The EOL plan needs to contain all the necessary information to ensure an effective implementation.

- Realistic — There is a tendency to be overly optimistic when drawing up end-of-life plans. The timeline for market withdrawal should be carefully vetted to ensure that the period of time allocated will allow deeply entrenched customers, who may use more than one of the company's products, sufficient time to migrate to another offering or be carefully terminated.

- Implementable — The plan must be able to be implemented with the existing technology, skills, and capabilities of the organization.

- Low impact — Eliminate or minimize the impact to customers and the organization. The plan needs to address overlapping customer relationships where clients may utilize more than one of the company's products as well as the impact to the company's revenue stream. It must also take into full account critical risk factors and address any gaps in the company's product portfolio.

Retiring a product from the market is one of the most difficult challenges a product manager will face.

17

Appendix A:
Contributors and Reviewers of ProdBOK® Guide – First Edition

The following individuals served as members of the project team for the inaugural edition of The Guide to the Product Management and Marketing Body of Knowledge. Each individual listed below played an important role writing or reviewing components of the ProdBOK manuscript.

Significant effort was undertaken to ensure a broad base of industry participation spanning academics, analysts, associations, authors, bloggers, consultants, thought leaders, and practitioners within the product management community.

Additionally, the editorial team worked closely with thought leaders from the adjoining professions to ensure a balanced view of how product management and the various disciplines of business analysis, product and program management, and user experience should interact in pursuit of an organization's product goals and objectives. Future editions will continue to expand upon these cross-functional interactions and additional functions that are not covered in this edition.

The editors would like to acknowledge Steven Starke and Don Vendetti for having made special contributions to this edition.

Contributors in Alphabetical Order

John Armstrong	Steven Eppinger	Jack Hilty
Jama Bradley	Mark Floisand	Peter Hiscocks
Kevin Brennan	Greg Geracie	Matt Jackson
Jose Briones	Stacy Goff	Steve Johnson
Hari Candadai	Linda Gorchels	Holly Joshi
Sharon Carmichael	Tom Grant	Lee R. Lambert
Sara Cleary	Paula Gray	Richard Larson
Greg Cohen	Rich Gunther	Jeff Lash
Bill Cohn	Ken Hanley	Edward MacBean
Nick Coster	George Hechtel	Neal McWhorter
Hector Del Castillo	Gary Heerkens	Linda Merrick
Jack Duggal	David Heidt	Rich Mironov

First Edition

Barbara Munderloh

Purnima Nath

Bill Needham

Therese Padilla

Roman Pichler

David Radzialowski

Kathleen Riley

Johanna Rothman

Trevor Rotzien

Guenther Ruhe

Frank Saladis

Jennifer Schroeder

Scott Sehlhorst

Carol Smith

Cindy F. Solomon

Steven Starke

Adrienne Tan

Sean Van Tyne

Don Vendetti

Nina Villacci

Beth Waibel

Steve Wells

Appendix B: References

Chapter 1. Introduction

No references for this chapter.

Chapter 2. Product Management and Product Marketing Management

1 Stewart, T.A. (2006, June). Growth as a Process, An Interview with Jeffrey R. Immelt. *Harvard Business Review*, 63–64.

2 Dyer, D., Dalzell, F., & Olegario, R. (2004). *Rising Tide: Lessons from 165 Years of Brand Building at Procter & Gamble*. Boston, MA: Harvard Business School Press.

3 McElroy, N. (1931). Procter & Gamble company memo, May 13, 1931.

4 Pepper, J. (2005). *What Really Matters*. Cincinnati, OH: Procter & Gamble Company.

5 Rutherford, D., & Knowles, J. (2007). *Vulcans, Earthlings and Marketing ROI*. Waterloo, ON, Canada: Wilfrid Laurier University Press.

Chapter 3. What Is a Product?

6 Kotler, P., & Keller, K. (2008). *Marketing Management* (13th ed.). Upper Saddle River, NJ: Prentice Hall.

7 Kotler, P., & Keller, K. (2008). *Marketing Management* (13th ed.). Upper Saddle River, NJ: Prentice Hall.

8 Ogilvy, D. (1985). *Ogilvy on Advertising*. New York, NY: Vintage Books.

9, 10 Kotler, P., & Keller, K. (2008). *Marketing Management* (13th ed.). Upper Saddle River, NJ: Prentice Hall.

Chapter 4. What Is Product Management?

No references for this chapter.

Chapter 5. Common Product Management Roles

11 Lysonski, S. (1985, Winter). The Boundary Theory Investigation of the Product Manager's Role. *Journal of Marketing*, 29–41.

12 Gemmill, G. R., & Willemon, D. L. (1972). The Product Manager as an Influence Agent. *Journal of Marketing*, 36, 26–30.

13 Schwaber, K., & Sutherland, J. (2009). *Scrum Guide*. Retrieved from http://www.scrum.org.

14 Pichler, R. (2010). *Agile Product Management with Scrum.* Boston, MA: Addison-Wesley.

15 Schwaber, K. (2007). *The Enterprise and Scrum.* Redmond, WA: Microsoft Press.

16 Leffingwell, D. (2011). *Agile Software Requirements.* Boston, MA: Addison Wesley.

Chapter 6. Aligning ProdBOK with Other Existing Processes (and Why It Matters)

17 Porter, M. E. (2006). What is Strategy. *Harvard Business Review*, 74(6).

18 Porter, M. E. (1998). *Competitive Strategy: Techniques for Analyzing Industries and Competitors.* New York, NY: Free Press.

19 OECD. (2005). *The Measurement of Scientific and Technological Activities: Guidelines for Collecting and Interpreting Innovation Data: Oslo Manual (3rd ed.).* Oslo, Norway: OECD.

20 Christensen, C. (1973). *The Innovator's Dilemma.* New York, NY: Harper Paperbacks.

21 Geracie, G. (2010). *Business value creation: Collaborating with project management and business analysts to achieve sustainable market success.* Chicago, IL: Presentation at the Project Summit and Business Analyst World.

22-25 Rothman, J. (2007). *Manage It! Your Guide to Modern, Pragmatic, Project Management.* Raleigh, NC; Dallas, TX: The Pragmatic Bookshelf.

26 Beck, K., Beedle, M., van Bennekum, A., Cockburn, A., Cunningham, W., Fowler, M...Thomas, D. (2001). *The Manifesto for Agile Software Development.* Retrieved from http://agilemanifesto.org/.

27 Schwaber, K., & Beedle, M. (2002). *Agile Software Development with Scrum.* Upper Saddle River, NJ: Prentice Hall. pp 24–25, 106–108.

28 Cohn, M. Retrieved from http://www.mountaingoatsoftware.com/topics/user-stories. To learn more on user stories, refer to Cohn, M. (2004). *User Stories Applied for Agile Software Development.* Boston, MA: Addison-Wesley.

29 Cohen, G. (2010). *Agile Excellence for Product Managers.* Cupertino, CA: Super Star Press.

30 Beck, K. (1999). *Extreme Programming Explained: Embrace Change.* Boston, MA: Addison-Wesley Professional.

31 Womack, J. P. Retrieved from http://www.lean.org/common/display/?o=1366. To learn more, refer to Womack, J. P., & Hones, D. T. (2003). *Lean Thinking: Banish Waste and Create Wealth in Your Corporation*. New York, NY: Free Press.

32 Reinersten, D. G. (2009). *The Principles of Product Development Flow: Second Generation Lean Product Development*. Redono Beach, CA: Celeritas Publishing.

33 Ibid, p. 56–57.

34 Ibid, p. 58.

35 Kanban, Japanese for "visual cards," is a Toyota-created visual scheduling system that outlines what to produce, when to produce it, and how much to produce.

36 Not to be confused with the Kanban Method, which also uses a kanban board. The Kanban Method is a Lean change management methodology developed by David Anderson and described in his 2010 book *Kanban: Successful Evolutionary Change for Your Technology Business*.

Chapter 7. Product Management's Relationship with Other Disciplines

37 Some of these other standards include Association for Project Management (U.K.) and International Project Management Association, or American Society for the Advancement of Project Management, IPMA-USA's ICB and National Competence Baselines.

38 North Carolina State University, Center for Universal Design, www.design.ncsu.edu/cud.

39 Norman, D. (1999). The Invisible Computer: Why Good Products Can Fail, the Personal Computer Is So Complex, and Information Appliances Are the Solution. Cambridge, MA: The MIT Press.

Chapter 8. Introduction to the Product Management Lifecycle Framework and Process Groups

40 Jacka, J. M., & Keller, P. J. (2009). *Business process mapping: Improving customer satisfaction* (2nd ed.). Hoboken, NJ: John Wiley and Sons Inc.

41 Geracie, G. (2010). *Take Charge Product Management*. Chicago, IL: Actuation Press.

Chapter 9. The Fundamentals

42-43 Kotler, P., & Keller, K. (2011). *Marketing Management* (14th ed.). Upper Saddle River, NJ: Prentice Hall.

44 Christensen, C. (1997). *The Innovator's Dilemma*. New York, NY: HarperBusiness.

45 Rogers, E. (2003). *Diffusion of Innovations* (5th ed.). New York, NY: Free Press.

46 Moore, G. (2002). *Crossing the Chasm*. New York, NY: HarperCollins.

47 Ansoff, I. (1957). Strategies for Diversification. *Harvard Business Review*, 35 (5), 113–124.

Chapter 10. The Conceive Phase

48 iTunes and iPod are registered trademarks of Apple Inc.

49 Actuation Consulting and Enterprise Agility. (2012). *The Study of Product Team Performance, 2012*. Chicago, Illinois: Actuation Press.

50 Consumer Reports is a registered trademark of Consumers Union of United States.

Chapter 11. The Plan Phase

No references for this chapter.

Chapter 12. The Develop Phase

51 Nielsen, J., & Landauer, T. (2000). Why you only need to test with 5 users. *Jakob Nielsen's Alertbox*. Retrieved from http://www.useit.com/alertbox/20000319.html.

Chapter 13. The Qualify Phase

No references for this chapter.

Chapter 14. The Launch Phase

No references for this chapter.

Chapter 15. The Deliver Phase

No references for this chapter.

Chapter 16. The Retire Phase

No references for this chapter.

Chapter 17. Product Management Tools

52 Isaacson, W. (2011). *Steve Jobs*. New York, NY: Simon & Schuster.

53 Osterwalder, A., & Pigneur, Y. (2010). *Business Model Generation: A Handbook for Visionaries, Game Changers, and Challengers.* Hoboken, NJ: John Wiley & Sons.

54 Moore, G. (2002). *Crossing the Chasm.* New York, NY: HarperCollins.

55 Amazon, Kindle, Kindle Fire, the Amazon Kindle logo, and the Kindle Fire logo are trademarks of Amazon.com, Inc. or its affiliates.

56 TurboTax is a registered trademark of Intuit Inc., registered in the United States and other countries.

Appendix C: Glossary of Terms

This glossary includes many terms that are unique or directly associated with the field of product management. As a result, all of the terms listed below are nuanced to reflect their connection with the product management profession and may vary from other definitions found in common everyday use.

Agile An umbrella term used to describe a group of iterative incremental product development principles and methodologies that support the Agile Manifesto.

Agile Manifesto A conceptual framework that emphasizes four central values and twelve supplemental principles encompassing an iterative and people-orientated approach to product development. (Also called the Manifesto for Agile Software Development.)

Agile Theory Holds that Agile is designed to follow a non-linear path more closely approximated to that of new product development instead of the more predictable path of manufacturing, which typically follows a serial process.

Alpha Test An initial in-house-only or controlled test of a product or a set of product capabilities.

Ansoff Matrix A tool designed to illustrate a range of possible corporate growth strategies for an organization's current and potential products/markets. These strategies include: market penetration, market development, product development, and diversification.

Behavioral Design Creating a cohesive conceptual model for the product that is easy to learn and understand. Behavioral design meshes the task requirements of a product with the skills, knowledge, and capabilities of the intended users.

Beta Plan Alignment around the purpose of the beta test; clarifies the goals of the testing to be performed and the logistics of how the test is to be conducted.

Beta Test A formal, structured, and controlled test of a new product or product capability in order to determine market readiness.

Body of Knowledge (BOK) A Body of Knowledge codifies the concepts, definitions, processes, and activities of a given profession.

Boston Consulting Group Market-Share Matrix (BCG Matrix) A commonly used growth-share framework that categorizes products within a company's portfolio according to growth rate, market share, and positive or negative cash flow.

Boundary Role A position or role that sits at the intersection of two points. In the case of product management, between the needs of the market and those of the organization.

Brainstorming A commonly used technique for developing creative solutions to problems or to generate new ideas.

Brand An identifying mark, label, trademark, imprint, or name that distinguishes the originator, creator, or manufacturer of a product or service.

Branding Originating, building, improving, and safeguarding a name or symbol representing a specific product or service.

Brand Equity The quality associated with a brand based on value assessed over a significant period of time; the affirmative perception of a brand or service based on customer loyalty and the positive reputation of a service or product.

Brand Extension Introducing a new or improved product by associating it with an established brand image.

Brand Identity A logo, slogan, moniker, or mark associated with a product or service by consumers that sets it apart from competitors.

Brand Positioning Optimizing a brand by having a clear concept of its strongest points and placing it among similar products to accentuate its superiority and uniqueness in relation to competitors.

Burndown Chart A visual tool used by Agile product development teams that represents the amount of work left to do versus time.

Business Analysis The practice of analyzing business needs and identifying viable solutions in order to enable organizational change and deliver value to stakeholders.

Business Analyst An individual that uses a prescribed set of business analysis tools and techniques to understand business needs and identify viable solutions that will maximize the value delivered by an organization to its stakeholders.

Business Case A well-structured document that provides the overall justification for a product or product investment and clearly demonstrates a cost-benefit analysis.

Buyer A person or organization that acquires or seeks to acquire a product or service in exchange for money or some other consideration.

Buyer Personas A representation of a specific group or groups of buyers who influence or make purchasing decisions about a product. Buyer personas are used to make informed product, marketing, and sales channels decisions.

Category Extension The use of an existing or parent brand to launch products in other categories.

Channel Conflict A situation resulting from the producer of a product competing, either inadvertently or through intent, with other parties distributing the same product to a targeted group of customers.

Closeout Refers to the processes used by a project manager to bring a project or project phase to an organized and well-planned conclusion.

Conceive Phase The first phase of the product management lifecycle where product ideas are generated and assessed for market viability. This phase is sometimes referred to as the fuzzy front end.

Concept Definition A set of activities that occur once a specific product concept has been identified for further exploration and analysis.

Concept Identification A set of activities focused on finding new market opportunities that may be addressed by a new product or product development activity.

Consumer Products Goods and services purchased by final consumers for personal consumption.

Convenience Products Items bought on a regular basis to meet immediate needs.

Corporate Strategy Defines the overall scope and direction of a company and details which markets the company competes in and how it will leverage company assets and capabilities to achieve success.

Customer Value Hierarchy A concept introduced by Philip Kotler that suggests that there are five levels of a product. These five levels include: the core benefit, the basic product, the expected product, the augmented product, and the potential product.

Daily Scrum A daily 15-minute stand-up meeting where team members share what they did since the last meeting, what they plan to do before the next meeting, and discuss any obstacles blocking progress.

Decision Matrix A tool used to evaluate a series of inputs in order to objectively prioritize a set of requirements or criteria for making a decision.

Decision Points Critical business decision-making junctures within the product management lifecycle used to optimize performance, scrutinize product development investments, and increase the quality of execution. Commonly referred to as gates.

Deliver Phase The sixth phase of the product management lifecycle where product managers seek to optimize the successful growth, profitability, and longevity of a product.

Develop Phase The third phase of the product management lifecycle where promising product concepts and plans are converted into a marketable product.

Disruptive Innovation An innovation that disrupts and eventually displaces entrenched products in established markets by creating a new market and value network. (Term originally coined by Clayton Christensen.)

Distribution Channel The path through which products and services travel from the producer to the consumer.

Downstream Activities focused on the active lifecycle management of existing in-market products.

Durable Goods Goods whose usefulness continues for a number of years and which cannot be consumed.

Early Adopters Customers that are willing to utilize a newly available or partial product that delivers a core benefit, and are willing to sacrifice attributes of the product or other commonly associated expectations in order to be first in obtaining the product.

Earned Value Management A technique that objectively compares planned and actual results to determine whether variances exist and what their magnitude is. Corrective actions are taken based on the outcome of variance analysis.

Elevator Pitch A quick but comprehensive statement of your product's or offering's intrinsic value.

End-of-Life Plan A retirement plan for a product nearing the end of its useful life.

Equitable Use A principle used to guide the design of a product that is both useful and marketable to people with diverse abilities. This includes providing the same means of use for all users—identical whenever possible and equivalent when not—and making provisions for privacy, security, and safety.

Estimating Analyzing components, circumstances, and characteristics to achieve specified product goals or features by fully taking into account effort, duration, cost, and benefits.

External Assessment Analysis focused on attempting to understand market trends and dynamics that have the potential to affect an organization's existing business or provide insight into new market opportunities.

External Product Roadmap Planned product development activities for the foreseeable future, normally on a rolling or calendar basis, and intended for external audiences.

Extreme Programming (XP) An iterative incremental approach to product development typically used by software development teams who face less-defined or rapidly changing requirements.

Feasibility Study Analysis and evaluation of a proposed effort to ensure that any product development activity undertaken is feasible on a technical, financial, and operational level and will result in a viable product or capability.

Finished Goods Products or services that are available for immediate sale.

Five Forces Model A strategy tool developed by Michael Porter that is commonly used to help evaluate market attractiveness and aid in decision making and planning. The five competitive forces are: supplier power, buyer power, competitive rivalry, threat of substitution, and threat of new entry.

Functional Requirement A document that clearly states the capabilities and functions that a system must be able to successfully perform.

Fuzzy Front End A term used to describe the early stage of product development where the outline of a future product is unclear. This term coincides with the Conceive phase of the product management lifecycle.

Gate Reviews Critical business decision-making meetings used to optimize product/portfolio performance, scrutinize development investments, and increase the quality of development execution. Also referred to as Decision Points.

GE-McKinsey Matrix A systematic portfolio management approach used to determine where cash should be invested for the best return based upon relative business strength and industry attractiveness.

General Management Encompasses strategizing, planning, organizing, staffing, executing, delivering, and providing the proper infrastructure to support the continued growth of the organization.

Graphic Design A creative process that combines words, symbols, and images to create a visual representation of ideas and messages.

Ideation The structured process of creating new ideas within an organization with the goal of bringing new capabilities or innovations to market.

Increment The quantifiable outcome of each iteration.

Incremental Innovation A small advancement beyond what already exists. Incremental innovations maintain or improve a product or service's competitive position.

Industrial Design Creating and developing concepts and specifications that improve the aesthetics, ergonomics, functionality, and usability of a product.

Industrial Products Goods used by an industry or business, rather than by an individual.

Information Radiator A wide range of visual tools that enable team members and management to see how Agile product development projects are progressing and act quickly when needed. The actual display can range from handwritten to more sophisticated electronic displays.

Initiation Refers to the activities associated with defining and approving a new project or determining whether a project should continue into the next phase as a current phase is nearing completion.

Intangible Product A product that lacks a physical presence.

Internal Product Roadmap Planned product development activities to be undertaken on a rolling or calendar basis, but used solely for internal purposes and not shared with external audiences.

Internal Assessment Internal analysis that reflects how the overall product, product line, or product category looks from the market perspective, specifically the customer perspective.

Internal Product Manager An individual that is responsible for a product or group of products and whose customers reside inside of the organization.

Iteration The cyclic nature of a process in which activities are repeated in a structured manner.

Iterative A product development method that timeboxes the length of the development cycle and produces an increasing set of capabilities with each successive cycle.

Iterative Incremental A product development methodology that produces the product in a series of short timeboxed cycles and in small, defined pieces until the fully envisioned product is constructed.

Joint Application Development (JAD) A method for implementing solution ideation through structured workshops, where a group composed of internal and external team members and market participants are brought together specifically to inform the design and development of a product.

Kanban A Lean scheduling system that is used to determine what to produce, when, and in what quantity.

Kanban Board A tool used by Lean product development teams to visualize flow through the system and enforce work-in-progress limits.

Key Performance Indicators (KPIs) Measurable metrics for tracking progress toward stated goals and objectives.

Latent Need Needs that customers are not consciously aware of or able to effectively communicate.

Launch Phase The fifth phase of the product management lifecycle, which is focused on the mechanics of successfully bringing a product to market.

Launch Plan The specific tactical activities to be undertaken in support of the launch of a product or service. Plan components include key messages and positioning along with the necessary tactical activities required to support a successful launch.

Launch Strategy The launch approach to be utilized; frequently coupled with a high-level set of tasks and costs to support the business plan objectives.

Lean A methodology whose central tenant is to create the most value for customers with the fewest resources by eliminating waste and implementing continuous improvement across entire value streams.

Line Extension Adding new versions, types, or varieties of existing branded products or services.

Market Anywhere buyers and sellers conduct transactions, and where the dynamics of supply and demand operate. From a marketing perspective, a market consists of groups of customers (current or potential) who have specific unmet needs that could be met by products or services.

Market Investigation Activities undertaken in order to understand, in detail, the overall needs of a targeted market segment and the market gap that's being addressed by the product concept.

Market Positioning Using research, trend analysis, and investigation of competitive products and services to set targeted products and services apart from and above the competition.

Market Requirements Document (MRD) Market segment-specific definition of needs, which focuses on describing the market problem, gap, or need to be addressed. Other common names for an MRD include: Business Requirements Document (BRD) and Customer Requirements Document (CRD).

Market Segment A targeted group of buyers that share some similar characteristic for which products and services are developed to meet their specific wants and needs.

Market Segmentation Segregating specific parts of a market based on criteria such as age, socioeconomics, behavioral patterns, or spending habits.

Market-Facing Product Manager An individual that is responsible for managing one or more products with customers outside of the organization and with whom they work closely to satisfy unmet needs.

Marketing The process of identifying unfulfilled needs and desires by defining, measuring, and quantifying market potential. Marketing narrows an organization's focus onto clearly defined market segments that can be served by its products and services.

Marketing Innovation Applying a new marketing method involving significant changes in product design or packaging, product placement, product promotion, or pricing.

Marketing Mix Controllable components of a product's marketing plan that can be adjusted until the right combination is found to efficiently deliver the optimal amount of value to both customers and the organization. Commonly referred to as the 4Ps: product, price, place, and promotion.

Marketing Strategy Enables an organization to concentrate its resources on the greatest opportunities to increase sales and achieve a sustainable competitive advantage.

Minimum Viable Product (MVP) The minimum amount of functionality that you deliver to the market with the specific intent of testing that you correctly identified the problem and core benefit with customers before investing more heavily in producing the full product.

Mission Statement The statement of a company's purpose; its reason for existence.

Mock Up Non-working models created early in the product development process to facilitate decision making or to illustrate how a product may eventually look or function.

Models Basic, visual guides used to suggest the layout and placement of fundamental design elements and elicit feedback on conceptual user interactions.

Non-Functional Requirements Qualities and constraints placed on a product in order to specify "how well" a system needs to perform.

Open Innovation A methodology that harnesses an open community of customers or partners to purposely capture and infuse knowledge in order to increase a company's rate of innovation.

Organizational Innovation Executing new methods in an organization's business practices, workplace organization, or external relations in order to achieve competitive advantage.

Penetration Pricing Setting a relatively low initial entry price, often lower than the market price, in an attempt to accelerate customer acquisition and penetrate a targeted market.

Perishable Products Goods that can spoil or decay easily and that do not have long shelf lives.

Personas Fictional representations of different types or groups of users being targeted in the design, development, and marketing of a product.

Phase-Gate A serial product development process that is broken into clearly defined phases utilizing gates as a means to control the exit from one phase of the process to the next.

Pilot A full end-to-end test of a product or system within a limited or controlled environment prior to full-scale deployment.

Portfolio Analysis An analysis of the components of a company's product and service mix to determine the optimum allocation of its resources.

Pre-Production Prototype A fully functional implementation that is still in the testing or validation stages prior to formal release. Often used for beta testing.

Primary Research Going directly to actual or potential customers in order to gain first-hand data or information.

Problem Scenarios A high-level method for describing the typical situation that a persona encounters and illustrates the market problem to be solved.

Process Innovation Implementing a new or substantially improved production or delivery method.

Product Can be either tangible or intangible. Tangible products have a physical presence. Intangible products lack a physical presence. Regardless of tangibility, products are purchased by consumers to meet needs and wants.

Product Backlog A term used by Agile product development teams to describe a prioritized list of user stories or features that have not yet been incorporated into a sprint cycle.

Product Concept A conceptual product or solution that addresses an identified and/or specific market need.

Product Lifecycle The evolutionary steps a product passes through beginning with market introduction and ending with decline.

Product Lifecycle Management The process of actively managing a product through its marketable life.

Product Line Extensions The creation of new products in the same category using the existing brand name.

Product Lines A group of products, categorized by a business unit or company that are closely related because they function in a similar manner, are sold to the same customer groups, are marketed through the same types of outlets, or fall within given price ranges.

Product Management The organizational function within a company dealing with the thoughtful and proactive management of a product or group of products throughout all stages and phases of the product management lifecycle.

Product Management Lifecycle An integrated framework of stages and phases that all successful products must progress through.

Product Manager An individual whose organizational responsibility is to create and maintain the optimal amount of value for a product or group of products throughout the entire product management lifecycle.

Product Marketing A set of responsibilities encompassing go-to-market activities, increasing the rate of product adoption, and supporting product management and the sales team's market-facing efforts.

Product Marketing Manager An individual that is primarily tasked with helping define and manage a product's image in the market. Product Marketing

Managers bring increased focus to "go-to-market" activities by supporting customer acquisition and in-market activities during the Launch and Deliver phases of the product management lifecycle.

Product Owner A clearly defined role on a Scrum team responsible for the success of the product. The product owner manages and prioritizes the requirements in the product backlog to maximize the value of the team's efforts and acts as the customer proxy.

Product Plan An integrated document suite that includes all the major components of a successful product.

Product Portfolio The entire range of products and services developed and distributed to consumers by an organization.

Product Portfolio Management Refers to the strategic process of proactively managing the overall health and value of a company's portfolio of products. Careful consideration is given to appropriately allocating investments in order to optimize the sustained growth of a company's revenue stream and profits.

Product Portfolio Manager An individual that is responsible for a group of products typically organized by business line or segment.

Product Production Process A structured process of documenting the stages, phases, owners, contributors, and deliverables required to bring a product to market in order to clarify roles and ensure smooth hand-offs between the various cross-functional parties.

Product Requirements Document (PRD) A document that contains product-specific definitions of the conceptual or planned product and thus is more focused on the solution to be delivered. Other common names for the PRD are Functional Requirements Document (FRD), Functional Requirements Specification (FRS), Functional Specification (FS), and Software Requirements Specification (SRS).

Product Roadmap The visual representation of a series of planned product development activities illustrating future product releases on either a calendar or rolling-year basis.

Product Strategy The strategic approach to be undertaken in order to achieve a product's goals in support of the overall business objectives of the organization.

Product Vision A defined, aspirational future state that a product manager wants the product to achieve in support of the overarching goals of the business.

Program Management The activity of actively managing a group of related projects coordinated to achieve benefits and control that could not arise from managing each project separately.

Program Manager An individual that is responsible for a group of related projects coordinated to achieve benefits and control that could not occur from managing each project separately.

Project A temporary effort undertaken to create, support, or retire a good, service, or result.

Project Execution The phase of a project that is focused on managing and controlling the underlying activities defined in the project plan in order to achieve a project's requirements.

Project Management The profession of applying a prescribed set of knowledge, skills, tools, and techniques to a specific project or set of projects to meet a set of defined requirements.

Project Manager The person responsible for ensuring that a project's scope, schedule, and cost are actively managed in support of the project objectives.

Project Planning Involves defining the scope of the project and the underlying actions that must be taken to achieve the established objectives codified in the project plan.

Project Portfolio Management A centralized approach to managing a group of current or pending projects based upon a predefined set of common characteristics.

Prototype A rudimentary working model of a product, usually built for demonstration purposes or as part of the product development process and used to elicit feedback from customers to validate that the model will meet their business needs.

Qualify Phase The fourth phase of the product management lifecycle, which outlines the steps that need to be taken to ensure that the product is ready to launch.

RACI Matrix A tool used by product and project managers to clearly define the parties that will be Responsible, Accountable, Consulted, or Informed on a particular activity or set of activities.

Radical Innovation A non-linear change that redefines the attributes concerning the way something is defined or that significantly transforms existing capabilities by a magnitude of five times or more. Other terms used to describe this type of innovation are discontinuous, breakthrough, transformational, or disruptive innovations.

Rapid Prototype A group of techniques used to quickly fabricate a scale model of a part or assembly using three-dimensional CAD data, such as through a 3D printer.

Rational Unified Process (RUP) An adaptable iterative software development framework that utilizes four phases of development. Each phase is organized into a number of separate iterations that must satisfy defined criteria before the next phase is undertaken. The phases are: inception, elaboration, construction, and transition.

Requirements A clearly defined set of actionable, measurable, and traceable criteria, typically distilled via customer engagement that is to be turned into a product or a set of product capabilities in order to capitalize on identified customer or business needs.

Retire Phase The final phase of the product management life cycle where a product is formally withdrawn from the market.

Retrospective A brief, dedicated period at the end of each sprint cycle used to reflect on the effectiveness of the sprint and to find ways to improve.

Rough-Order-of-Magnitude (ROM) An initial high-level estimate of the cost and timeline for a particular product development project. Typically expressed in terms of months or quarters for the project to deliver to some milestone, and often contains ranges or confidence level of the estimates.

SMART An acronym used to set and define organizational objectives that meet five criteria. The criteria need to be: Specific, Measurable, Achievable, Relevant, and Time-bound.

Secondary Research A method of collecting information that relies upon indirect methods, such as published reports, public or commercial databases, websites, agencies, etc.

Scrum An iterative incremental software product management methodology that utilizes small teams composed of a product owner, scrum master, and team members.

Scrum Master A person who ensures scrum practice is followed and facilitates so the team can identify areas of improvement and remove roadblocks to its progress.

Serial Process A product development process that proceeds through a series of linear steps commonly associated with manufacturing processes. These types of processes are often referred to as Waterfall.

Serviceable Available Market (SAM) An estimate of how much of the market an organization can realistically access. Also called Served Available Market.

Services Intangible products sold to meet a customer's needs.

Shopping Product Goods that require research and analysis before purchase.

Single Piece Flow The ideal state in Lean product development where parts are manufactured one at a time and flow throughout the manufacturing and supply chain as a single unit.

Soft Launch A controlled or limited launch with the objective of assessing the product, its performance, and some adoption and conversion factors before moving to the more formal broad launch.

Solution Scenarios Illustrates the user activities that would result from each of a selected set of candidate solutions.

Specialty Product Goods and services that are either unique or have such a clear brand identification that a consumer is willing to make a significant effort to purchase them.

Sprint A term used by Scrum product development teams to describe a timeboxed and protected unit of development that lasts no longer than 30 days.

Sprint Burndown Chart A publically displayed graphical representation of the work remaining in a Sprint.

Statement of Direction A document that contains a high-level narrative discussion of planned product development activities. An alternative to the traditional tactical product roadmap.

Storyboard A visual representation of the intended use of a product that people from different functional backgrounds can intuitively understand.

Story Point A method used by a Scrum product development team to estimate the relative amount of effort required to complete a work effort as compared to other possible work efforts that could be undertaken.

Strategy A method or plan chosen to bring about a desired future, such as achievement of a goal or solution to a problem.

SWOT Analysis A strategic planning tool used to identify the Strengths, Weaknesses, Opportunities, and Threats that exist inside and outside of the organization.

Task Board An Agile product development tool designed to help the team self-manage the workload and monitor the status of each requirement.

Technical Product Manager A product management role that typically requires a detailed understanding of the technological aspects of a product. In certain organizations the technical product manager has both market- and internal-facing responsibilities. In others, the technical product manager is more internally focused and partners with a market-facing product manager to serve the needs of the market.

Technical Support Services Services that often accompany complex products. These services are offered either directly from the manufacturer or through a third-party provider.

Technical Writing A form of written communication that presents technical information about a product or service in a manner that is clear and easy to understand by a user.

Test Plan Details how the product will be verified and ensures that the requirements have been met. It may also include the test cases used to verify the product. The test plan should provide specific reference back to the product requirements for traceability.

Total Available Market (TAM) An estimate of the maximum revenue number or total customers available to all competitors in the segment for all competing solutions. Also called Total Addressable Market.

Unsought Product Goods and services that a consumer either doesn't know about or want to think about.

Upstream A term used to describe a set of activities, including portfolio management, product strategy, and new product development, which commonly concluding at product launch.

Usability The ease of understanding and learnability inherent to an experience or a product.

Usability Engineering The field of developing effective usability for a product by systematically approaching, improving, and (if possible) measuring usability.

Use Case A discreet unit of interaction between users and the product (system) in order to achieve a goal that is well-defined and meaningful from the user's perspective.

User The person who will directly use or interact with a product's functionality or capabilities.

User Acceptance Testing (UAT) The final phase of the testing process where actual users test the product to make sure it can handle required tasks in real world scenarios and according to specifications prior to market introduction.

User-Centered Design A multi-stage problem-solving process that not only requires designers to analyze and predict based on ergonomic design principles and likely usage of a product, but also to test the validity of their assumptions in real-world tests with end users.

User Experience (UX) A person's perceptions and responses resulting from the use or anticipated use of a product, system, or service. User experience includes all of a person's physical and psychological responses that occur before, during, and after use. UX also refers to the concept of placing the end-user at the focal point of design and development efforts.

User Persona A fictional representation of a specific group of users that will use a product in different ways or have different expectations of it.

User Research A range of methods utilized to gain insight into user needs and behaviors.

User Stories An Agile product development method of capturing functional requirements by succinctly outlining the who, what, and why from the user's perspective.

Value Creation Process A term used to describe the way the product manager and the product team organize around the work that needs to be completed in order to create the most value for the customer and the organization across the span of the product management lifecycle.

Value Proposition A statement that summarizes the value a customer will receive by buying and using a product in comparison to other available options.

Voice of the Customer A widely practiced market research approach that relies on seeking direct input or data from customers in order to create new products or improve existing products.

Waterfall The name given to a serial product development process that follows a series of prescribed linear steps.

Wireframe A guide that visually represents the structural or skeletal framework of an emergent product. Wireframes are often used to lay out base functionality or content early in the product development process.

Work in Progress (WIP) Partly finished products that are at various stages of the production process, but are not yet finished. Excess WIP is viewed as an indicator of bottlenecks in the production process and/or supply chain that can lead to undesirable waste and inefficiencies.

Working Prototype A functioning item that may not be fully operational, be designed and engineered for manufacturability, or have the final appearance required.

About the Editors

Greg Geracie is a recognized thought leader in the field of product management and the President of Actuation Consulting, a global provider of product management training, consulting, and advisory services to some of the world's most well-known organizations. Actuation Consulting provides popular training courses for product managers and product teams and publishes the global *Study of Product Team Performance* annually.

Greg is also the author of the global best seller *Take Charge Product Management* and led the development of *The Guide to the Product Management and Marketing Body of Knowledge (ProdBOK)* as editor-in-chief. He is also an adjunct professor at DePaul University's College of Computing and Digital Media where he teaches graduate and undergraduate courses on high-tech and digital product management.

Greg is a regular contributor to a wide variety of industry publications and a former board member of the Business Architecture Guild. As a Guild member Greg actively contributed to the development of the product chapter of the BIZBOK™ Guide. Greg has also been asked to contribute his product management knowledge to a growing list of other professional bodies of knowledge, including the Institute of Electrical and Electronics Engineers (IEEE) first ITBOK and the latest BABOK Guide. Greg's articles have been published by the Silicon Valley Product Management Association, the Boston Product Management Association, the Association of International Product Marketing and Management, Project Times, the American Society for the Advancement of Project Management, the International Project Management Association, and the Business Analyst Times.

Greg earned his undergraduate degree from the University of Vermont and continued his executive education at Harvard University, the Massachusetts Institute of Technology (MIT), and the Wharton School.

You can learn more about Greg and Actuation Consulting at www.ActuationConsulting.com.

Steven D. Eppinger is professor of management science and innovation at the Massachusetts Institute of Technology (MIT) Sloan School of Management. He also holds the General Motors Leaders for Global Operations chair and has a joint appointment in MIT's engineering systems division. He is the co-director of MIT's system design and management program, and served as deputy dean of the MIT Sloan School from 2004 to 2009. Before joining the faculty, he received bachelor's, master's, and doctoral degrees from MIT in mechanical engineering.

Professor Eppinger has created an interdisciplinary product development course in which graduate students from engineering, management, and industrial design programs collaborate to develop new products. He also teaches MIT's executive programs in product development and complex project management. Professor Eppinger has co-authored a leading textbook entitled *Product Design and Development* (5th edition, 2012, McGraw-Hill) that is used by hundreds of universities around the world.

Professor Eppinger is a renowned researcher specializing in development of complex technical systems. He has published dozens of articles in academic journals and technical conferences, including many papers that have advanced the design structure matrix methodology. His book based on this research is titled *Design Structure Matrix Methods and Applications* (2012, MIT Press).

Have comments or feedback for the Editors? You can contact us at Editors@ActuationConsulting.com.

INDEX

A

Acceptance Criteria 47, 48, 67, 170, 188, 189, 208, 210

Agile 17, 48, 49, 51, 58, 64-70, 73, 74, 188, 189, 194, 206, 208, 209, 280, 283, 319

Agile Manifesto 51, 170, 319

Agile Release Burndown Chart 68

Agile Theory 66, 319

Alpha Test 215, 291, 319

Alternatives Analysis 163

Analyst Briefing Plan 301

Analyst Strategy 306

Ansoff Matrix 130, 131

"As-is" and "To-Be" Process Modeling 98

Augmented Product 124, 246, 321

B

BABOK® Guide 2, 94, 336

Basic Product 123

Behavioral Design 103, 104, 319

Beta Plan 213, 215-217, 224, 225, 291, 292, 319

Beta Test 64, 109, 167, 196, 207, 213-215, 219, 223-225, 231, 232, 291, 292, 319

Body of Knowledge (BOK) 16, 23-25, 94, 120, 121, 195, 319

Boston Consulting Group Market-Share Matrix (BCG Matrix) 133, 260, 319

Boundary Role 43, 320

Brainstorming 94, 97, 129, 161, 162, 320

Brand 23, 25, 28-31, 33, 34, 37, 41, 54, 126, 129, 133, 139, 174, 177, 243, 244, 246, 247, 298, 308, 320

Brand Equity 262, 320

Brand Extension 34, 320

Brand Identity 34, 302, 320

Brand Positioning 236, 320

Brand Promise 29, 298, 299

Burndown Chart 68, 69, 72, 74, 320

Business Analysis (BA) 93-95, 97, 100, 117, 312, 320

Business Analysis Techniques 97

Business Analyst 16, 25, 48, 62, 93, 94, 99, 117, 152, 171, 195, 210, 336, 320

Business Case 47, 63, 64, 77, 93, 148, 165, 171, 173, 180-187, 195, 198, 200, 201, 202, 208, 219-221, 227, 230, 232, 280, 295, 320

Business Case Activities 186, 200

Business Plan 205, 206, 216-218, 220, 221, 226, 229, 230-232, 292, 305

Business Requirements Document (BRD) 149

Business-to-Business 32, 193, 252

Business Workflow 98

Buyer 53, 103, 106, 125, 144, 151, 153-157, 160, 193, 266, 269, 270, 274, 276, 306, 320

Buyer Personas 153, 269, 320

Buyer Power 323

C

Cash Flow 319

Category Extension 34, 35, 321

Change Management 63, 212, 213, 288, 316

Channel Conflict 321

Channel Launch Preparation 228, 229

Channel Plan 304, 305

Channel Strategy 304, 305

Closeout 81, 321

Competition 27, 53, 108, 124, 125, 142, 152, 155-157, 174, 177, 231, 236, 237, 242-246, 264, 274, 277, 279, 299, 303, 307, 326

Competitive Advantage 65, 92, 99, 158

Competitive Analysis Matrix 272

Competitive Position 60, 133, 189, 254, 262, 307

Competitive Rivalry 323

Competitive Strategy 53

P

Penetration Pricing 327

Perishable Products 32, 327

Personas 107, 153, 154, 157, 166, 189, 190, 208, 214, 216, 268, 269, 270, 274, 282, 289, 298, 327

PEST analysis 134

Phase-Gate 58, 60, 61, 62, 327

Pilot 179, 199, 200, 213, 224, 327

Place 2, 21, 26, 46, 55, 84, 92, 99, 125, 126, 137, 141, 142, 151, 158, 160, 175, 181, 183, 216, 263, 274, 289, 294, 295, 296, 300, 308, 309

Planned Obsolescence 252

Plan Phase Activity Groups 185

PMBOK® Guide 2, 75, 76, 77, 94

Portfolio Analysis 133, 252, 254, 327

Portfolio Management 75, 91-93, 132, 146, 254, 259, 262

Positioning 28, 46, 60, 108, 173, 175, 176, 177, 179, 180, 181, 186, 189, 199, 202, 214, 217, 234, 236, 239, 240, 254, 273, 279, 280, 292-294, 297-299, 307

Positioning Statement Framework 279

Post-Launch 226, 235, 239, 240

Potential Product 124

Pre-Production Prototype 167, 327

Price 29, 31, 33, 34, 53, 54, 126, 139, 141, 155, 160, 176, 219, 224, 225, 228, 242-246, 248, 272

Pricing Comparison Chart 305

Primary Research 126, 269, 327

PRINCE2 75-77

Probe-and-Learn 64, 65

Problem Scenarios 154, 157, 162, 169, 270, 274, 298, 327

Process Innovation 54, 328

Product 2-347

Product Backlog 48, 68, 69, 71, 189, 194, 208, 210, 328, 329

Product Concept 135, 136, 143-147, 149, 151, 157, 160, 161, 166, 168, 173, 185, 189, 198, 263, 266-268, 328

Product Concept Approval 145, 147

Product Concept Identification 135, 263

Product Concept Investigation 147, 160, 268

Product Concept Statement 266

Product Concept Team 147, 149

Product Definition 10, 69, 185-187, 193, 194

Product Demos 12, 228, 305, 306

Product Development 8, 10, 28, 37, 38, 51, 56-59, 66, 73, 76, 82-86, 94, 114, 115, 129, 131, 135, 163, 191, 192, 196, 205-207, 216, 239, 277, 280, 285, 292, 319-335

Product Development Activities 10, 205, 206, 323, 324, 329, 332

Product Development Method 111, 206, 324, 334

Product Documentation 11, 15, 211, 217, 219, 220, 226, 230, 231, 275

Product Implementation 10, 14, 206, 208, 220

Product Innovation 54

Product Launch Activity Groups 11, 234

Product Launch Plan 12, 296, 297

Product Lifecycle 9, 11, 17, 37, 43, 46, 51, 82, 84, 116, 124, 125, 127, 128, 132, 136, 152, 174, 233, 241, 242, 244, 248, 252, 277, 296, 302, 318, 328

Product Lifecycle Management 82, 252, 328

Product Lines 7, 34, 41, 91, 129, 130, 132, 133, 304, 328

Product Management 2, 3, 5-11, 13, 16, 17, 19, 21, 23-29, 37-40, 42, 111, 113, 114, 328

Product Management Framework 7, 8, 13, 24, 51, 52, 75, 86, 92

Product Management Lifecycle 9, 13, 19, 26, 55, 75, 76, 82, 83, 86, 94, 95, 97, 99-111, 113-118, 120, 121, 135, 145, 147-150, 153, 164, 172, 177, 181, 233, 241, 251, 257, 302, 317, 321, 322, 328-330, 334

Product Management Lifecycle Phase 26, 111, 233

68286062R00190

Made in the USA
Charleston, SC
09 March 2017